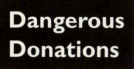

Dangerous
Donations

Dangerous Donations

Northern Philanthropy and
Southern Black Education, 1902–1930

Eric Anderson and Alfred A. Moss, Jr.
With a Foreword by Louis R. Harlan

University of Missouri Press

Columbia and London

Copyright © 1999 by
The Curators of the University of Missouri
University of Missouri Press, Columbia, Missouri 65201
Printed and bound in the United States of America
All rights reserved
5 4 3 2 1   03 02 01 00 99

Library of Congress Cataloging-in-Publication Data

Anderson, Eric, 1949–
    Dangerous donations : northern philanthropy and southern Black
education, 1902–1930 / Eric Anderson and Alfred A. Moss, Jr. ; with
a foreword by Louis R. Harlan.
        p.   cm.
    Includes bibliographical references (p.   ) and index.
    ISBN 0-8262-1226-3 (cloth : alk. paper)
    1. Afro-Americans—Education—Southern States—Finance—
History.   2. Endowments—Southern States—History.   I. Moss,
Alfred A., 1943–   . II. Title.
LC2707.A53   1999
370'.8996'073—dc21   99-28263
                                                                CIP

♾™ This paper meets the requirements of the
American National Standard for Permanence of Paper
for Printed Library Materials, Z39.48, 1984.

Designer: Elizabeth K. Young
Typesetter: Bookcomp, Inc.
Printer and binder: Thomson-Shore, Inc.
Typefaces: Goudy, Gill Sans Bold

For
John Hope Franklin

Contents

Foreword

by Louis R. Harlan

When African Americans gained their freedom from bondage in the 1860s, they recognized immediately that education of themselves and their children was one of the vital necessities for the full realization of that freedom. Skills and broader understanding through education could place them on a higher plane of independence, racial pride, and self-improvement. They gratefully accepted financial aid from federal and state governments and northern private philanthropy, but sought whenever possible to control the administration of their own education so as to direct it toward the achievement of their own goals.

Even under the relatively benign influence of Reconstruction governments in the South and of church-oriented missionary societies of the North, there were undercurrents of struggle between the conflicting agendas of whites and blacks and between racial stereotypes and racial realities. Reconstruction soon ended in failure and missionary zeal gradually waned, but the missionary societies continued to impose their educational programs on black colleges and schools. This struggle between giver and given entered a new phase around 1900. The new industrial age concentrated vast wealth in the coffers of corporate millionaires who developed a sudden interest in reforming the backward South through black and white education. This latter phase of the ongoing struggle over the direction of black education is the central topic of *Dangerous Donations*, written by Eric Anderson and Alfred A. Moss, Jr., two seasoned scholars in midcareer.

Other scholars have written about the Ogden Movement of the first decade of the twentieth century, and about its executive arm, the Southern Education Board and the closely allied General Education Board. None, however, have so thoroughly mined the Rockefeller Archives at North Tarrytown, New York, locus of the General Education Board Papers, as well as the rich holdings of the correspondence of the Southern Education Board philanthropists at the Library of

Congress and the Southern Historical Collection of the University of North Carolina Library at Chapel Hill. And no others have examined the controversial role of philanthropy with the coolness, analytical skill, and persistent search for the truth as Eric Anderson and Alfred Moss. There is some narrative and sense of development in their history, but the essence of it is close examination of the major, controverted questions in order to set the record straight.

The organizations of the "new philanthropy" had an interlocking directorate similar to those of monopolistic corporations, and on occasion they worked so closely together that some contemporary critics charged them with creating an educational monopoly. When the Southern Methodist Bishop Warren A. Candler warned of "dangerous donations and degrading doles," it was because he believed that the northern philanthropists threatened both southern religious independence and southern white supremacy. Anderson and Moss examine the controversy surrounding this charge. They also apply the test of the documentary evidence to my own assertion in my first scholarly book, *Separate and Unequal*, written some forty years ago, that the motives of the leaders of the Ogden Movement were essentially benign but that these motives were bent to the stronger will of racist southern whites. I do not come out of this analysis unscathed.

More recently, several African American scholars have put forward a conspiracy theory of the history of black industrial education in the South. This theory places Booker T. Washington in unholy collusion with the railway magnate William H. Baldwin, Jr., the Rockefellers, and other corporate philanthropists to profit directly from the promotion of black industrial education. As this argument runs, these philanthropists would use Tuskegee Institute and other industrial schools to train a subservient, cheap black labor force for the corporations. Thus they would break the unions and make millions for southern industry and its absentee owners. Anderson and Moss examine the evidence for and against this theory and reach conclusions. In all of the scholarly controversies they deal with, they fairly state the best arguments of both sides and settle a number of scholarly controversies that have puzzled scholars for decades. I believe that other readers will be as persuaded, as I have been, that Anderson and Moss have made an outstanding contribution to the history of education for both races in the segregated South of 1900 to 1930.

Moss and Anderson do not neglect the important though waning influence of the church-based missionary societies on southern African American education. Rather than seeking to treat all of the missionary societies in a superficial way, they study one of them in monographic depth because it is the only major society that has not been the subject of an earlier history. The Episcopal Church had taken part in the Reconstruction Era home mission movement for black schools, but not until 1906 was the American Church Institute for Negroes founded to coordinate its efforts. Two chapters trace its history of inadequacy until 1929, showing how northern indifference and southern white recalcitrance prevented it from reaching its goal of achieving high-quality education of blacks in Episcopal schools. The book ends with a masterful statement of the maturing and transformation of northern philanthropy for "the black South" between 1900 and 1930, with particular credit to the philanthropist Julius Rosenwald and the philanthropic agent Thomas Jesse Jones. The rehabilitation here of the reputation of Jones by resort to the documentary evidence is sure to provoke controversy of its own, for Jones has been vilified in several recent scholarly works. This is a most stimulating book for anyone interested in southern educational history or historical controversy.

Acknowledgments

Our work on this book has been supported by many individuals and institutions. We are particularly grateful to the Ford Foundation for the fellowships that allowed us to do some of the most important basic research. Other financial support came in the shape of a grant from the Earhart Foundation that provided the authors released time from academic responsibilities to complete the final research and writing. Eric Anderson also received several forms of financial support from Pacific Union College, including a rare full-year sabbatical arranged by Lorne Glaim, chairman of the history department. Alfred Moss was supported by aid from the General Research Board of the University of Maryland, College Park campus.

In the course of our research we were fortunate to benefit from the services of a number of fine archivists and librarians. We acknowledge a special debt of gratitude to H. G. Jones, now retired but for many years director of the North Carolina Collection at the University of North Carolina, for his interest in the project and helpful suggestions; to Michael R. Winston, former Director of the Moorland-Spingarn Research Center, to Esme Bahn, a former curator there, and to current curators Donna Wells, Dean C. Harris, and Joellen ElBashir, each of whom brought important collections and historic photographs to our attention; to Shawn McDermott, periodicals librarian at the Virginia Theological Seminary, who made it possible for us to secure copies of rare photographs, and to his colleagues Carol Cummins, Otey Swoboda, and Martha Taylor, all of whom were unfailingly gracious and knowledgeable resources; to Mark Duffy, Archivist of the Episcopal Church and his associate, Jennifer Peters, Assistant Archivist for Reference and Public Services, whose graciousness and assistance made our busy week in Austin, Texas, such a pleasant and productive time. We are grateful to Thomas E. Rosenbaum, who assisted us in the selection of photographs from the collections of the Rockefeller Archive Center; to Deborah Price, librarian of St. Paul's

College, Lawrenceville, Virginia, whose extraordinary efforts to locate and reproduce photographs for this book took place during a period when her mother died and she was mourning her great loss; and to Loretta O'Brien Parham, director of Hampton University's Harvey Library, T. J. Hunter Hayes, assistant director, and Frank Edgecombe, librarian, for locating a rare photograph and granting permission for its reproduction and use in this book. We also wish to thank Clifton Johnson of the Amistad Center, Richard Schrader of the Southern Historical Collection, and William Hess of the Rockefeller Archive Center, as well as their invariably helpful staff members. We are also greatly indebted to the archivists at the University of Chicago, Fisk University, Duke University, Atlanta University, the Library of Congress, and the Schomburg Research Center.

We were fortunate to have colleagues and friends who assisted us in practical ways and by their interest and encouragement. Louis R. Harlan, Keith Francis, Keith Olson, Herman Belz, Robert C. Morris, Diane Ravitch, Walter Rundell, Robert Durden, Marilyn Glaim, Elizabeth Jacoway, and Joseph Reidy critiqued papers, drafts, or proposals that shaped the development of our study, offering helpful suggestions. Although the authors alone are responsible for the contents of this book, we are deeply grateful to them for suggestions that have improved our study. Jonathan Watts, Craig Donegan, and Jeremy Warnick provided crucial research assistance at various points. Melinda Smith and Lionel Lee helped prepare the final manuscript of *Dangerous Donations*. Vernon Horn pointed us toward a valuable resource he had found as part of his own research and he, Richard Bankhead, Kathleen Russell, and Jon Boone were always available to assist and advise the authors in finding new and better ways to make computers facilitate their labors. The late Walter Utt, John and Cassandra Pyle, Nathan and Charlotte Scott, Reginald Blaxton, Marcie Rickun, and Robert Steele took an enthusiastic interest in the progress of the study, shared ideas and offered encouragement. Our editor John Brenner helped us through the final preparation of *Dangerous Donations* with good sense and serenity. Our friend Beverly Jarrett, editor-in-chief at the University of Missouri Press, never lost faith during the years of research, writing, and rewriting.

We are both men whose lives are centered in our families and, as such, Eric Anderson acknowledges with the deepest gratitude the love, support, and forbearance of Loretta, Matthew, and Seth Anderson, and Alfred Moss the love, support, and forbearance of Daniel Moss. (It is sobering to consider that we have been researching this book for most of our children's lives.)

Our book is dedicated to John Hope Franklin, a great scholar and teacher, under whose tutelage we are proud to have learned our craft.

Dangerous Donations

Introduction

P hilanthropy for black education has been described in two ways. It is either an example of the richness and vitality of American life, a sign of the nation's potential for renewal, or it is an illustration of America's broken promises, a crafty form of "generosity" designed to prevent real reform.

Scholars who support the first view are likely to cite Alexis de Tocqueville. "No sooner do you set foot upon American ground," observed this famous foreign visitor to the United States, "than you are stunned by a kind of tumult"—the clamor of Americans engaged in their voluntary associations for social improvement. "The Americans make associations to give entertainments, to found seminaries, to build inns, to construct churches, to diffuse books, to send missionaries to the antipodes; they found in this manner hospitals, prisons, schools."[1] From this point of view, philanthropy for black schools (whether generated by Yankee do-gooders or blacks pursuing self-help) is a good illustration of the same restless spirit, the same energetic community building observed by Tocqueville. The fact that private giving played a key role in the establishment of black educational institutions (as well as churches and hospitals) is simply part of a national pattern.

The contrasting view describes philanthropy in ambivalent, ironic, even hostile terms. Philanthropists created and supported schools, argue some scholars, as a means to achieve larger goals, particularly the maintenance of social peace after the Civil War and the creation of a class of submissive workers. Proponents of this position remember, no doubt, a passage from Ralph Ellison's *Invisible Man*, in which a student at a Tuskegee-like school contemplates a statue of the school's founder:

> Then in my mind's eye I see the bronze statue of the college Founder, the cold Father symbol, his hands outstretched in the breathtaking gesture of lifting a veil that flutters in hard metallic folds about the face of a

1. Alexis de Tocqueville, *Democracy in America*, Richard D. Heffner, ed. (New York: New American Library, 1956), 108, 198.

1

kneeling slave; and I am standing puzzled, unable to decide whether the veil is really being lifted, or lowered more firmly into place; whether I am witnessing a revelation or a more efficient blinding.[2]

Neither view does full justice to the variety of philanthropic experiences, nor to the permutations of donors' motives and ideals. Both views may be correct, depending on which philanthropists are examined—and when. For example, W. E. B. Du Bois, the distinguished African American scholar-activist, both praised and blamed philanthropy. The northern educational crusade in the Reconstruction South was, he said, the "finest thing in American history, and one of the few things untainted by sordid greed and cheap vainglory." Yet he was a relentless critic of the motives and ideals of twentieth-century foundation philanthropists—though in 1930 he grudgingly admitted that, despite its "past mistakes," the Rockefeller-funded General Education Board had "been the salvation of education among Negroes."[3]

In *Dangerous Donations*, we have not written a defense of the philanthropists, though we repeatedly challenge some of the conclusions of the radical revisionists of educational history. (Revising revisionists is, of course, an old game among historians.)[4] If our own loyalties are relevant, let it be noted that neither of us is entirely comfortable with the worldview of the men of the General Education Board, the Southern Education Board, and kindred organizations. In fact, if we had to choose for ourselves, our students, or our children, we would prefer the humanities-oriented education championed in *The Souls of Black Folk* to Booker T. Washington's industrial education or the vision of Progressive education articulated by Thomas Jesse Jones. Politically, each of us would prefer a form of philanthropy more respectful of local and private institutions, less certain of the future, and more skeptical of the conventional wisdom of the early twentieth century.

Both celebrators and critics of philanthropy have sometimes treated blacks as more or less helpless victims or mostly passive objects of charity. Influenced by the scholarship of John Hope Franklin, August Meier, Louis R. Harlan, J. Carleton Hayden, James McPherson,

2. Ralph Ellison, *Invisible Man* (New York: Vintage Books, 1972), 36.
3. W. E. B. Du Bois, *The Souls of Black Folk: Essays and Sketches* (Greenwich, Conn.: Fawcett Publications, 1961), 82. Du Bois, "The General Education Board," 229–39.
4. For an important example, see Diane Ravitch, *The Revisionists Revised: A Critique of the Radical Attack on the Schools*.

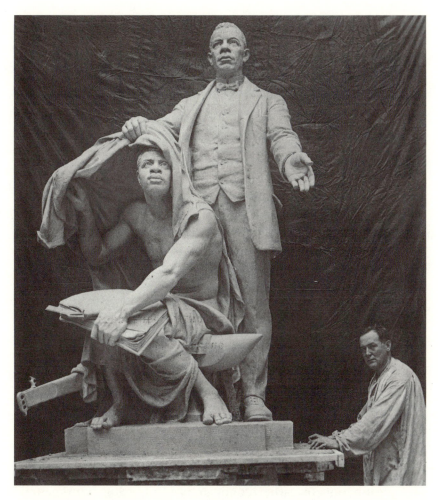

Statue of Booker T. Washington at Tuskegee Institute, with sculptor. Division of Photographs and Prints, Library of Congress.

and Robert Morris, among others, we think that the demands and expectations of black students, teachers, parents, and donors must be recognized in any complete assessment of this topic. Thus we begin our work with an examination of "the African American agenda" for education, believing that the full story of philanthropy and black education cannot be written from the perspective of the philanthropists. The plans, motives, and ideology of the major donors and their advisers in the great foundations must be studied in the context of all the evidence, especially including the hopes of the recipients of philanthropy. It is inaccurate to think of southern blacks as mere receivers of charity. Not only were northern donors often forced to take into account the educational goals of African Americans, but black communities were also donors, contributing millions of dollars in educational self-help.

In the first half century after the Civil War, northern philanthropy for blacks was primarily motivated by religion and distributed through Protestant denominations seeking to "elevate the freedmen." Far from "melting away" after Reconstruction, this sort of private giving reached new highs in the early twentieth century. The four dominant missionary societies (Congregational, Methodist, Presbyterian, and Baptist) spent four times as much on black education in 1906 as they had in 1876.[5]

The work of the missionary societies was at first supplemented, and then ultimately overshadowed, by secular foundations. The Peabody Fund (established 1867) and the Slater Fund (created in 1881) promoted southern education as "a patriotic duty that could not well be shirked without disaster," in the words of millionaire merchant John F. Slater. This more secular motivation for educational philanthropy reached fuller elaboration, under more complex organization, in the early twentieth century. The establishment of the General Education Board in 1902 marked a new phase in foundation philanthropy. Endowed with $33 million in Rockefeller gifts during its first decade of operation, the GEB was committed to an ideal of "scientific" and efficiently organized philanthropy significantly different from the goals and organization of earlier donor groups. Rejecting "sentimental" giving that responded to mere symptoms, these "new philanthropists" believed that they could eliminate the root causes of social problems through research and the careful application of insights.

Thanks to the GEB's focused goals, immense resources, and energetic officers—men who were both creative and well connected with business and political leaders in North and South—the board quickly became more influential and visible than any other philanthropic group supporting black education. Other foundations, such

5. James M. McPherson, *The Abolitionist Legacy: From Reconstruction to the NAACP,* 147.

as the Southern Education Board (established in 1901), Jeanes Fund (founded in 1907), Phelps-Stokes Fund (established in 1911), and the Julius Rosenwald Fund (organized in 1917), worked closely with the GEB, imitating its organization, responding to its initiatives, and sharing trustees in an "interlocking directorate" of calculating altruism.

At a time when the gifts of missionary societies and individual donors to black schools far outstripped GEB contributions to black education, the GEB acquired immense prestige, enabling its planners and theorists to set the philanthropic agenda. In 1910, for example, the primary missionary societies and donors to Hampton and Tuskegee Institutes contributed about $2 million to black education—compared with less than $90,000 from the GEB. Yet when GEB officers called a conference on Negro education in 1915, they did not even invite the leaders of missionary philanthropy. By the 1920s, as GEB spending for black education dramatically increased, the board's support of particular schools or programs had become a kind of imprimatur, a warrant of worthiness for other givers interested in black education.

Instead of challenging the new philanthropy, missionary philanthropists gradually adopted the key positions of the GEB and other foundation philanthropists—including the idea that private education for Negroes should be replaced wherever possible by public schools, supported by taxation and controlled by whites. One of the oldest missionary societies, the American Missionary Association, moved from supporting forty secondary schools in the early twentieth century to maintaining only one in 1950. Reflecting upon the results of this policy, the head of the American Missionary Association recognized that every decision to turn over an AMA school to the public school authorities had been received by black parents and students as "a death sentence." The policy would never have been adopted if AMA leaders had based their policy on the counsel of "principals, teachers, parents and patrons" in the South.[6]

A newer missionary society, the Episcopalian American Church Institute for Negroes, was also deeply influenced by the ideals and practices of the GEB. In chapters 5 and 6, *Dangerous Donations* provides an extended review of the early history of the ACIN, an organization previously neglected by historians. Unlike other Protestant denominations, the Episcopal Church entered the twentieth century without

6. See chapter 7.

Class of 1903, Morehouse College (then known as Atlanta Baptist College).
Photograph courtesy of John Hope Franklin.

a long-established organization dedicated to southern black educational philanthropy. Founded by men who saw the GEB as the model
for their work, the ACIN lacked a strong tradition of independent operation, and was especially receptive to the GEB's efforts to standardize
southern black education. Thus the institute's development provides
an illustration of the impact of the secular foundations beyond their
own operations.

Yet while northern philanthropy shaped the ACIN from the outside,
southern whites were gaining control of the organization from within,
as the resourceful churchman Robert W. Patton revised the tactics
and rhetoric used by Samuel H. Bishop, first director of the institute.
Patton's success should be contrasted with the failure of George Foster
Peabody, who had once declared privately, "We cannot afford to let
the present generation of the south control negro education."[7] A
philanthropist of great prestige, longtime treasurer of both the GEB
and the Southern Education Board, Peabody strove for nearly three

7. Peabody to Ida Mason, March 26, 1912, in George Foster Peabody Papers, Library
of Congress.

decades to implement his dream of a powerful, nationally influential ACIN, supported by direct grants from the GEB and major gifts from the national Episcopal organization.

Students of northern philanthropy have often emphasized the power of the great foundations. We have sought to balance this insight with a recognition of the limits on their power. Rich and influential as the northern philanthropic agencies were, they did not enjoy unlimited freedom. As Judith Sealander has perceptively observed, it is possible to exaggerate the power of philanthropy both for good or ill. Foundation initiatives did not automatically become government policy, nor could philanthropists be sure that a program would be eliminated if they "retracted their endorsement."[8]

From the beginning, GEB-style philanthropy sought to placate southern white critics. (Our title is, in fact, borrowed, with an ironic tip of the hat, from Methodist Bishop Warren A. Candler, an important critic of northern philanthropy, who penned in 1909 a powerful tract with a striking title—*Dangerous Donations or Degrading Doles, or A Vast Scheme for Capturing and Controlling the Colleges and Universities of the Country.*) As early as 1903, Booker T. Washington protested to Wallace Buttrick, a key board officer: "We have already gone as far as decency permits in our attempt to avoid stirring up southern feeling." But in the early twentieth century's atmosphere of deteriorating race relations, even the mildest program of reform met intense opposition from many white southerners, who suspected that the reformers intended to elevate blacks at their expense. In its vigor and anger this opposition was, according to James W. Patton, "comparable in some respects to the Southern [white] reaction to the anti-segregation decisions of the Supreme Court in the 1950s." White extremists denounced both Washington and his northern friends, accusing the promoters of black schools of failing to prepare African Americans for their subordinate place in a segregated society and, indeed, "training the negroes to the vain hope of social equality with whites." Reporting in 1904, W. T. B. Williams, a black field agent for the GEB, found "but little interest in negro education among the whites, save in the cases of the very best element. . . . But the mass of whites actually believe that by educating the negro they are putting

8. Judith Sealander, *Private Wealth, Public Life: Foundation Philanthropy and the Reshaping of American Social Policy from the Progressive Era to the New Deal,* 8–9, 242–43.

African American members of the Faculty, St. Augustine's School, Raleigh, N.C.
1902. Archives of the Episcopal Church, Austin, Texas.

him in a position [in] which he will be of less material advantage
to them."[9]

Southern opposition to northern philanthropy was most intense in
the first fifteen years of the twentieth century, though it broke out
with unpredictable intensity at various later dates. The opposition
created an indelible impression upon the foundation executives. "The
Board was aware from the start," wrote Raymond B. Fosdick, GEB
officer and author of an official history of the board, "of the dangers
inherent in a Northern institution working in the highly charged
emotional atmosphere of a biracial South. . . . A single misstep could
be disastrous."[10]

9. See chapter 2.
10. Raymond Fosdick, Henry F. Pringle, and Katharine Douglas Pringle, *Adventure
in Giving: The Story of the General Education Board, a Foundation Established by John D.
Rockefeller*, 320.

Based on our study of internal policy papers and private correspondence, we have concluded that fear of southern white opposition played an important role in the structuring of northern philanthropy for the South. This is especially true of the GEB's decision in 1911 to endorse the "policy of cooperating with the white people of the South in promoting Negro education," thus making the stimulation of government spending on public education the first priority of its programs for black education—with aid for private and denominational schools a distinctly secondary emphasis. Other foundation initiatives suggested a similar strategy of countering opposition by avoiding direct confrontation as much as possible. For example, the GEB's program of appointing state supervisors of Negro rural schools minimized opposition by making these supervisors subordinate to the state superintendent of public instruction, by recommending no blacks for these positions, and by simply not making an appointment where significant opposition existed. In other cases, the GEB attempted to forestall criticism by using indirect funding and euphemisms such as "county training school" in place of "high school." The Rosenwald Fund's famous school-building program employed similar defensive methods. By supporting schools only where white authorities would help, the Rosenwald Fund gave local opponents of black education veto power. No school would be built in a community that harbored determined opposition to northern philanthropic activity.

Perhaps most important of all, southern white opposition helped shape the decision by the GEB, the Southern Education Board, and other philanthropic agencies to promote the development of a comprehensive educational system for whites, rather than focusing primarily on blacks, as the abolitionists and neo-abolitionists of the missionary societies had done. The secular philanthropists assumed that southern whites would not tolerate large-scale aid to blacks until whites had an adequate educational system. Although the GEB began as an outgrowth of John D. Rockefeller, Jr.'s concept of a "Negro Education Board," in the end only 19 percent of the board's gifts went to black education.

From the start, the foundation philanthropists were much less concerned about black criticisms of their activities. They expected black leaders to be disappointed with the pace of progress and were prepared to be "greatly misunderstood" by "our colored friends" as they cautiously sought to awaken southern whites to their responsibilities.

Calculating that their scientific philanthropy would "take years and perhaps even successive generations" to achieve appropriate results, the philanthropists (with few exceptions) did not share the sense of crisis felt by most African American educators, nor did they see a need for urgent, even desperate, action. Instead, they feared provocation, overextension, and unwise spending.

By the 1920s, foundation philanthropy was directed, for all practical purposes, by foundation staffs rather than the original donors. Many of these philanthropic bureaucrats were primarily interested in black educational experiments for their relevance to the overall Progressive educational agenda, including the elimination of "dead languages," the introduction of "practical" vocational training, and reformation of the curriculum to promote "life adjustment." As Abraham Flexner of the GEB put it, "The effort of those who think they are progressive in education is to modify the existing curriculum . . . very much in the direction of what is . . . proposed in the South as especially fitting for colored children."[11] Educational innovation was easier to carry out in weak and underfunded black schools than in more secure white schools.

The philanthropists' early commitment to "the Hampton-Tuskegee idea" faded even before the death of Booker T. Washington. As the foundations intensified their support for black education in the late 1920s, black collegiate education increased dramatically and small private industrial schools modeled on Tuskegee largely disappeared. Hampton and Tuskegee themselves evolved into little more than cautious imitations of the standard American college. By 1930, Washington's philosophy and network of influence were no longer preeminent in black educational philanthropy.

These changes are illustrated well in the careers of two important philanthropists: William H. Baldwin, Jr., a reform-minded businessman who was the first chairman of the General Education Board; and Julius Rosenwald, the Jewish entrepreneur famous for his creative plan to build southern rural schools. Committed to a variety of Progressive reforms, Baldwin's understanding of black education changed in important ways as he was tutored by Booker T. Washington. By the end of his life, Baldwin was increasingly out of step with his fellow philanthropists, who did not share his sense of urgency nor

11. See chapter 4.

his continuing belief in the value of establishing "other Tuskegees." Rosenwald, though initially inspired by Washington and Baldwin, eventually moved along a path blazed by the GEB. His benefactions were organized in a thoroughly modern manner, with the formation of the Rosenwald Fund in 1917 and its reorganization in 1928 on the model of the Rockefeller Foundation, with a former Rockefeller Foundation vice president as its head. The famous school-building program moved from being a Tuskegee-administered project to being one controlled by the experts of an outside foundation.

Further research will be necessary before historians can offer a comprehensive judgment on the ultimate impact of northern educational philanthropy in the South. Undeniably, the foundation philanthropists excused or accepted many injustices by placing their confidence in gradual change or "the slow processes of evolution." The foundations did little to attack directly segregation, poverty, or disfranchisement. Believing "our work is education not agitation," they did, however, greatly strengthen selected black colleges and universities, and advocate, with some success, increased public support for black education.

The whole South (including the black South) experienced striking educational progress in the early twentieth century, despite the fact that dominant whites treated black schools with high-handed inequity. Between 1900 and 1930, black literacy jumped from 50 percent to 80 percent, the proportion of black children in school reached nearly 90 percent, and, for the first time, black public high schools became common. The number of African American college students increased at a spectacular rate, rising from a mere sixteen hundred circa 1914 to eight times as many twelve years later. The gifts that encouraged these changes were "dangerous donations" in a sense that Bishop Candler did not understand, perhaps, since the new educational opportunities, even at their most uneven, created new expectations and new frustrations.

In spite of their compromises and ulterior motives, the foundation philanthropists had a vision of race relations (and black potential) that was significantly different from the ideas of the South's white majority. Unlike some of their public utterances, their private correspondence is full of comments on the narrowness and bigotry of the white South and earnest hopes for change. "It is extremely stupid on the part of the Southern people," declared Robert C. Ogden in a representative letter to an associate, "that they fail to perceive the injury they are inflicting upon themselves by surrendering their entire section of the country to crazy prejudice."[12]

The themes of *Dangerous Donations* are widely significant. Historians researching race relations, students of the role of philanthropy in the United States, and scholars examining the social philosophy underpinning American education are all required to understand the evolution of education for black Americans. Our research on philanthropy and black education raises, we believe, questions central to American history as a whole, including the role of private fortunes in shaping public policy, the place of education in the nation's social order, and the changing influence of religious and other private institutions on cultural values. We have examined black education in the South as both a central political issue and an urgent social question. Seeking to do justice to the complex objectives of both donors and recipients, we have written *Dangerous Donations* as a study of the paradoxical impact of mixed motives and unintended consequences.

12. Ogden to William H. Baldwin, Jr., February 12, 1903, Ogden letterbook, in Robert C. Ogden Papers, Library of Congress.

The African American Agenda for Education

[The] man who holds that all I need is to be a good servant is not fit to teach me.

—Charles Grandison[1]

Even before the Emancipation Proclamation, as northern reform-ers and missionaries began creating schools for African Americans, southern blacks sought education with an enthusiasm that amazed white observers. From the start, black students and parents registered their own distinctive demands and expectations. They were confident that schools would provide them and their children the skills necessary to develop racial pride, economic mobility, and political freedom. Without waiting for white encouragement, blacks sought to administer Negro schools, staff them with teachers of their own race, and supplement outside philanthropy with community self-help.[2]

So persistently did black southerners seek a voice in their own education in the late nineteenth century that it is possible to speak of an African American agenda in education, though in fact the most consistent black demand was that their education should be

1. American Association of Educators of Colored Youth, Minutes of Meeting Held at Baltimore, July 24–27, 1895, 9.

2. Joe M. Richardson, *Christian Reconstruction: The American Missionary Association and Southern Blacks: 1861–1890*; Robert C. Morris, "Educational Reconstruction," 144, 147, 151; Robert C. Morris, *Reading, 'Riting, and Reconstruction: The Education of Freedmen in the South, 1861–1870*, 1–14, 17, 22, 120–21; Robert C. Sherer, *Subordination or Liberation?: The Development and Conflicting Theories of Education in Nineteenth Century Alabama*, 2; Ronald E. Butchart, *Northern Schools, Southern Blacks, and Reconstruction: Freedmen's Education, 1862–1875*, 175, 177; James M. Smallwood, "Early 'Freedom Schools': Black Self-Help and Education in Reconstruction Texas, A Case Study," 790; Jacqueline Jones, *Soldiers of Light and Love: Northern Teachers and Georgia Blacks, 1865–1873*, 61–86, 84.

similar to everyone else's. Whenever white educators argued that Negroes were "not yet ready" for some role, or advocated curricular experiments not standard in white schools, they could count on clear and steadily increasing black resistance. The most bitter arguments between blacks and whites involved issues of practical control, not educational philosophy.

Although black educational objectives were often frustrated by powerful whites, the black community was not powerless. Their hopes played an important part in shaping southern black educational institutions. The black agenda for education is revealed in thousands of small choices, including parents' decisions about whether and where to send their children to school, decisions by churches and local communities starting new schools, and the choice by beneficiaries of philanthropy to oppose, on occasion, the policy decisions of donors and their agents.

The role of black teachers in black schools was a perennial issue. Southern blacks expressed a steady hunger for racial role models and authority figures in their schools, stimulating growth in the number of black schools at all levels, especially schools that offered teacher training. Though the public and private educational resources for southern blacks were never adequate, there was a steady expansion in the number of black teachers. As early as 1869, blacks were a majority of the teaching force, dominating, in particular, the primary schools. By the early twentieth century blacks also outnumbered whites among post-primary teachers. This expansion also opened the way for growing numbers of black women to enter the profession. North Carolina's black female and male public school teachers were almost equal in number by 1902, a situation that may have been true in other parts of the South. James McPherson's research indicates that by 1915 blacks made up 60 percent of the teachers in secondary schools and colleges aided by northern missionary societies. On the college level, black faculty members rose from 27 to 51 percent during the years 1895 to 1915. Among school administrators, eight of the thirty presidents of colleges and professional schools were blacks, while the comparable figure for secondary school principals was fifty-two blacks out of eighty-five.[3]

3. Morris, "Educational Reconstruction," 151. Glenda Elizabeth Gilmore, *Gender and Jim Crow: Women and the Politics of White Supremacy in North Carolina, 1896–1920,* 157.

The demand for black teachers was not simple racial chauvinism. From the earliest appearance of schools for former slaves, some black communities made it clear that, whenever possible, they wanted black teachers for their children. Yet other communities were equally adamant in their preference for white teachers under some circumstances. Throughout the Reconstruction Era and later, the African American community was divided on this issue. For almost all southern blacks, Negro teachers were visible examples of the potential of their race. Some went further, doubting that any white teacher was capable of providing former slaves and their children with race pride, education, and the drive for mobility their situation required. As North Carolina educator and clergyman James W. Hood put it, white teachers could not "enter into the feelings of colored pupils as the colored teachers did."[4] In specific situations, some black parents and students preferred white teachers, believing them to be better trained and more capable educators than the available black instructors. There were even a few places where, after whites were replaced by blacks, the community demanded the return of the old teachers, convinced that the quality of the schools had plummeted. Those African Americans who argued, as a matter of principle, that teaching positions should go to the best qualified, regardless of race, added to the complexity of the discourse.

Among the strongest proponents of Negro teachers were black ministers and other black leaders of the first postslavery generation, men and women motivated by a mixture of race pride and ambition. The position of the black clergy connected with the black Baptist and Methodist denominations also reflected the commitment of their religious organizations to independent black-run and supported educational institutions. Whatever position the various segments of the black community took on the issue, as the numbers of black graduates of normal schools and colleges expanded during the last decades of the nineteenth century, northern missionaries and philanthropists had increasing difficulty arguing for their exclusion as teachers.[5]

Gilmore finds that in 1902 there were 1,325 black women and 1,190 black men teaching in the public schools of North Carolina. McPherson, *Abolitionist Legacy*, 293.

4. John Haley, *Charles N. Hunter and Race Relations in North Carolina*, 84.

5. Jones, *Soldiers of Light*, 65; McPherson, *Abolitionist Legacy*, 274–74.

These sentiments were strengthened by the competition between the schools established and run by black religious communities and those administered and run by white churches and missionary societies. To call for black teachers was to support black institutions and black jobs. Other members of the black community may have called for black teachers as part of the effort to get more instructors of their race hired in schools run by whites. And some may have been motivated by fear that blacks taught by whites would no longer support black institutions or pay heed to black leaders.

One white observer noted "that blacks will accept white teachers in virtue of their superior qualifications, but whenever they can get black ones really competent they receive them with great satisfaction." Another white educator summarized the strong campaign for black educational leadership in Savannah, Georgia, in words that apply in many places: "What they want is assistance without control." Here, as in other places where blacks expressed a preference for schools run by members of their race, northern educational missionaries sometimes perceived racial "ignorance and ingratitude," an opinion some did not hesitate to make public.[6]

Between 1865 and 1880, approximately 39 secondary schools and colleges for blacks were established, nine of which offered college courses. By 1915 that number had tripled to 117, with 27 schools offering collegiate studies. Among these 27 were the state-funded agricultural and mechanical colleges for Negroes that began to be established during the last decade of the nineteenth century. While most of these institutions had black heads and predominantly black faculties, they were dependent on usually hostile or indifferent white legislatures, which provided minimal funds and discouraged the development of serious college-level programs.[7]

Local black congregations in the South and historically black denominations were among the earliest participants in the creation of educational institutions for Negroes during and after the Civil War. Many local congregations established literacy schools as soon as federal troops arrived, some with the aid of the Freedmen's Bureau or northern aid societies, some without. While local initiative on

6. Morris, *Reading, 'Riting, and Reconstruction*, 90, 120, 124–25; Haley, *Charles N. Hunter*, 36; Butchart, *Northern Schools, Southern Blacks, and Reconstruction*, 173; Jones, *Soldiers of Light*, 74, 50–51.
7. McPherson, *Abolitionist Legacy*, 143, 268–69.

the part of black congregations of all religious persuasions created "freedmen's schools" throughout the South, this pattern was most typical of black Baptists from 1865 until well into the twentieth century, a consequence of their slowness in developing denominational structures and the absence or weakness of their local and regional organizations. The African Methodist Episcopal (AME) Church, the African Methodist Episcopal Zion (AMEZ) Church, and the Colored Methodist Episcopal (CME) Church (later renamed the Christian Methodist Episcopal Church) were better prepared to enter the educational arena because they possessed denominational structures that facilitated the establishment and systematic funding of institutions. For much of the nineteenth and early twentieth centuries the AME Church was the most effective of the three. The educational work of these religious organizations was complemented by the African Civilization Society (ACS), in many ways another expression of the black religious communities, for the bulk of its founding members were northern black evangelical clergy who were members of denominations active in southern black education. The ACS would remain active until approximately 1875, after which it disappeared. That black Baptists and Methodists should take the lead in this work was not surprising, for they were the largest religious communities among Negroes. In 1890, 53 percent of African Americans who claimed church membership listed themselves as Baptists, 44 percent as Methodists.[8]

The black congregations, the black denominations, and the African Civilization Society brought similar convictions to their educational endeavors, beginning with the certainty that Christian beliefs, manners, and morals were the keys to black survival and development

8. Ira Berlin, Barbara J. Fields, Steven F. Miller, Joseph Reidy, and Leslie S. Rowland, *Slaves No More: Three Essays on Emancipation and the Civil War*, 111; Reginald F. Hildebrand, *The Times Were Strange and Stirring: Methodist Preachers and the Crisis of Emancipation*, 24–27, 59–63; William J. Walls, *The African Methodist Episcopal Zion Church: Reality of the Black Church*, 201–332; Dwight Oliver Wendell Holmes, *The Evolution of the Negro College*, 138–49. For additional information on the educational work of black Baptists, see the biography of Edward McKnight Brawley in the Benjamin G. Brawley Papers, Moorland-Spingarn Research Center, Howard University; June O. Patton, "The Black Community of Augusta [Georgia] and the Struggle for Ware High School, 1880–1899," 45–49. John Hope Franklin and Alfred A. Moss, Jr., *From Slavery to Freedom: A History of African Americans*, 265, 285–86. James D. Anderson, *The Education of Blacks in the South: 1860–1935*, 67, 135, 240. Morris, *Reading, 'Riting, and Reconstruction*, 13–14, 116–19, 190; Butchart, *Northern Schools, Southern Blacks, and Reconstruction*, 7; McPherson, *Abolitionist Legacy*, 149.

in freedom. This theologically grounded sense of purpose, as well as an unwavering commitment to the belief that their central purpose was to provide students in their schools with a liberal arts education, was reinforced by the fact that often the earliest educational goal of these schools was preparing students for the ministry. Most of these black church institutions resisted white dominance, carrying on their educational work despite the negative assessments they regularly received from northern missionary societies and secular foundations.[9]

As a result, from 1865 to 1902, the black denominational schools and colleges were the ones that can be most accurately described as controlled by African Americans. Some white and black observers felt these institutions were less effective, often pointing to black control as the basic problem. Writing in a later period, B. C. Caldwell, white field officer of two influential philanthropic agencies, the Jeanes and Slater Funds, perceived both weakness and vitality in such institutions. Caldwell always distinguished between two kinds of Negro church schools: "1st, the missionary kind, established and maintained by white churches of the north, and usually taught and controlled by white people, necessarily northern white people; and 2nd, the niggery kind, established and maintained by negro church boards, taught and controlled entirely by negroes."[10]

Caldwell's reports made clear his belief that schools for blacks run by white churches were superior: they had the "advantage in buildings, equipment, sanitation, refinement of surroundings, quality of teaching and wholesomeness of living conditions." Yet the students at the black-controlled schools were superior to their counterparts at richer, more refined schools. In "general personal worth," Caldwell asserted, students at a school such as the AME's Allen University "would compare with advantage" with those at Fisk or Shaw or St. Augustine. He noted, without fully understanding or appreciating its importance, how attractive some African Americans found black denominational schools precisely because of their freedom from white control. It pained Caldwell that "schools controlled entirely by negroes" were

9. Anderson, *The Education of Blacks in the South*, 66–67.

10. B. C. Caldwell, Report to Conference of State Agents for Negro Rural Schools, Battery Park Hotel, Asheville, North Carolina, November 26–28, 1921, in General Education Board Papers, Box 28, Folder 1998, Rockefeller Archive Center, Pocantico Hills, New York.

"marked by detachment, isolation, frequently carried to the point of open hostility toward contact with white people, and a more or less skeptical attitude toward public schools controlled by white officials." While he pointed to an occasional black Baptist institution as an example, he judged the AME and AMEZ schools to be the worst in this regard, largely due to their bishops, most of whom Caldwell described as "autocrats," with "no more religion than the law allows." Grudgingly conceding them to be of some value, Caldwell noted that schools run by the black churches had "close, direct relations with the great body of negro population," which drew "the sturdiest students to their classes."[11]

The schools of the various black religious communities were from the start in competition with each other, and with schools established by predominantly white churches and missionary societies. Each of the black denominations touted aggressively its brand of Christianity as the one most suitable for moving the former slaves and their progeny "from slavery to freedom." Yet despite their differences, the two most fundamental tenets of educational philosophy in schools for blacks founded and directed by the black churches were the certainty that educated blacks could best instruct, direct and elevate their race, and a belief that the inculcation of race pride was an indispensable element in the curriculum of any truly effective school for African Americans.[12]

The rivalry between the various black and white denominations helped also to stimulate this expansion in the number of schools, creating situations in several parts of the South where competing colleges for blacks were literally neighboring institutions. Numerous black and white educators pointed to the poor stewardship of limited resources this indicated, urging the creation of a master plan for consolidating black collegiate education as an essential step toward increased effectiveness. Within the African American community, members of the American Negro Academy, a black learned society, were among the most important voices calling for reform in this regard.[13]

11. Ibid.

12. Hildebrand, *Times Were Strange*, 24–27, 59–63; Walls, *African Methodist Episcopal Zion Church*, 201–332; Holmes, *Negro College*, 138–48; Edward McKnight Brawley biography in the Benjamin G. Brawley Papers.

13. McPherson, *Abolitionist Legacy*, 143, 151–52, 268–69; Alfred A. Moss, Jr., *The American Negro Academy: Voice of the Talented Tenth*, 48.

For many black schools inclusion of "college" or "university" in their name was more an expression of hope than reality. Between 1880 and 1915 few black schools with this designation awarded undergraduate degrees, and the percentage of their students taking college-level courses was small. The struggle of these schools to strengthen their college work was seriously burdened by the need to also offer primary and secondary education programs. The low standard of black public education, particularly "the virtual absence of public high schools for Negroes in the South" until the post–World War I period, meant that black colleges had to function as their own feeder institutions.[14]

Beginning in the 1870s, the problems of the white-run colleges for blacks were compounded by intense demands for increased black presence in their administrations and on their faculties. Among black colleges, Howard University in Washington, D.C., experienced the greatest pressure to expand the number of Negroes on its teaching and administrative staffs. Howard's location in the nation's capital and its federal subsidy gave it greater public visibility than most other institutions of higher education for Negroes and, to a certain degree, exempted those African Americans who sought to make it an example of "Negro self-reliance" from the most extreme forms of retaliation employed by white supremacists in other parts of the South.

Articulating the opinions of many black alumni and supporters of Howard, John W. Cromwell, editor of *The Peoples Advocate*, one of the local black newspapers and a graduate of Howard's Law School, produced a series of articles in 1875 that were blistering attacks on the whites who controlled Howard. In his opening salvo he denounced Erastus M. Cravath, a white trustee of Howard University who was president of Fisk University, for dismissing a petition from a group of black Washingtonians who urged the appointment of African American John Mercer Langston as permanent occupant of that office. At the time the petition was presented to the trustees, Langston, a lawyer and former dean of Howard's law school, was acting president of Howard. Cromwell expressed outrage at reports that Cravath not only opposed Langston's selection but also scolded the petitioners for their temerity, telling them, "you colored men are failures in the

14. McPherson, *Abolitionist Legacy*, 205, 206.

management of enterprises and institutions." Cromwell denounced Cravath as an enemy of "Negro progress," and launched a general attack on whites involved in black education who refused to share their responsibilities with blacks of equal or superior ability.[15]

Ten years later, the death in 1885 of Wiley Lane, an African American who had been professor of Greek at Howard University, moved his eulogist, prominent black Presbyterian clergyman Francis J. Grimké, to recount the fight waged by blacks on Howard University's trustee board to secure Lane's appointment in 1881. Lane, who held A.B. and A.M. degrees from Howard, also earned an A.B. degree from Amherst College, where he was elected to Phi Beta Kappa. Grimké used the eulogy to argue strenuously that qualified blacks must be allowed to teach in the schools conducted for them. Perhaps speaking especially to white officers of Howard present at the funeral, Grimké recalled that in the debate over the Lane appointment only one white trustee had expressed unequivocal support for an expanded role for blacks, through his statement, "We must decrease in these institutions, but they [Negroes] must increase."[16]

In 1887, the editor of the *Raleigh* [North Carolina] *Outlook*, a black newspaper, used similar words to denounce the white head of St. Augustine's Normal and Collegiate Institute for his dismissal of African American Anna J. Cooper from the school's faculty. Cooper's firing, attributed to "incompatibility of temperament," immediately drew attention because she was widely respected throughout the black community for her writings and speeches on racial and women's issues as well as her abilities as a teacher. The sense of outrage was compounded by the fact that the person who fired her had earlier "praised her work repeatedly." "In spite of the fact that St. Augustine's was "founded for the benefit of the Negro," the editor of the *Outlook* charged, "we are fully cognizant of the fact that the united voice of the entire race is not . . . heard" in this and many other schools for blacks "conducted in utter and contemptible ignorance of the very race for whose elevation noble philanthropists reared them."[17]

15. Cromwell, letter to the editor, *National Republican*, June 29, 1875, in John Mercer Langston Papers, Moorland-Spingarn Research Center.

16. Francis J. Grimké, *Address of Rev. F. J. Grimké In Memoriam Prof. Wiley Lane of the Howard University, Washington, D. C.*, 27.

17. *Raleigh* [N.C.] *Outlook*, June 24, 1887, Charles Norfleet Hunter Papers, Perkins Library, Duke University. In addition to being a respected teacher of mathematics,

Howard University students in biology lab, early 1900s. Moorland-Spingarn
Research Center, Howard University Archives.

In 1895 the need for more African American teachers at all levels
of black education was the central theme of the "Address to the
Public" from the American Association of Educators of Colored Youth
(AAECY). The address demanded an expansion of employment options for "colored" teachers, not "simply because they are colored
but because they are qualified, and we challenge contradiction to the
statement that there can *now* be found perfectly well qualified teachers
for *all* of the colored primary schools and for most of the higher positions in the universities and professional schools." These statements,
endorsed by the membership of the AAECY, were formal phrasings
of sentiments voiced by delegates throughout the annual meeting.
One of the most outspoken was Charles Grandison of Delaware, who

Latin, and Greek at St. Augustine's College from 1885–1887, Cooper was an alumna
of the school who was repeatedly pointed to, by both black and white supporters
of St. Augustine's, as one of its finest products. See Paul Phillips Cooke, "Anna J.
Cooper, Educator and Humanitarian," *Negro History Bulletin;* Anna Julia Cooper Papers,
Moorland-Spingarn Research Center.

during a heated discussion shouted that he "would rather men of my own race . . . teach my children than a white man who is not in sympathy. . . . [The] man who holds that all I need is to be a good servant is not fit to teach me."[18]

Numerous speakers during the various AAECY sessions and the organization as a whole, through its published "Address to the Public," voiced support for a curriculum that was in essentials similar to that offered in schools for whites. Grandison argued that blacks needed instruction in basic literacy and "the trades." Since both races must "traverse the same paths," Negroes "must be taught all things." In a separate discussion, Professor Richard Foster of Howard University urged that Negro children be provided with "kindergarten . . . schools" and sent to them when they are "three years old." At another point in the meeting, Kelly Miller, also a member of the Howard faculty, stressed the importance of ancient history and classical languages in producing leaders. And "if any race needs leaders we do." The AAECY's "Address" called for "a more hearty support" of "our industrial schools," but immediately followed the appeal with a caution of the need to maintain a balance between vocational and classical education: "It is of the highest importance that academic studies should be pursued at the same time as the manual training." This message was reinforced by the "Report of the Committee on Educational Exhibit," which endorsed courses for Negro students in business ("especially necessary for the success of our youth who do not get this training"), penmanship, science, mathematics, classical and modern languages, civics, economics, English, and geography.[19]

Black teachers shared many of the same goals as their white counterparts. The fact, however, that they were of the same race as their students caused most to feel that their professional credibility rested on the ability of their students to demonstrate that they were as educable as whites, and that they could use whatever education they received to good effect. A diverse group, black teachers brought many goals to their work, but eight seem to have been paramount. The first four—all related to their work as educators—included the desire to instill in their students racial pride, self-respect, Christian beliefs and behaviors, and "civilized" values and actions. Those teachers in

18. *Minutes of the American Association of Educators of Colored Youth, 1895*, 9–10, 24–26.
19. Ibid., 9, 12, 13, 25–26.

post-secondary education concentrated on training their students for "practical occupations," introducing them to the liberal arts, and preparing them for racial leadership and uplift. An eighth goal— one related to teachers' own well-being—was the establishment and expansion of the prestige, rewards, and influence of black teachers in the South. One of the clearest statements of the last goal was a report endorsed by the 1894 AAECY meeting:

> It is the sense of this Association that where there are separate colored public schools, in the appointment of teachers for such schools the preference should be given to efficient colored teachers. . . . and where there are mixed schools there should be no discrimination in the appointment of teachers for such schools solely on the ground of color, and that all appointments should be tried by the same rules and judged by the same standards.[20]

Racial pride, the conviction that people of African origins had distinctive positive characteristics, as well as the same capacities as whites, had been identified as early as the 1850s by many black teachers in the North as a key component in the education of black youth. As numbers of northern black teachers went south to become educational missionaries following the Civil War, for many this conviction was a prime tenet. Martin R. Delaney, a black physician and Civil War veteran, used his position as an officer of the Freedmen's Bureau in South Carolina to encourage black teachers and students "to put their faith in themselves rather than whites." When Charlotte Forten, a member of a distinguished northern black family, went south to be an educational missionary, she made the inculcation of racial pride a major component of her teaching, using the Haitian insurrectionist Toussaint L'Ouverture and other blacks who resisted enslavement as historical models for her students. And the African Civilization Society, the leading northern black aid organization for former slaves, stressed the importance of ensuring that southern blacks were taught to take pride in themselves and their race, in addition to modeling it by the employment of black teachers only in an effort to "prove the complete fitness of the educated negro . . . to teach and lead his own race." Yet the teaching of race pride was also done by numbers of white instructors and by white authors of textbooks for Negroes,

20. Ibid., 27.

members of both groups believing it to be an indispensable part of the education of former slaves who were now free Americans.[21]

The efforts of black teachers "to develop self-respect" in their students constituted an assault on slave culture's legacy of sexual permissiveness, casual work habits, individual and communal boisterousness, and its discouragement of frugality and delayed gratification. This was a large part of what was meant by teachers' injunctions to those in their classrooms to live quiet, respectable, sober lives for their own benefit and to raise the race in the estimation of whites. Most black teachers, like most of their white colleagues, sought by injunction and example to instill in their charges values that would set them on the road to "respectability," as defined by nineteenth-century European American society, and to cultivate in them behavior conducive to success in a competitive economic order.

In both academic and industrial schools, as well as colleges for Negroes, a strict Victorian code of behavior prevailed, whether the faculty was predominantly black or mainly white. Students were discouraged from all forms of unsupervised association between females and males. Dress, language, and manners that deviated from a "genteel," "Christian" norm were both unacceptable and grounds for dismissal. Specific injunctions against gambling, alcoholic beverages, tobacco, and firearms were standard. Fraternization between individual teachers and students was forbidden. The rigidity of these norms was reflected in the response of Tuskegee Institute's dean of women to a suggestion in 1902 by Booker T. Washington, the school's founder, that female students be allowed to dance with each other as a form of exercise and training in deportment. Arguing that to do so would lead to a breakdown of order, the dean successfully quashed the idea. Such rules were also in force at white schools and colleges during this period. But in black schools the need of teachers, administrators, and students to demonstrate the capacity of those enrolled for "civilization," of which education was considered to be only one component, added to their intensity.[22]

---

21. Butchart, *Northern Schools, Southern Blacks, and Reconstruction*, 70; *The Journals of Charlotte Forten*, ed. Brenda Stevenson, 397–98; Morris, *Reading, 'Riting, and Reconstruction*, 9, 116, 199; *National Freedman*, February 15, 1866.

22. Louis R. Harlan, *Booker T. Washington, The Wizard of Tuskegee, 1901–1915*, 115–57; Gilmore, *Gender and Jim Crow*, 41–42.

Laundering: Kowaliga School, 1909. Rockefeller Archive Center.

Several forces impelled black teachers to stress the crucial role of Christian beliefs in the education of their students. Many were themselves devout Christians who believed that their ability to achieve in a racist society was directly traceable to the "hand of God" and fidelity to "Divine Will." Northern white denominations and religious aid societies, black denominations, and southern black congregations were in the forefront of those organizations establishing, funding, and staffing educational institutions for former slaves, an involvement that gave them, for much of the late nineteenth and early twentieth centuries, a major role in the selection of the blacks who taught in schools for Negroes. It is not surprising, therefore, that educational institutions established at the initiative of churches and missionary societies should often have drawn into their service blacks who took religious beliefs seriously, frequently infusing these beliefs into every aspect of the educational and social life of their schools.[23]

23. Morris, *Reading, 'Riting, and Reconstruction,* 1–2, 86; Richardson, *Christian Reconstruction.* See Francis Louis Cardozo to George Whipple, October 21, 1865, F. L. Cardozo Papers, Amistad Center, Tulane University.

Few black teachers employed the term "civilization" when discussing their work, but their regular identification of moral and spiritual uplift as a basic educational need of former slaves indicated a belief that the "civilization" of American blacks was one of their main concerns. The concepts of "civilized" and "uncivilized" societies had been shaped and defined by white thinkers in Europe and the United States, many of whom argued that people of African descent were incapable of civilization.[24] The particular understanding, however, that African American educators brought to the term was shaped by the discourse of nineteenth-century black intellectuals, particularly the ideas and writings of Alexander Crummell (1819–1898), who used it to assert the potential of the "Negro race" and as an incentive to blacks to adopt selectively the best of "Western civilization."

In a series of books, pamphlets, lectures, and sermons that deeply influenced the thinking of literate nineteenth-century blacks, Crummell identified the highest forms of civilization as embodied in the cultural, political, and religious institutions, beliefs, and behaviors of Europeans, especially English-speaking white Protestants in Great Britain and the United States. For much of the nineteenth century and the first decade of the twentieth century, such ideas were common currency in the African American community and constituted bedrock convictions among black teachers, many of whom believed, as Crummell stated in one of his best-known published works, that "civilization" was "the primal need of the [Negro] race." Such ideas, which Wilson J. Moses usefully describes as "civilizationism," integrated several goals of black teachers, including racial pride, self-respect, and the need for Christian beliefs, values, and actions.[25]

By the last two decades of the nineteenth century, black teachers in the South were using Crummell's interpretation of civilization and loosely evolutionary ideas to argue "that in the struggle for life only the fittest survived and they and other blacks who educated themselves were assuming the important responsibility of 'making the weakest struggle successfully so as to become the fittest.'" Many of these ideas

24. George Frederickson, *The Black Image in the White Mind: The Debate on Afro-American Character and Destiny, 1817–1914*, 98–102, 228–55.

25. Wilson Jeremiah Moses, *The Golden Age of Black Nationalism, 1850–1925*, 201–21, 59–82, 84–85; William Jeremiah Moses, *Alexander Crummell: A Study of Civilization and Discontent*, 97, 132–33, 262–63.

were embodied in the "talented tenth" theories of W. E. B. Du Bois, who in the 1890s and the first decades of the twentieth century stressed the preeminent role of educated blacks in promoting the advancement of their people. As the number of educated blacks grew, Du Bois believed, so also in direct proportion did his race's prospects for social and economic advancement. Another equally influential proponent of civilizationism was the black educator Booker T. Washington, who believed African Americans who committed themselves to an ethic of hard work, investment, and self-improvement soon left behind the debilitating effects of the race's slave past.[26]

The emphasis among educated blacks on training members of their race for practical occupations preceded the Civil War. As early as the 1830s the various national conventions of free blacks in the North called for a program of training in the skilled trades for Negroes, which they envisioned as the best way to promote the development of a business class able to support itself independent of the white community. The original educational concept can be traced to antebellum white abolitionists and educational reformers who believed that "manual-labor schools" were ideally suited for the lower classes, black and white. Persuaded by these theories, black teachers in the South, along with most of their white colleagues, were convinced for almost fifty years after the Civil War that for the majority of African Americans training in the skilled trades, artisanship, and "efficient scientific agricultural methods" would provide the tools for economic mobility. Vocational training was seen by those who taught blacks as the way to provide their students an economic alternative to "Negro work," i.e., poorly paid jobs in domestic service, unskilled labor, and the crude farming most southern blacks had learned in slavery.[27]

Francis Cardozo, W. E. B. Du Bois, and Anna J. Cooper, however, were typical of black teachers who insisted that, in addition to vocational courses, their students had to be taught the liberal arts. These teachers stressed the importance of a classical or liberal arts curriculum in black schools as the means of ensuring that the most intellectually

26. *North Carolina Teachers Association, Proceedings of the 20th Annual Session Held at Kittrell College, Kittrell, North Carolina. June 12, 13, 14, 15, 16, 17,* 1901, 25–26; August Meier, *Negro Thought in America, 1880–1915,* 100–118, 103, 117, 97–98; Moses, *Alexander Crummell,* 292–93.
27. August Meier and Elliott Rudwick, *From Plantation to Ghetto,* 126–27.

able students received the same kind of higher education provided at the best white schools, colleges, and universities.[28]

By the end of the nineteenth century, these trends had produced elementary and secondary schools for blacks that combined vocational training with lessons in basic reading, writing, and mathematics. In the institutions that conducted college-level education, a vocational program often existed alongside a liberal arts program. For most of the period 1865 to 1902, schools for blacks offered some variant of this mixed curriculum. The sharp and acrimonious debate waged by W. E. B. Du Bois and Booker T. Washington from 1903 to 1915 over what constituted an appropriate education for the masses of Negroes symbolized a disagreement that in some degree affected every southern black educational institution in the late nineteenth and early twentieth centuries. Sometimes this issue was engaged with great intensity locally, surfacing in the form of a power struggle between a school's administration, faculty, and local supporters on one side and its white benefactors on the other. At other times the struggle was between various factions of all these groups. Three examples from the period 1890–1910 make the point.

Avery Institute in Charleston, South Carolina, established in 1868 by the American Missionary Association (AMA) and from its earliest days a college preparatory and normal school, became a flash point in this struggle after 1883. Paying lip service to the growing force of industrial education theories, Avery's administrators introduced courses in stenography and bookkeeping. No offerings, however, appeared in the catalogue for woodworking, bricklaying, farming, housekeeping, sewing, or the like, standard courses at industrial education flagships Hampton and Tuskegee. Avery's "classical tradition was not abandoned . . . but . . . modified and enlarged to fit the changing times." In 1890 when the AMA "mandated industrial education at all its schools . . . Avery complied by renovating a separate building to house an industrial department and by requiring that all of its students have some kind of industrial training." Black trustees, faculty, and alumni,

28. Morris, *Reading, 'Riting, and Reconstruction*, 157–72; Meier, *Negro Thought*, 85–99; Cynthia Griggs Fleming, "The Plight of Black Educators in Postwar Tennessee, 1865–1920," 358–60; Anna J. Cooper, "The Ethics of the Negro Question, Delivered at the Bi-ennial Session of Friends General Conference at Asbury Park, New Jersey, September 5, 1902" in Anna Julia Cooper Papers, Moorland-Spingarn Research Center; Anna J. Cooper, *A Voice from the South*; Paul Phillips Cooke, "Anna J. Cooper," 12–13.

reflecting strong sentiment in Charleston's African American community, employed these maneuvers in their successful effort to maintain the school's college preparatory and teacher training curriculum.[29]

In a struggle with a different outcome, Fort Valley High and Industrial School in Georgia's black belt was transformed from "a good liberal arts secondary and normal school for the training of black teachers" to a Hampton-Tuskegee style of industrial school. John W. Davison, the black who founded the school in 1895 and was its first principal from 1895 to 1904, attempted to maintain a mixed academic-vocational school curriculum with the greater emphasis on the academic program. By 1900 he was being pressured by the northern white industrialists on his trustee board to make Fort Valley an institution devoted to industrial education. Similar pressures also came from the officers of the Rockefeller-financed General Education Board (GEB), who left the impression that such a shift would bring Fort Valley substantial and much-needed funding from the GEB. In an effort to please the trustees, the GEB, and his original supporters in the local community, Davison introduced various industrial education programs while preserving the old curriculum. What he did, however, was convince the advocates of industrial education he was making cosmetic changes in an effort to attract funds that he would divert to the school's liberal arts program. With the local black community only able to contribute tiny sums, in 1904 Davison resigned to ensure the survival of the school, leaving the way open for his critics on the trustee board, working in cooperation with the GEB, to select a new principal whose philosophy of education was more in accord with theirs.[30]

In Southern Virginia the resourceful black Episcopal clergyman James Solomon Russell—shrewdly shifting his public posture from accommodationist to assertive race leader as it suited his purposes—shaped the development of St. Paul's Normal and Industrial School, which he founded in 1888. Russell's original intent was to establish a college that provided liberal arts education and vocational training, but he altered his plans in the face of prevailing trends. To placate local whites and encourage contributions from agencies and individuals

---

29. Edmund L. Drago, *Initiative, Paternalism, and Race Relations: Charleston's Avery Normal Institute*, 84–85, 94–95.
30. Anderson, *The Education of Blacks in the South*, 114–21.

advocating industrial education for Negroes, he "carefully avoided highlighting liberal arts," while ensuring that "every student learned a trade and received a basic liberal arts education." Between 1906 and 1914, Russell successfully fought off repeated attempts by the American Church Institute for Negroes (ACIN), his predominantly white denomination's national funding agency for black Episcopal schools and colleges, to wrest control of St. Paul's from him. ACIN efforts to reduce Russell to a figurehead derived from the white director's and the all-white ACIN board's doubts about the genuineness of the minister's commitment to industrial education and their low regard for his administrative abilities. Russell was so skillful, however, in fending off his detractors that he remained head of the school until his retirement in 1929. Under his leadership St. Paul's produced numbers of graduates who went on to become "successful farmers, teachers, businessmen, and clergy."[31]

Along with vocational training and the liberal arts, education for racial leadership and uplift of the black masses constituted the third major emphasis and concern of most black teachers. Charles N. Grandison, a black clergyman and educator from Delaware, declared the promotion of "Negro political liberty" to be one of his race's educational goals; "God never elevated a slave people," he added. According to Kelly Miller, professor of mathematics at Howard University, the goals of education were "to plant the seeds of intelligence" and to "produce leaders."[32] Repeatedly, during the years 1865–1902, black teachers at all educational levels stressed the necessity of cultivating students who through action and word would be leaders in defending black Americans and improving their situation.

Black teachers also took a healthy self-interest in their own well-being, seeking individually and through professional associations to promote, in both the black and white communities of the South, respect for themselves as professionals. They also sought to provide information to each other on employment opportunities, social networks,

---

31. James Solomon Russell, *Adventure in Faith: An Autobiographic Story of St. Paul's Normal and Industrial School, Lawrenceville, Virginia and James S. Russell, Founder*, 31–51, 82–87, 104; J. Carleton Hayden, "James Solomon Russell (1857–1935): Missionary and Founder of St. Paul's College," 10–11; Frances A. Thurman, "The History of St. Paul's College, Lawrenceville, Virginia, 1888–1959," 82–125, 178.

32. *Minutes of the American Association of Educators of Colored Youth*, 1895, 9–10, 13–15.

and continuing education experiences.[33] During the disfranchisement movement of the 1890s, with its patterns of increasingly restrictive legal segregation, widespread violence against blacks, and wholesale disparagement of educated blacks by leaders of the white South, some black teachers joined other elite African Americans in attempting to turn racist reasoning to their benefit. In several southern states, as political campaigns to deny blacks the right to vote moved toward victory, a number of black teachers supported a limited suffrage based on education. They believed that, in a rigidly segregated South, this change would enhance the prestige of black teachers, who expected to pass an educational test easily and thus claim the right to vote. Some black teachers hoped this not only would assert their worth and the potential of uneducated members of their race but also would be a clear assertion of their superiority over poor whites, whose access to the ballot box came not through merit but through the machinations of white supremacist politicians.[34] The success of southern white politicians in eliminating virtually all black votes proved them wrong.

When, in 1897, forty prominent black intellectuals formed the American Negro Academy, the new organization's goals included a commitment "to aid youth of genius in the attainment of the higher culture, at home or abroad." The ANA, formed, led, and supported by African Americans who encouraged scholarship and learning among their people, committed itself to strengthening the intellectual life of the black community to "insure that henceforth arguments advanced by 'cultured despisers' of their race were refuted or at the very least challenged."[35]

These educational goals were articulated in several lively discussions at the initial meeting of the society. Speaking in support of an ANA-funded scholarship for exceptional blacks, Crummell proposed "an annual survey of the various colleges and university campuses to discover students who could profitably be sent abroad for further study." He believed black men and women whose education was enhanced by study at centers of learning outside the United States

33. For two significant examples, see *The Memphis Diary of Ida B. Wells: An Intimate Portrait of the Activist as a Young Woman*, ed. Miriam Decosta-Willis, and *The Journals of Charles W. Chesnutt*, ed. Richard Brodhead.

34. For two careful discussions of these dynamics see Fleming, "The Plight of Black Educators in Postwar Tennessee," and Haley, *Charles N. Hunter*.

35. Moss, *American Negro Academy*, 2.

had the potential to elevate the intellectual climate of the Negro community and expand its resources for countering racist ideas. It was equally important, Crummell argued, that the costs of their studies be paid for by a black organization such as the American Negro Academy. In a related discussion on the quality of colleges for blacks and the adequacy of the financial resources available to them, W. E. B. Du Bois expressed the opinion that sufficient resources existed for the "development of 'Negro intellect,' but they were 'dissipated' by being scattered among so many small, poor schools none of which could afford to do first class work. Put this money into one institution, he urged, and something significant can be done."[36]

The comments of Crummell and Du Bois, laying out principles endorsed by most of the founding members of the society, pointed the Academy toward the creation of an educational foundation controlled by blacks, with resources sufficient to contribute financially to the education of the most promising of their race and to influence the educational policies of the schools that existed for African Americans. Barely able to sustain itself for the thirty-one years it existed, the ANA would never garner the financial resources needed to pursue successfully these educational goals.

The members of the American Negro Academy also took a forth-right position in the rancorous debate between proponents of industrial and academic education for blacks. William S. Scarborough, a classics scholar and founding member, spoke for them in his essay, "The Educated Negro and His Mission," published by the society in 1903 as its eighth occasional paper. That same year *The Souls of Black Folk*, written by Du Bois, president of the Academy, appeared. Du Bois's chapter three, "Of Mr. Booker T. Washington and Others," offered a blistering indictment of Washington as a tool of racist whites whose educational and political "programme practically accepts the alleged inferiority of the Negro races." Scarborough's article, in effect an official statement of the ANA, did not mention the principal of Tuskegee Institute, but it was equally uncompromising in its opposition to the growing popularity of industrial training as the panacea for black education.[37]

36. Ibid., 42, 48.
37. William S. Scarborough, *The Educated Negro and His Mission*; Du Bois, *Souls of Black Folk*, 48, 42–54.

Scarborough conceded that some blacks needed "manual educa-tion" but used the greater part of the essay to warn that industrial education threatened continued growth in the number of educated Negroes equipped with the knowledge and understanding necessary "to lead and . . . influence" their race "to live better lives . . . to get the most and best out of life." Voicing the concerns of many black community leaders, teachers, and intellectuals, he argued that Negro institutions of higher education, the training centers for the race's future leaders and scholars, were in danger of being "abandoned." Perhaps, Scarborough speculated, the fear is that African Americans "may go too far—excel or equal the Anglo-Saxon—and that fear is prime motive in the minds of many who seek to hedge the onward path of the race."[38]

For Scarborough and the membership of the ANA, continued and expanded black access to higher education was crucial to the well-being of the African American community and that of the United States. Black college and university graduates were a "reforming" force for the world's "betterment" because of their ability to provide enlightened race leadership in the effort to improve the quality of black life in rural communities and urban ghettos, to check vice, and to fight political corruption. This same group also produced the small but growing body of black scholars such as Scarborough, Du Bois, and other members of the Academy whose efforts promoted the "civilization" of the black masses. "No," Scarborough concluded,

> The race is in no danger of going "college mad." . . . the early schools [of higher education for Negroes] . . . were generally established upon the broad university plan, yet their work has been largely basic; and they have done far more in laying foundations than in producing a surplus of graduates. . . . It is an absurdity to claim there can be too many of the race with learning enough and discipline enough to make themselves useful leaders.[39]

Despite the widely publicized debate between Washington and Du Bois over the best type of education for African Americans, there was general agreement among the majority of black intellectuals as to the need for the availability of both vocational ("industrial") and liberal arts (referred to variously as "academic," "classical," and "collegiate") education for black men and women. Most agreed with

38. Scarborough, "The Educated Negro," 3, 4, 7, 8–9, 10.
39. Ibid., 4, 5, 7, 8–9.

Washington that vocational education stressing the willingness and ability of students to work with their hands built character. Indeed, this was a message that Frederick Douglass and Alexander Crummell had sounded before the Civil War.[40] Both men also believed that an academic education—as opposed to industrial education—produced individuals with the kind of personal discipline that allowed the intellect to rule the emotions, thus promoting in these persons the ability to exercise legitimate authority through leadership, as well as to respond to the directions of others who were exercising legitimate authority.

Even Du Bois agreed with Washington's proposition that "industrial education" met the practical needs of the black masses for the foreseeable future. His opposition to the proliferation of schools that were clones of Hampton and Tuskegee arose from the conviction that these kinds of institutions were useless in preparing the most talented and able African Americans for the intellectual tasks they would face as leaders and defenders of the race. Du Bois and those who shared his opinions sought through their attacks on industrial education to preserve the more balanced perspective of earlier leaders such as Douglass and Crummell. John W. Cromwell, a strong supporter of Du Bois and a teacher and journalist, put it this way: "The great work of black education has two focuses: first to eliminate illiteracy and, second, to counter the 'absence of a spirit of independence in the Negro.'"[41]

African American leaders early recognized that the poverty of their people was a great obstacle to efforts to create and sustain schools, colleges, and universities to meet the needs of their race. This reality threatened the survival and sometimes compromised the quality of the schools established by the black churches and local black

40. For Frederick Douglass's views, see his editorials in *Frederick Douglass's Paper* in March 1853; *The Frederick Douglass Papers*, ed. John W. Blassingame, vol. 2, 443; and William S. McFeeley, *Frederick Douglass*, 359, 363. For Crummell's views, see the following writings: "The Necessities and Advantages of Education Considered in Relation to Colored Men," 1844, in the Crummell Papers, Schomburg Research Center of the New York Public Library; "The Destined Superiority of the Negro," 1881, in *The Greatness of Christ and Other Sermons*, 382–402; and "Common Sense in Common Schooling," 1886, in *Africa and America*, 350–54.

41. See Du Bois, "A Rational System of Negro Education," W. E. B. Du Bois Papers, University of Massachusetts at Amherst, Files for 1897–1900; Du Bois, ed., *The College-Bred Negro*, 29. [John Wesley Cromwell], "The Virginia Normal and Collegiate Institute—A Brief Sketch of the Summer Session," [Alexandria, Virginia] *Peoples Advocate*, September 11, 1886 in Scrapbook 2, John Mercer Langston Papers, Moorland-Spingarn Research Center.

communities. It also weakened the force of black demands for a larger role in the operation of white-established educational institutions for Negroes. In response, numerous black leaders issued appeals from 1865 to 1902 for "sacrificial giving" in support of schools by all members of the race, especially the more affluent and those with steady incomes. In 1875 an article in the *Christian Recorder*, an organ of the African Methodist Episcopal Church, discussed pointedly the difficulties created by the scarcity of black philanthropists. While acknowledging that it would have been an honor to African Americans if John Mercer Langston had been appointed president of Howard University, the writer of the piece was certain Langston's selection would not have increased giving by blacks to the school. Indeed, the appointment might have been a step backward for Howard, leading to less white giving and no increase in black support, for "colored men of means show very little heart in the matter of giving to educational institutions." Twenty years later, delegates to the 1895 meeting of the Association of Educators of Colored Youth expressed the same opinion. In their "Address to the Public," however, they sought to counter it with a declaration that the tools of black educational advancement were now in the hands of those members of the race who were accumulating wealth, thus giving them the means for providing adequate support for black educational institutions. There is no evidence that this and similar statements produced an increase in black contributions to schools.[42]

Despite the inability of African Americans to finance their schools generously, blacks contributed $25 million during the years 1865 to 1915 to educational institutions. Over the same time span northern philanthropic sources provided $57 million.[43] Those schools most drastically undernourished financially were the ones largely dependent on the black community. As a consequence, throughout this period the black schools considered generally the best or most prestigious were those supported by whites. Thus, the black community was doubly victimized by its poverty in that it was too poor to support adequately the educational institutions controlled by black organizations and unable to gain control of the white-run institutions judged its best schools.

42. A.M.E. *Christian Recorder*, July 1, 1875; *Minutes of the American Association of Educators of Colored Youth, 1895*, 24–26.
43. Monroe N. Work, ed., *The Negro Yearbook, 1915*, 235.

George William Cook, dean of Howard University's commercial department, was one of the leading members of the African American community who labored during the late nineteenth and early twentieth centuries to remedy this situation. In words repeated on almost every occasion when he had the opportunity to address members of the black upper classes, he declared: "When along with the request for preferment will come endowment; when the black philanthropist can with a princely gift turn an unpopulated district into a center of learning; when Negro wealth can make benefactions like those of Peabody and Slater, then honest demands will have more weight."[44]

A related though distinct hope of many blacks who thought, wrote, and talked about "Negro education" was the desire to ensure that black educational institutions were anchors and stimulants for the economic life of the African American communities in which they were situated, particularly those in rural areas. James T. Gregory, another black Howard University professor who, like Cook, constantly preached the "gospel of Negro education," repeatedly assured black audiences that property near black schools was among the most valuable in their communities. The same certainty provided considerable motivation for T. S. Inborden, an enterprising black who founded North Carolina's Brick Industrial School in 1902. Toward the end of his career, Inborden would recall, with a sense of accomplishment, that

> When the Brick School began, there was not a single Negro owning land within five miles of the institution. Now every piece of land . . . adjacent to Brick School is owned by Negroes. There are thirteen of them who own their farms of various sizes from 150 acres down to a city lot. These farms are occupied by people who were influenced to come here by Brick School activities and attitudes.[45]

The black agenda for education, as of 1902, could almost be summarized as consistent opposition to the idea of a distinct and separate black agenda for black education. Although black leaders had high expectations for education—and recognized the special need of a group long denied education—they persistently rejected the idea that

44. McPherson, *Abolitionist Legacy*, 268; Cook, "Money Our Need," n.d., in George William Cook Papers, Moorland-Spingarn Research Center.
45. *Minutes of the Association of Educators of Colored Youth, 1895*, 13; Inborden, "History of Brick School" (Typescript, 1934), Perkins Library, Duke University.

African Americans required white teachers or a unique curriculum. Much of the educational development of the years between 1865 and 1902 was a matter of blacks insisting that their education follow national standards, not excluding blacks from leadership nor implementing curricular experiments disdained in white schools.

The African American desire for more black teachers and administrators steadily advanced during the late nineteenth century. The fact that blacks were moving toward the majority among post-primary teachers in the 1890s—they outnumbered whites in this field by 1906—and expanding their numbers in post-secondary education at the same time, made issues of control and representation particularly critical at the time the General Education Board was formed in 1902.

Despite their difficult cooperation in some areas, black and white educators were in agreement on certain fundamental issues. Most shared the belief that the building of "Christian character" was a central part of education. There was strong consensus that black students had the right and ability to participate in the advanced culture of the English-speaking world. Their success in mastering this culture or "civilization," as it was often termed, was deemed a refutation of hostile critics of the Negro race. Teachers of both races in black schools were agreed that a highly trained elite was essential to the progress of any group, though there were differences between both black and white teachers and among black educators as to how large that elite should or could be. From 1865 to 1902 black and white teachers accepted industrial education of some sort as part of the schooling of the black masses. Debates on this subject, before and after the clash between supporters of Washington and Du Bois, centered on the relative mix of classical and industrial elements in the curriculum. All involved in black education were convinced by 1902 that the disconnected but overlapping system of private and public schools and colleges for Negroes lacked organization, was wasteful, and needed direction. Neither blacks nor whites disputed there were too few—not too many—genuinely learned people among African Americans. Teachers of both races believed that African Americans needed to do more in the way of self-help, that black students ought to be made aware of distinctive positive characteristics of their group—though there were often different perspectives on what those characteristics were—and that education was a means of challenging and transforming the legacy of slave culture.

2

Ogdenism and Its Enemies

We must earnestly desire to disarm all criticism, intelligent or ignorant. . . . I am gladly willing to adapt policy to prejudice, upon the principle of St. Paul, "All things to all men if thereby some may be saved from ignorance."

—Robert C. Ogden[1]

In the first six decades after Emancipation, schooling for black southerners was always a matter of some controversy. In periods of crisis, such as the beginning of Reconstruction or the era of white supremacy excess in the early twentieth century, zealots were ready to turn access to common education into an explosive political issue, even a dangerous sign of black assertion. At other times, when there were fewer open challenges to black education, there was a persistent undercurrent of resentment and resistance on the part of at least a significant minority of whites. The "naked truth," according to Tar Heel editor Josephus Daniels, was that much of the money appropriated for Negro education was "given against the judgment of Southern taxpayers."[2]

Speaking among themselves, supporters of black education admitted the challenge of developing "right thinking among white people in the South." At almost any point between 1865 and 1925, one can find some educational crusader, white or black, northern or southern, making comments similar to those of Methodist clergyman Atticus G. Haygood in the 1880s. Writing to his friend Rutherford B. Hayes, Haygood compared his work as agent of the Slater Fund for black education to the slow, arduous work of "draining the Everglades of

1. Robert C. Ogden to Charles W. Dabney, January 4, 1902, in Dabney Collection, Southern Education Papers, Southern Historical Collection, University of North Carolina, Chapel Hill.
2. *Proceedings of the Conference for Education in the South, the Sixth Session,* 143–44.

Florida." Assuming that destroying useless wetlands was a form of progress, Haygood wrote to former President Hayes: "There is much to do before sugar cane will grow where lagoons now cover the earth." He argued, as most of his successors in educational philanthropy for the South would also argue, that only the most cautious and patient methods could be used to promote black education. "My work seems so slow," he wrote, "but there is no other way. This work must take *root* in the South—& in Southern white consciences—Else, some day, it will die."[3]

Black education, and anyone who supported it, came under particularly strong attack after 1900, as the white South sought to enforce white supremacy and segregation in all areas of life. In response to this crisis in race relations, northern philanthropists were forced to consider a new approach to the South. The familiar phrases about the importance of tact and caution took on added urgency, of course, in an environment of increasing southern white intransigence and fading northern interest in "the Negro question" and other vestiges of Reconstruction. But more importantly, key northern leaders began to challenge the policy of focusing northern philanthropy upon black education. Beginning about 1900, a new group of philanthropic leaders developed a strategy for changing the South—and sought to impose this strategy on all supporters of African American education.

Though they have often been accused, then and now, of capitulating to southern racism, or, even worse, enthusiastically sharing in it, the new educational philanthropists were definitely committed to the idea of reforming the South.[4] They believed that the status quo was not only unjust but also a deadly threat to the future security and prosperity of the whole nation. Yet the old ways of promoting black education, the supposedly outmoded methods of the neoabolitionist

3. Haygood to Hayes, February 5, 1885, and January 12, 1887, in Louis D. Rubin, Jr., ed., *Teach the Freeman: The Correspondence of Rutherford B. Hayes and the Slater Fund for Negro Education, 1881–1887*, vol. 1, 133, 191.

4. Louis R. Harlan describes the philanthropists as "yielding reluctantly to the superior power of the White Supremacy movement." Harlan, *Separate and Unequal: Public School Campaigns and Racism in the Southern Seaboard States, 1901–1915*, 97. James D. Anderson claims that the northern philanthropists were "white supremacists themselves," as committed to the goal of a "second-class education to prepare blacks for subordinate roles" as the so-called extreme racists of the South. Anderson, *The Education of Blacks in the South*, 80, 92.

Protestant missionary societies, would only make matters worse. In the future, they asserted, the growth of black education must be tied to the expansion of white education—an idea that, in many minds, quickly degenerated into the notion that white educational needs must be met *before* black needs. Those who really wished to change the South, the argument ran, should learn to work with white southerners of goodwill and moderation to mitigate the power of ill-informed extremists. Only with the help of this minority of fair-minded southern whites could northern educational reformers effectively make the case that black education was in the long-term interest of all southerners, white as well as black. Patient, calm appeals to common sense and the mutual benefits of economic growth would be more effective in building support for black education, the reformers assumed, than "sentimental" or idealistic arguments based on the rights of man or human brotherhood.

The new philanthropists recognized that black leaders would probably be disappointed with the slow pace of progress, as well as the new emphasis on white education, but considered their criticisms less important, under the circumstances, than the views of the "best whites." As Robert C. Ogden, one of the most influential northern friends of Negro education, put it, "We cannot meet the views of our colored friends and must be content to be greatly misunderstood for the sake of the largest usefulness."[5]

With crucial support from northern donors and promoters, the South experienced a remarkable "educational revival" between 1901 and 1915, complete with emotional public evangelism, sweeping promises of social renewal, and specific legislative action to support and reorganize public schools. By 1920 federal census statisticians found evidence of dramatic change. Though the region still lagged behind the nation, every southern state sharply increased its spending on education, extended school terms, and cut illiteracy rates. In North Carolina, for example, from 1900 to 1920, white illiteracy fell from about 19 percent of the population ten years of age and older to 8 percent. The percentage of black illiterates dropped almost as quickly, from 48 percent to approximately 25 percent. Public school expenditures per pupil increased more than ninefold in two decades,

5. Robert C. Ogden to Oswald Garrison Villard, March 10, 1905, in Oswald Garrison Villard Papers, Houghton Library, Harvard University.

and the average school term nearly doubled. Even in Mississippi, where per pupil spending was the lowest in the region in 1920, school statistics showed striking progress, with per pupil spending increasing by 247 percent and black illiteracy falling by 40 percent.[6]

The symbolic leader of the educational revival was Ogden. Merchant and philanthropist, friend and admirer of both Samuel C. Armstrong, the white founder of Hampton Institute, and Armstrong's protegé Booker T. Washington, Ogden served as a trustee of Hampton and Tuskegee, vigorously supporting the ideal of "character-building" industrial education for black southerners. Ogden's interest in Negro education led him to a wider interest in the problems of the whole South, which, he came to believe, sorely needed Armstrong's educational philosophy. Though he attended only one of the three annual Capon Springs Conferences on Christian Education in the South, Ogden was elected president of this organization in absentia in 1900. Even before he took command, the Capon Springs educators were moving in a direction of which he approved. The 1898 conference had recommended that "Industrial Education" be "encouraged in all schools," white as well as black. Each of three conferences expressed concern about the need for coordinating giving for black schools, so that donations might not be wasted on "worthless enterprises." The 1899 conference called for "a general committee of direction . . . to guard against the haphazard, and in some cases harmful, use of money contributed at the North for negro education." Already these friends of black education had concluded that "the education of the white race in the South is the pressing and imperative need."[7]

Under Ogden's leadership, the Capon Springs Conference dropped the word "Christian" from its name, emphasized public education over private schools, and scheduled its annual meeting for a different southern city each year. Ogden helped to draw attention to southern

6. Dewey W. Grantham, *Southern Progressivism: The Reconciliation of Progress and Tradition*, 248–53, 256–58.

7. On Ogden, see "Robert Curtis Ogden," *Dictionary of American Biography*; Philip Whitwell Wilson, *An Unofficial Statesman—Robert C. Ogden*; Ralph E. Luker, *The Social Gospel in Black and White: American Racial Reform, 1885–1912*, 125–28, 144–58; Harlan, *Separate and Unequal*, 74–83. Quotes are from *Proceedings of the First Capon Springs Conference on Christian Education in the South*, 1898, 35; *Proceedings of the Second Capon Springs Conference for Christian Education in the South*, 1899, 7–8; *Proceedings of the Third Capon Springs Conference for Christian Education in the South*, 1900, 6.

education with a brilliant publicity stunt: he invited a group of fifty wealthy and influential northerners to accompany him on a railway excursion through the South, visiting white and black schools in order to see the needs of the region firsthand. Chartering "as elaborate a special train as the Pennsylvania Railroad could supply," Ogden spent about twenty-five thousand dollars from his own pocket. In 1901, Ogden's luxurious train included among its passengers John D. Rockefeller, Jr.; William Henry Baldwin, Jr., president of the Long Island Railroad; Georgia-born Wall Street financier George Foster Peabody; editor Walter Hines Page, a transplanted North Carolinian; and leading social gospel advocates the Rev. Charles H. Parkhurst of New York, Professor Francis Greenwood Peabody of Harvard, and Lyman Abbott, editor of *Outlook*.[8]

These annual railway trips, which Ogden continued to sponsor until 1906, are a good illustration of his leadership style. Never the intellectual leader of the education revival nor a really large-scale donor, Ogden was a courtly promoter and impresario, a genius at bringing together donors and educators, idealists and practical men of affairs. He had a knack for focusing public attention upon a problem, though he had no detailed program for solving it. John D. Rockefeller, Jr., a young man "only four years out of college," remembered the 1901 excursion years later as "one of the outstanding events in my life." As a result of this trip, the younger Rockefeller helped organize the General Education Board a few months later. Though he and his father had originally been thinking of establishing a Negro Education Board, the discussions on Ogden's excursion led the young man to conclude "that an educational program geared to the needs of a particular race, would represent an unfortunate and perhaps impossible approach."[9]

For both friends and critics, it seemed perfectly appropriate to speak of the educational revival as "the Ogden movement" or, less respectfully, "Ogdenism." Ogden and his associates were so eager to promote consensus and cooperation that their public statements were often bland and platitudinous, much like the pronouncements of diplomats after a "full and frank discussion" between suspicious

---

8. Wilson, *An Unofficial Statesman*, 205; Luker, *The Social Gospel in Black and White*, 147–48; Fosdick et al., *Adventure in Giving*, 4–8.

9. Fosdick et al., *Adventure in Giving*, 7–8.

Booker T. Washington and distinguished guests, including Robert C. Ogden (to the left of Washington) and Andrew Carnegie (to the right of Washington). Division of Photographs and Prints, Library of Congress.

rivals. On the basis of the Ogden movement's public positions, it is easy to dismiss Ogden as a thinker of "the Sunday School type," a "philosopher of sunny faces and well-filled bellies," as historian John Spencer Bassett did in 1907. "He has no more concept of what the South needs than that he knows the situation is happy when men like one another," Bassett commented in a letter to a fellow historian.[10] But if the Ogden movement really stood for little more than the idea that education was a Good Thing, historians would be hard put to explain why anyone would oppose it.

Yet "Ogdenism" had bitter enemies, and their opposition reveals much about the movement. In fact, a careful study of the opponents of the Ogden movement is essential to understanding the ideas and tactics of northern philanthropy in the South. Using loose, polemical shorthand, many influential southern voices, white and black, attacked "Ogdenism"—meaning the whole interlocking directorate of calculating altruism clustered around the person of Robert Ogden and the money of the Rockefeller family, including the Southern Education Board, the Conference for Education in the South, and the General Education Board. The opposition also touched other foundations, especially the Carnegie Foundation, and occasionally struck the long-established northern missionary societies. In its vigor and anger this opposition was, according to historian James W. Patton, "comparable in some respects to the [white] Southern reaction to the anti-segregation decisions of the Supreme Court in the 1950s."[11] The critics expressed themselves in newspaper editorials, pamphlets, speeches, even novels and, in one case, a popular play.

It is important to distinguish between white and black critics of the education movement, though their complaints were sometimes similar and the philanthropists themselves treated the two sets of opponents as morally equivalent, and equally irresponsible. The white opponents of the Ogden movement were more influential, at first, than black critics of northern philanthropy, and the "everglade drainers" were far more worried about them. Yet in the long run the black skeptics may have been more important. The survival and expansion of black higher education would eventually make it more difficult to ignore their questions.

Certainly historians studying this turbulent era have paid more attention to white resistance to northern philanthropy. In his indispensable monograph *Separate and Unequal: Public School Campaigns and Racism in the Southern Seaboard States, 1901–1915*, Louis R. Harlan

10. John Spencer Bassett to William E. Dodd, May 7, 1907, in William E. Dodd Papers, Library of Congress.
11. James W. Patton, "The Southern Reaction to the Ogden Movement," 71.

Ogden, William Howard Taft, Washington, and Carnegie. Division of
Photographs and Prints, Library of Congress.

has shown how the philanthropists equivocated and compromised as
the educational revival progressively downplayed black education in
an attempt to placate or forestall criticism. In this respect, Harlan's
book is an elaboration of Booker T. Washington's 1903 lament to
Wallace Buttrick: "We have already gone as far as decency permits in
our attempt to avoid stirring up southern feeling." Raymond Fosdick's
official history of the GEB, *Adventure in Giving,* made frequent passing
reference to southern white opposition, but gave few details. "The
Board was aware from the start," he wrote, "of the dangers inherent
in a Northern institution working in the highly charged emotional
atmosphere of a biracial South. . . . A single misstep could be disastrous." Henry Snyder Enck devoted an entire chapter in his carefully
researched doctoral dissertation to white and black press attacks on
the educational philanthropists. The southern white criticism, he
concluded, was ignorant and "unfounded," often "carefully calculated
to sell papers" or score points in local and state newspaper rivalries.

By about 1910, according to Enck, "the Southern white press came to realize the extent to which the philanthropists had been won over and ended their harangues." Most other historians of southern education, from Charles W. Dabney to James Anderson, have also noted the white opposition to the "Ogden movement," though in most cases they have not given enough attention to the content of the criticism, or its power.[12]

In fact, the opponents of the "Ogden movement" could plausibly present themselves as spokesmen for the majority of white southerners. Although they would not admit it, northern philanthropists frequently felt inhibited by criticism, and devoted much energy to responding to critics whom they longed to ignore but were unable to do so. "The opposition is amusing," wrote Ogden in 1903 to the white president of a Negro college, "and the discussion in Southern circles created by unfair attack is one of the helpful influences for the cause we have at heart."[13] This lofty disdain was simply a pose, and did not represent the real actions or concerns of Ogden and the other reformers.

Even as Ogden was dismissing the critics as "amusing," he had already made plans that showed how seriously he took them. Writing to a fellow northerner on the Southern Education Board, Ogden urged that careful thought be given to organization, elections, and resolutions at the 1903 Conference for Education in the South. "These are all extremely important," he wrote,

> for nothing would be more disastrous to the proceedings of the Conference than to let them loose upon a miscellaneous and ill-informed audience. I think it not impossible that there may be some enemies present who may claim the rights of delegates for the purpose of fomenting trouble. There is certainly an opposition developing through the "Manufacturers

12. Harlan, *Separate and Unequal*; Booker T. Washington to Wallace Buttrick, November 27, 1903, Box 722, GEB Papers; Fosdick et al., *Adventure in Giving*, 320; Henry Snyder Enck, "The Burden Borne: Northern White Philanthropy and Southern Black Industrial Education, 1900–1915," 361–403; Charles W. Dabney, *Universal Education in the South*; Henry Allen Bullock, A *History of Negro Education in the South: From 1619 to the Present*; Anderson, *The Education of Blacks in the South*.

13. See Anderson's judgment, *The Education of Blacks in the South*, 94. Ogden to A. B. Hunter, May 13, 1903, in Ogden letterbook, Ogden Papers, Library of Congress. See also Ogden to Alexander Purves, July 17, 1902, in Ogden Papers. (All references to Ogden Papers are from Special Correspondence, unless otherwise noted.)

Record," "The Farm Magazine," "The Charleston News & Courier," "The New Orleans Picayune" and other papers.

About the same time, Tulane University awarded Ogden an honorary degree. Although his original intention was not to accept the degree in person, the opposition caused him to change his mind. "I went to New Orleans for one special and only reason," he admitted. "Some of the Southern attacks upon myself and our cause are very violent. I thought, under the circumstances, it might be evidence to the effect that we are not Northern intermeddlers when an important institution of learning recognizes and compliments our movement."[14]

Ogden showed his concern in other ways—sending copies of one of the harshest attacks on him to a number of his friends, wondering at one point in 1905 if criticism might force him to resign from leadership of the Conference for Education in the South, and by 1907 even responding directly to his most vocal critic, Richard H. Edmonds of the Baltimore *Manufacturers' Record*. The decision to meet in Pinehurst, North Carolina, for the 1907 meeting of the conference— in order to have a real conference of specialists rather than a public propaganda meeting as before—provoked worries among several of the everglade drainers that this change would be interpreted as a "retreat," a "surrender to the Manufacturers' Record and other ignorant and prejudiced forces," intimidation "by some do-nothing politicians and a few reactionaries."[15]

The philanthropists—using the term to include donors and their agents, northern promoters and their southern allies—faced a wide range of criticism, including some charges that were simply fatuous or sensational. Robert Ogden was "a Negro worshipper, pure & simple," a man who "hugged" Booker T. Washington as he toured Ogden's place of business. "The whole tendency of the proceedings" at the 1909 meeting of the Conference for Education in the South

14. Ogden to H. B. Frissell, April 13, 1903, and March 18, 1903, in Ogden letterbook, Ogden Papers.

15. Ogden to Walter Hines Page, June 1, 1905, Booker T. Washington to Ogden, June 5, 1905, A. J. Montague to Ogden, June 8, 1905, Charles D. McIver to Ogden, June 13, 1905, Ogden to Oswald Garrison Villard, February 27, 1905, in Ogden letterbook; Sidney J. Bowie to Ogden, January 14, 1907, Ogden to Edgar Gardner Murphy, January 4, 1907, S. C. Mitchell to G. S. Dickerman, January 6, 1907, all in Ogden Papers. For a direct criticism of Edmonds, see *New York Times*, February 16, 1907.

was "paganistic," according to an Atlanta Baptist preacher. Another Georgian warned that a northern educational monopoly could lead to social equality and intermarriage in the nation's colleges. "The south means to be Anglo-Saxon forever! Do they imagine that, for money, we are going to imprison the blood of kings in the veins of mulattoes?" The philanthropic movement, said others, was a scheme conceived by insincere northerners to keep blacks concentrated in the South. "The Atlanta tragedy"—the 1906 race riot—was the ultimate responsibility of the spirit of "Ogdenism."[16]

It would be a mistake, however, to concentrate on these colorful or extreme criticisms. Through the choking smoke and the incredible noise of the opponents' barrage there were some real cannon balls flying, and not infrequently these projectiles hit their targets.

The arguments of the most influential white critics of northern philanthropy may be boiled down to three basic assertions. First, the critics claimed, the philanthropists had a hidden agenda for the Negro that would result in the ultimate subversion of "white supremacy"— that is, the current pattern of southern race relations. Second, the philanthropists had a patronizing attitude toward the South, believing it to be backward and inferior to the North. Third, northern philanthropy threatened to create an educational "monopoly" that would discourage southern self-reliance and try to close schools of which it disapproved. Oddly enough, some black observers made opposite charges: the philanthropists *accepted* white supremacy, had a patronizing attitude toward African Americans, and sought centralized power to discourage black autonomy.

Stripped of the invective with which they were usually adorned, the white critics' charges emerge as fundamentally accurate. Consider, for example, the charge that the philanthropists thought the South primitive, and gazed with a certain condescension upon the region "as upon a helpless minor needing . . . guidance or a benighted sinner needing . . . missionary efforts." As the *Norfolk Landmark* commented: "The trouble is that some of these men—not all, but maybe

16. Thomas Dixon, Jr., to J. C. Hemphill, May 9 [1905] in Hemphill Family Papers, Duke University Library; clipping from unidentified Atlanta newspaper [1909] in Ogden Papers; *Atlanta Journal*, May 24, 1909, Box 262, GEB Papers; *Manufacturers' Record*, September 27, 1906, August 13 and September 3, 1908.

the dominating ones—believe that the South is the abode of barbarism, and they would reclaim it along lines utterly mistaken and repulsive."[17]

If the critics had had the opportunity to peek into the private correspondence of major philanthropists and their agents, they would certainly have felt justified in their charges. The people of the South "need our help to a far greater degree than they comprehend," wrote Ogden to William H. Baldwin, Jr. "The miserable condition of the race question, the prevalent ignorance, the prejudiced public opinion, the suspicion that prevents individuals from speaking frankly with each other—have created an abnormal and hyper-sensitive condition throughout the South." In a later letter, he added:

> After all, when we look at the circumstances of the case we may easily ask, Why should not the Southern people be narrow and prejudiced. They have never had a chance at anything else. . . . Sparse populations, widely scattered, the dull and dreary lives and no leaven of general information to inspire the mass—the more sanely I see it, the deeper becomes my pity.

Baldwin thought southerners were "like children in their sentiment," and did not expect them to speak "the 'whole truth.'" Charles W. Dabney, one of Ogden's southern allies, summed up this negative image of the South by referring to the "almost insurmountable prejudice, narrowness, sectarianism, sectionalism, demagoguism [sic], and profound stupidity of the leaders of these people & of the masses of the people themselves."[18]

The view that the South was benighted and backward came through most clearly in the philanthropists' statements on race relations. "The South is insane upon the Negro question," wrote Ogden in a confidential outburst. "Not one Southern man in ten thousand approaches correct views." As southern opposition intensified, he wrote to Dr. James E. Russell of Columbia University: "The South

17. Bishop Warren A. Candler, *Dangerous Donations and Degrading Doles, or A Vast Scheme for Capturing and Controlling the Colleges and Universities of the Country*, 37; *Norfolk Landmark*, March 6, 1907, in G. S. Dickerman scrapbooks, Southern Education Papers, Southern Historical Collection, University of North Carolina at Chapel Hill.

18. Ogden to William H. Baldwin, Jr., March 1, 1904, and April 12, 1904, in Ogden letterbook, Ogden Papers; Baldwin to Charles Francis Adams, Jr., September 1, 1903, in Booker T. Washington Papers, Library of Congress; Charles W. Dabney to George Foster Peabody, January 8, 1904, in George Foster Peabody Papers, Library of Congress.

is not yet through with the effort to reenslave the Negro." Arguing for "right feeling" and "education of sentiment" toward blacks, Edgar Gardner Murphy of the Southern Education Board declared, "The fundamental problem in our public opinion is not ignorance but perversity," then, exhibiting his typical caution, crossed out "perversity" and substituted the words "something more formidable." George Foster Peabody, who served as treasurer for both the General and Southern Education Boards, told a correspondent in 1912 "that the present generation of Southerner's [sic] do not believe the negro capable of the highest attainment either of morality or intellectual ability and they unconsciously resent the criticism of methods and standards."[19]

Such sentiments, needless to say, were seldom expressed in public. In fact, the philanthropists went to great lengths to reassure white southerners that they were not seeking to impose alien ideas about the race question. In 1903 GEB executive secretary Wallace Buttrick told a conference of county educational superintendents in New Orleans: "The negro, if he is to be educated at all, is to be educated by the people of the South and in the way they may prescribe. We, as a General Education Board, have no suggestions to offer." Going a step further, Buttrick asserted, "We come to you with no notions of our own upon the subject at all."[20]

One would not need to be as belligerent a racist as novelist Thomas Dixon or rabble-rouser James K. Vardaman to be skeptical about Buttrick's claim, which was certainly inconsistent with the private comments of the philanthropists. Even the statement Buttrick made at a Nashville conference of school superintendents might not have been completely satisfying: "I recognize the fact that the negro is an inferior race, and that the Anglo-Saxon is the superior race." A critic might well ask: Was Buttrick speaking of a permanent, inherent condition of black inferiority, or was he referring to temporary "facts" that might change over time? His deceptively clear statement may have been designed to obfuscate the issue. Perceptive racial radicals

19. Ogden to Baldwin, February 26, 1904, in Ogden letterbook, Ogden to James E. Russell, March 27, 1906, "Mr. Murphy's Report of his Remarks at Abenia, August 7th, 1907: Statement," all in Ogden Papers. Peabody to Henrietta Gardiner, April 29, 1912, in Peabody Papers.

20. Transcript of Conference of County Superintendents, New Orleans, La., November 25–27, 1903, Box 209, GEB Papers.

were not satisfied with anything less than the dogma that Negroes were by their nature doomed to eternal inferiority, if not imminent extinction. It is worth noting that such southerners were enraged a few months later by a John Spencer Bassett essay which, while referring to whites as "the superior race," predicted that blacks in America would "win equality at some time."[21]

In short, southern white critics were certain that the philanthropists did, indeed, have notions about Negro-white relations and black education, and they were irritated both by the content of these ideas and by the fact that the philanthropists were so disingenuous about their real program. The *Charlotte Observer* responded angrily when, during the presidential campaign of 1904, Robert Ogden deplored "the introduction of the negro question into national politics" because doing so might undo the "large amount of good" then being done "by the white people North and South working in harmony for the political and intellectual advancement of the negro in the Southern states." The *Observer* editorialized: "If this means that Mr. Ogden's efforts are mainly toward uplifting the negro, let him go ahead, as he has a right to do. In the meantime, however, the Ogden movement should take the Southern people into its confidence and be candid about what it is up to." The *Charleston News and Courier* found similar ground for suspicion in a comment by Booker T. Washington: "His statement that 'the movement which is fathered and guided by the General and Southern Education Boards has already gone far in laying the foundation for helpful service to both races' would appear to justify much of the criticism with which this movement has been received in the South."[22]

"There is suspicion among some of the Southern people," said the *Richmond Times* in 1902, "that these Northern philanthropists are endeavoring to elevate the negro and bring him into a closer social relationship with the Southern people." Believing "such a thought is utterly foreign to Mr. Ogden and his friends," the *Times* supported the "Ogden Movement" until 1905, when the editor learned

21. Conference of County and City Superintendents, Nashville, April 8–9, 1903, Box 209, GEB Papers; John Spencer Bassett, "Stirring Up the Fires of Race Antipathy," 304–5. For the furor this article ignited, see Joel Williamson, *The Crucible of Race: Black-White Relations in the American South since Emancipation*, 261–71.

22. *Charlotte Observer*, August 20, 1904, in Ogden scrapbooks, Ogden Papers; *Charleston News and Courier*, October 18, 1904.

that Ogden had often had Washington as a guest in his home. The newspaper then promptly withdrew its support for the educational movement.[23]

Though the charge that the philanthropists would undermine the southern system of white supremacy was often expressed in feverish hyperbole, and despite the fact that the philanthropists were less radical than the critics believed, it was true that the northern-backed reformers had a vision of just race relations that differed significantly from current southern practices. They did hope to change the South, albeit by subtle, indirect, and slow methods. In his usual rambling style, George Foster Peabody made the point to a northern donor to the Episcopal American Church Institute for Negroes: "I am constantly in touch with my old school mates and others at the south who as a rule can be carried only so far and *we cannot afford to let the present generation of the south control negro education* without definite cooperation with those of us who believe in the negro as a man and child of God." (When he sent a copy of this letter to the executive secretary of the American Church Institute, Peabody instructed: " . . . do not leave on your desk at the office because I do not want to distress any Southerner who might not readily understand it.") "It is extremely stupid on the part of the Southern people that they fail to perceive the injury they are inflicting upon themselves by surrendering their entire section of the country to crazy prejudice," wrote Ogden to an associate. "The South needs to learn its immense obligation to Negro education."[24]

In short, the northern philanthropic agencies *did* want to reform southern race relations in ways unpopular with the majority of southern whites. This truth should not be obscured by the correlate fact that the northerners involved in the educational revival generally held views different from the most liberal contemporary northern opinion, as well as from present-day antiracist thought. Like most people at most times, they fancied themselves moderates. They believed they were more open-minded than even the best-intentioned

23. *Richmond Times*, May 15, 1902, in Ogden scrapbooks, Ogden Papers; *Richmond Times-Dispatch* quoted in *Norfolk Landmark*, March 6, 1907, in Dickerman scrapbooks, Southern Education Papers.

24. Peabody to Ida Mason, March 26, 1912 (emphasis added), Peabody to Rev. S. H. Bishop, March 26, 1912, in Peabody Papers; Ogden to Baldwin, February 12, 1903, in Ogden letterbook, Ogden Papers.

white southerners but more sensible than enthusiasts such as white editor Oswald Garrison Villard, and far from the really loathsome extremes. A jocular Slater agent wrote a satiric litany a few years later that perfectly illustrates this self-perception:

> From the Ku Klux Klan and N. A. A. C. P., and all other common asses,
>   Good Lord deliver us!
> From northern negrophiles and southern hill-billy negrophobes,
>   Good Lord deliver us![25]

The white critics' third major assertion against northern philanthropy was that it would lead to an unwarranted "concentration of power" in educational matters. The most effective champion of this charge, Methodist Bishop Warren A. Candler, wrote a 1909 tract (*Dangerous Donations and Degrading Doles*) in which he declared: "An educational trust has been formed, and is operating to control the institutions of higher learning in the United States, and to dominate especially the colleges and universities of the South." At first favorably inclined toward the benefactions of Rockefeller and Carnegie, Candler turned against the philanthropists when the Carnegie Fund offered Vanderbilt University one million dollars "with the stipulation that the institution not be bound by denominational control," an offer Candler saw as a "bribe," sure to work "a revolution in behalf of secularism." In his broadside against "degrading doles," Candler questioned whether "it is good for the country to have its educational work determined" by the fifteen trustees of the GEB, who, whatever their motives, were not responsible to any "authority civil or ecclesiastical in the land." Citing northern press reports, Candler warned that the GEB would cause many colleges to close by refusing them aid while supporting their rivals. "In other words the 'General Education Board' proposes to both kill and make alive, to make and unmake colleges at will," he stated, accurately perceiving an element of coercion in systematic, large-scale philanthropy. He predicted that the ultimate result of the board's activities would be a revival of plans for federal aid to education—and even a cabinet-level department of education. In the meantime, he warned, the GEB "may be able to do in our country

25. B. C. Caldwell to James H. Dillard, July 15, 1923, Box 268, GEB Papers.

Warren A. Candler. Special Collections
Department, Robert W. Woodruff Library,
Emory University.

what the government does in France or Germany, but without the
government's responsibility to the people."[26]

The charges about philanthropic plans for consolidation and concentration, like the charges on the philanthropists' views about the
South and race relations, had some basis in fact. The idea that there
were too many southern colleges was a common theme among educational reformers, with consolidation and higher standards frequently
suggested as the remedy. A few weeks after publication of Candler's
attack, his fellow Methodist clergyman James Cannon, Jr., wrote
to Buttrick requesting a copy of a private policy paper written by
Frederick T. Gates, GEB chairman. Gates directed Buttrick to refuse
the request. Among other reasons for this course of action, he noted
one which would not have startled Candler: "Our policy, any sound

26. Candler, *Dangerous Donations*, 11, 15–17, 19, 32–35; Mark Keith Bauman, "Warren
Akin Candler: Conservative amidst Change," 187–93.

policy we think, will cut off three-fourths of the present colleges. Publication might arouse the hostility of many of these and would not be likely to bring us the least compensating advantage . . . either in money or information of value."[27]

African American critics, North and South, also saw potential danger in northern philanthropic activity, and expressed profound skepticism about the foundations' endeavors. Black criticism of the northern philanthropists, though often ignored at the time, proved to be highly influential over the long term. In addition, these black opponents of the "new philanthropists" offer an ironic counterpoint to the suspicions of white southerners. As Ogden pointed out to one of his confederates: "The Negro press is charging us with surrendering to the South and the Southern press charges us with being simply friends of the Negroes in disguise."[28]

Consider, for example, the case of William Edward Burghart Du Bois, by 1916 one of the most significant spokesmen for African Americans. Although his reasons were completely different from Bishop Candler's, Du Bois denounced the philanthropists' dangerous donations with a vigor and persistence nearly equal to that of the Wesleyan prelate. In his fear that the Ogden movement represented concentrated power pursuing a secret agenda, Du Bois was almost as vehement as Thomas Dixon.

In fact, Du Bois and Dixon published novels at about the same time, both attacking the Ogden movement, but for opposite faults. In Du Bois's 1911 novel, *The Quest of the Silver Fleece*, a northern cotton speculator becomes cynically involved in philanthropy for black education. In conversation with a white southerner, the speculator learns to his surprise that "educating, or rather *trying* to educate niggers" will make them discontented, thereby undermining "cheap cotton." He then concocts a plan for a "Negro education steering committee" made up of philanthropists, tycoons, and selected southerners. "We'll see that on such committee you Southerners get what you want—control

27. Wallace Buttrick to Frederick T. Gates, June 7, 1909, Gates to Buttrick, June 8, 1909, Box 716, GEB Papers. For an example of the consolidation theme, see the letter from E. B. Craighead, president of Tulane, to Buttrick, December 22, 1905, in Peabody Papers.

28. Ogden to Charles W. Dabney, May 21, 1904, in Dabney Collection, Southern Education Papers.

of Negro education," he assures a southern collaborator. After this "Negro Education Board" has been duly organized, the members steam south on a special railway excursion, uttering a stream of ill-informed judgments and half-baked racist bromides on their way to the black school where the protagonist is a student.[29]

In 1912 Dixon published a novel that made an opposite claim. In an overheated tale about miscegenation and secret "taint" of Negro blood entitled *The Sins of the Father*, the preacher-turned-novelist imagined a confrontation between a character based on John Spencer Bassett and a crusading white supremacist editor. "Professor Alexander Magraw" is a flabby, effeminate supporter of "the great Educational Movement in the South" who has made himself famous in the North by his "fulsome eulogy" of "a notorious negro" who really never accomplished anything "except to demonstrate his skill as a beggar in raising a million dollars from Northern sentimentalists" (read Booker T. Washington). Representing the northern educational philanthropists, Magraw attempts to bribe or cow the editor into suspending his "agitation of the so-called negro problem." Dixon's hero responds with denunciation of the true goals of the northern "Poor Funds." Dominated by Washington (mentioned only as a Negro "of doubtful moral character" and "fertile brain"), the educational philanthropists sought "the ultimate complete acceptance of the black man as a social equal," asserts the author's mouthpiece. The results of northern philanthropy, he added, could only be "degradation of the white race" and the "pauperizing" of the South's educational system.[30]

Unlike Dixon, Du Bois was open to new evidence, and willing to revise his judgments in the light of new policies. Looking backward, years later, he perceived major changes in the policies of the GEB beginning about 1919, as "the old heads of the General Education Board who believed in the Baptist faith, white supremacy, and industrial training for Negroes" were gradually "gathered to their fathers," and a "more liberal element of young Southerners became members of the board." By 1930, Du Bois saw the GEB as "the salvation of education among Negroes"—despite the board's earlier egregious mistakes.[31]

29. W. E. B. Du Bois, *The Quest of the Silver Fleece*, 158–65, 174–80.

30. Thomas Dixon, *The Sins of the Father: A Romance of the South*, 197–210.

31. Du Bois, "The Negro Since 1900: Progress Report"; Du Bois, "A Graduate School"; Du Bois, "The General Education Board," 229–30.

Du Bois's reservations about the actions of the philanthropists were shared, to some extent, by all African Americans. As an editorial in Oswald Garrison Villard's *New York Evening Post* observed in 1914, "the colored people and those working on their behalf in the South" believed that the General Education Board was "indifferent, if not hostile, to them." Even Booker T. Washington was quietly critical of the work carried on by whites who admired him. As early as 1904, in a candid letter to his aide Emmett J. Scott, Washington expressed his concern about open criticism of the Ogden movement, though privately he had his own doubts: "While there are many things in connection with Mr. Ogden's work with which I cannot agree, at the same time on the whole I think it is helpful and it is certainly better than no work."[32]

Most black critics of the philanthropists were circumspect in expressing their disappointment. No one involved in southern education, and longing for outside help, dared to attack the Ogden movement with the zeal of editor Monroe Trotter, whose *Boston Guardian* ran an angry cartoon showing Ogden and associates joining with Booker T. Washington in mourning over the graves of "Negro Vote," "Negro Social Rights," and "Higher Education." More representative was the editorial comment in J. Max Barber's *The Voice of the Negro*. The Ogden movement was "bound to do good," yet "no Negro who lives in the south can afford to agree completely with Mr. Ogden." The educational philanthropy generated by Ogden's group went mostly to whites, the editorial noted, and Ogden himself was a " 'conservative' northerner" who was "willing to let the south work out its own problems."[33]

Even newspapers controlled by Booker T. Washington were sometimes critical of northern educational philanthropy. The *New York Age*, for example, criticized the Peabody Fund's discriminatory distribution of funds for southern schools and condemned the Southern Education Board for its lack of black representation. "A very queer and ominous condition of affairs has developed in the working out of the ideas of these Education Boards," declared an editorial in 1907.

32. *New York Evening Post*, July 13, 1914. Washington to Emmett J. Scott, July 9, 1904, in *The Booker T. Washington Papers*, vol. 8, 13. On Washington's frustrations with the SEB, see Harlan, *The Wizard of Tuskegee*, 187–91.

33. Luker, *The Social Gospel in Black and White*, 208; cf. Enck, "The Burden Borne," 391–92. "The Ogden Educational Conference," 219.

After the GEB published its first annual report in 1914, the *Age* noted that only 4 percent of the board's philanthropic dollars had gone to black education.[34]

One black journalist adopted the creative tactic of praising "the pure and disinterested philanthropy" of Rockefeller and other "Christian philanthropists," but condemning the "misuse" of these donated funds by the "Southern education movement." Confusing the Southern Education Board and the General Education Board, the editor of the *Atlanta Independent* complained that the money was going to rich schools, not "those who needed assistance most." Why was a "rich institution" such as Agnes Scott College given $100,000 while Spelman College (a "poor negro school, entirely dependent upon the cold charity of the public") given only $10,000? Surely the original donors did not envision "that their benevolence would be used to make the wealthy more wealthy while those who are famishing in ignorance and darkness grow more unfortunate." Joining with an unlikely ally, the editor declared: "We agree with Bishop Candler, your money is a curse and the South should refuse it."[35]

Perhaps the most important question about opposition to northern philanthropic activity is "How much impact did the critics have?" Was it true, as the *Manufacturers' Record* claimed, that as early as 1906 "Ogdenism" had been "compelled to walk so warily" that it was "practically standing still"?[36]

The answer, like everything else in the early-twentieth-century South, has two parts, one black and the other white. In the first two decades of the century, black critics had little impact on the plans of the philanthropists. Only in the 1920s, as educational opportunities for southern blacks expanded and black students and alumni showed their ability to demand changes at several institutions, did the northern foundations begin to engage seriously the primary black criticisms of their activities. Until then their concern was to counteract the relentless white opposition.

Certainly it is wrong to picture white opposition as steadily declining, simply fading away as the activities of the philanthropists became better known in the South. If anything, opposition intensified between

34. Enck, "The Burden Borne," 398–402.
35. *Atlanta Independent*, June 12, 1909, in Ogden Papers, Container 26 (Clippings).
36. *Manufacturers' Record*, April 5, 1906.

1907 and World War I, with some former supporters turning against the "Ogden movement" and a powerful debater in the person of Bishop Candler entering the discussion. Eventually the opposition began to be expressed in national terms, rather than strictly southern terms, and foundations found themselves under attack in such national forums as the National Education Association and the U.S. Congress.

In 1914 one leader in the southern education movement warned: "Just now . . . we are facing the danger of an agitation that will check all benefaction and thus set back progress for a decade or longer, making the work of the Southern Board or any other Board impossible." The political unpopularity of John D. Rockefeller, *père et fils*, and specifically public anger over the brutal tactics of a Rockefeller-controlled company in a Colorado coal mine strike, led to strong congressional criticism of the GEB. Senator William S. Kenyon of Iowa even introduced a bill to repeal the act incorporating the GEB. This bill never came to a vote, but other legislation forbidding continued GEB funding of farm demonstration work did pass. Senator James K. Vardaman observed: "I think it is very proper for this Government to put the stamp of its disapproval upon the methods by which the great fortunes of John D. Rockefeller and men of his class were made."[37] It is significant that the law which emerged from the debate, the Smith-Lever Act of 1914, was the work of two southerners—Senator Hoke Smith of Georgia and Representative A. F. Lever of South Carolina.

No doubt influenced by the congressional discussion, the normal school department of the National Education Association adopted a resolution attacking "the Carnegie and Rockefeller Foundations"—meaning in fact the GEB and the Carnegie Foundation. According to the resolution, these two philanthropic groups, "agencies not in any way responsible to the people," threatened academic freedom and democracy by their efforts to "control" state educational institutions and standardize curriculum.[38] These were sentiments Bishop Candler and Richard Edmonds could heartily endorse.

As the Southern Education Board faded into insignificance, after the death of Ogden in 1913 and changes in GEB policy, its leaders

37. A. P. Bourland to W. K. Tate, May 18, 1914, in A. P. Bourland Collection, Southern Education Papers. Fosdick et al., *Adventure in Giving*, 58–60; *Congressional Record*, 63d Cong., 2d sess., 7530, 7675–85, 8093–8103.

38. "Draft Reply to Resolution of National Education Association," Box 329, GEB Papers.

continued to respond to criticism in much the same way as the organization had a dozen years earlier. "Information has recently come to me that the feeling against the Conference for Education in the South is still strong among some of our industrial leaders in the South," wrote A. P. Bourland, executive secretary of what was now known as the Southern Conference for Education and Industry, in 1915. He urged North Carolina educator J. Y. Joyner, president of the conference, to find ways to enlist the cooperation of these businessmen. He suggested that the organization make plans for a careful discussion of the race issue at the following year's meeting. "My feeling is that it is not an opportune time to make the race question prominent in our programs," Bourland wrote, adding that "possibly in one more year we can come to the front in such a way as to benefit the entire Southern situation."[39]

It is possible to see permanent effects on northern educational philanthropy from the storm of criticism in the years 1901 to 1915. By 1911 the GEB and other funding agencies were structuring their aid in ways that seemed particularly designed to preempt opposition from white southerners. The philanthropists were trying to apply the lessons of the southern war against "Ogdenism."

Several of the most important initiatives of the GEB fit this apparent strategy of presenting a smaller target, of countering opposition by avoiding direct confrontation as much as possible. For example, the GEB's program of appointing state supervisors of Negro rural schools minimized opposition by making these supervisors subordinate to the state superintendent of public instruction, by recommending no Negroes for these positions, and by simply not making an appointment where significant opposition existed. (South Carolina, Louisiana, Mississippi, and Florida were the last states to have supervisors of Negro schools because of unsympathetic or unreliable state officials.) The "county training schools" (a less controversial name than "high schools") established by the GEB and the Slater Fund were another example of trying to forestall criticism by relying on public authorities— as well as by employing euphemisms and indirect funding. The money channeled through the Jeanes Fund for supervising industrial teachers also kept the GEB somewhat in the background. The GEB countered

39. A. P. Bourland to J. Y. Joyner, January 27, 1915, in J. Y. Joyner Collection, Southern Education Papers.

charges that it was seeking to dominate the schools to which it donated by gradually lifting most conditions on its gifts.[40]

A similar defensive strategy is evident in the workings of the Rosenwald Fund in the years after 1917. By supporting schools only where white authorities would help, the fund gave opponents of Negro education veto power. No school would be built in a community that was overwhelmingly opposed to northern philanthropic activity. As black historian Carter G. Woodson explained in an unpublished history of the Rosenwald school-building program, it was "unwise" to build a Rosenwald school in a community until "at least an enthusiastic minority" of whites "could grasp the new idea of democratic education." "To ignore these antagonisms . . . might result . . . in the burning of the schoolhouses after they had been completed." As the school-building program gained the support of many southern whites, however, "cases of incendiarism" were "much less than one might expect," he reported.[41]

Southern white opposition to northern philanthropy was, in short, sustained and effective, shaping northern reform efforts for years to come. The study of these critics of everglade draining—to use Haygood's metaphor again—is essential to any complete understanding of the philanthropists themselves. For rich and influential as the northern philanthropic agencies were, they did not enjoy unlimited freedom. Their choices were limited in important ways by people who feared their power, questioned their motives, resented outsiders, and suspected that they were failing to educate blacks for servitude. If nothing else, the fervor of these naysayers should remind us that southern education, especially for blacks, did *not* flow simply and "directly from the interests and views of the philanthropists of the industrial Northeast and the professional reformers and emerging businessmen of the New South."[42]

40. Wallace Buttrick to John D. Rockefeller, Jr., February 5, 1914, Box 203, GEB Papers. Fosdick et al., *Adventure in Giving,* 318–19.

41. Carter G. Woodson, manuscript history of Rosenwald school program, chap. 5, pp. 1–2, in Julius Rosenwald Papers, University of Chicago.

42. James D. Anderson, "Education for Servitude: The Social Purposes of Schooling in the Black South, 1870–1930," 4.

3

The Education of a Philanthropist
William H. Baldwin, Jr., 1898–1905

You have never doubted the advisability of giving your own children a reasonable education—are not such doubts always about the children of others?

—W. H. Baldwin, Jr.[1]

F rom the outside, to critics and beneficiaries, "Ogdenism" appeared strong and consistent. From within the philanthropic movement, however, it was easier to perceive the uncertainty, shifting options, and development incident to any reform movement. The career of William Henry Baldwin, Jr., Tuskegee trustee, member of the Southern Education Board, and first chairman of the General Education Board, is both a good illustration of the philanthropists and their ideals, and, at the same time, a revealing example of failure, the representation of an important "road not taken."

Baldwin was a wealthy, reform-minded businessman whose philanthropic activity has been explained in two ways. According to one interpretation, his commitment to reform was the direct product of economic motivation, with calculating self-interest lying behind his concern for black education. He was, in short, a pseudo-reformer. The alternative explanation for Baldwin's philanthropy is even simpler. Here was a good man, an exemplary American citizen, who provided inspirational (or "sentimental") leadership purely out of a sense of duty. Good deeds, from this perspective, require no explanation, nor is there anything mysterious about philanthropic motivation. Neither explanation is entirely satisfactory nor completely wrong.

1. William H. Baldwin, Jr., "Why a Businessman Should Be Interested in Public Education," November 22, 1902, speech to the Richmond Educational Association, in William H. Baldwin [III] Papers, State Historical Society of Wisconsin.

The most influential of the "self-interest" interpretations of Baldwin was offered by the scholar-activist W. E. B. Du Bois, who claimed years later (after his conversion to Marxism) that Baldwin's "philanthropy" had as its real goal the creation of two equally skilled groups of southern workers, one white and the other black. Baldwin calculated (according to Du Bois) that if appropriately trained black workers were available in large enough numbers, then northern capitalists could use them "to break the power of the trade unions."[2]

A recent student of black educational history has endorsed Du Bois's claim and, indeed, carried it several steps further. According to James D. Anderson, Baldwin was a "railroad entrepreneur who employed thousands of black laborers" and a man who strongly opposed labor unions. In less than a decade as an active educational philanthropist, Baldwin somehow came to dominate Booker T. Washington, the most prominent black educator of the day. Despite what friends and foes believed, Washington was not "the dominant voice" in his own Tuskegee "machine." Instead, Baldwin "was the chairman of the Tuskegee machine and the mind behind the economic philosophy," according to Anderson. He used Washington and educational philanthropy to promote the economic stability necessary for the capitalist development of the South. For Baldwin "economic stability" meant, above all, subservient Negroes, shaped by what Anderson has called "education for servitude."[3]

The evidence for any interpretation of Baldwin's life is limited, since most of Baldwin's personal papers have not survived. Aside from a few papers preserved by his son, Baldwin's direct, pithy letters are mostly to be found scattered in the manuscripts of his associates such as Washington, Robert Ogden, and Wallace Buttrick. An early biography, written five years after his death, provides useful information, but ignores some questions of interest to scholars.[4]

The available evidence contradicts the Du Bois–Anderson interpretation at almost every point. During the time he was chairman of the General Education Board, Baldwin, who was president of the Long

2. Merle Curti to W. E. B. Du Bois, December 14, 1932, in W. E. B. Du Bois Papers, Library of Congress. See also Curti, *The Social Ideas of American Educators*, 299n.
3. James D. Anderson, "Northern Foundations and the Shaping of Southern Black Rural Education, 1902–1935," 373–74, 376–77; Anderson, "Education for Servitude," 225–26. Cf. Anderson, *The Education of Blacks in the South*.
4. John Graham Brooks, *An American Citizen: The Life of William Henry Baldwin, Jr.*

William H. Baldwin.
Rockefeller Archive Center.

Island Railroad, was not a large-scale employer of African Americans and had no important investments in the South. Throughout his business career, he was a supporter of labor unions, even gaining something of a "radical" reputation among his fellow businessmen for his attitudes and practices. He opposed corporate efforts to eliminate unions "as the gravest social danger," in the words of his biographer. "Labor, to protect its rights and standards, needs organization, at least as much as we need it," said Baldwin. "For capital to use its strength to take this weapon from workingmen and women is an outrage." Furthermore, far from dominating Booker T. Washington, or serving as "the kind overseer Booker had been too young to know in slavery," Baldwin was closer to a disciple of the Wizard of Tuskegee, admitting on one occasion, "I almost worship this man." Certainly neither man was the puppet of the other, though there was a strong bond of mutual admiration between the young executive and the black educator, seven years his senior. If Washington's memory was accurate, the two men felt immediate rapport at their first meeting. Washington had the impression "that I had met a man who could thoroughly understand me and whom I could understand."[5]

But if the Marxist analysis is weak, to say the least, in its supporting evidence, it does ask some of the right questions. The motives of long-term, organized philanthropy require careful study. It will not do to say simply that Baldwin and other donors (and organizers of donors) were good people, moved solely by high idealism or strong emotion. The good deeds of men such as Baldwin must be examined in the light of their political philosophy and economic values. One does not debunk or explain away altruism by assuming that it has some practical connection to other goals important to the philanthropist, that there is a coherent rationale behind the generosity.

Baldwin's influence as a philanthropist was out of proportion to the length of his career. Born in 1863 into an old Massachusetts family with roots extending back to the earliest days of the colony, Baldwin grew up in an atmosphere of intense idealism. His father, a supporter of abolition and other reforms, founded the Young Men's Christian Union of Boston, and, when young Baldwin was five years old, retired from a successful mercantile career to serve as president of this "center for adult education, recreation, and social service," a forerunner of the YMCA.[6]

After preparatory education in Boston's public schools and Roxbury Latin School, Baldwin enrolled at Harvard College, where he was an outstanding student leader but a merely satisfactory scholar. After graduation in 1885, he studied law for a few months before coming to the attention of Charles Francis Adams, Jr., president of the Union Pacific Railroad. Identified by Harvard president Charles W. Eliot as a young man of unusual promise, Baldwin was offered a position in 1886 as, in effect, a management trainee at Union Pacific.

After three years in various positions with the railroad, Baldwin had gained a reputation as an executive of great energy and talent, who

5. See Louis Harlan's comment on Baldwin in *Separate and Unequal*, 76n: "By 1901 his business life was apparently divorced from the South." Brooks, *An American Citizen*, 169, 147, 150, 165. David Levering Lewis, *W. E. B. Du Bois: Biography of a Race*, 240. Nancy J. Weiss, *The National Urban League, 1910–1940*, 36. Booker T. Washington, *My Larger Education: Being Chapters from My Experience*, 16.

6. Weiss, *The National Urban League*, 34.

had "quite a remarkable ability for getting on with men," as Adams put it. In rapid succession he became general manager of the Montana Union Railroad, an assistant vice president at Union Pacific, general manager of Michigan's Flint and Pere Marquette Railroad, and a vice president of the Southern Railway. In 1896 he became president of the Long Island Railroad, a position he held for the rest of his life.[7]

Baldwin might be described as the model of a Progressive business-man. Asserting that "there is a higher law than supply and demand," he strongly supported the idea of railroads run in the public interest, welcoming public scrutiny of their operation and making the common good a higher priority than the wishes of the stockholders. Though he was not, as some of his colleagues jested, "a sort of socialist," he saw his own industry as requiring a large degree of government regulation.[8]

Baldwin's interest in southern black education ought to be seen as part of a wider commitment to reform, as it was understood in his lifetime. In addition to championing new principles of business ethics and Negro schools, Baldwin was interested in several other reforms, the most significant of which was curbing prostitution in New York City. For five years he was chairman of the Committee of Fifteen, a group of New York civic leaders who sponsored a thorough investigation of "the social evil" in the nation's largest city and issued the first of many Progressive-era vice commission reports.

Baldwin was so committed to Progressive ideals that he considered abandoning his business career. "I . . . have three possible roads to follow," he wrote to his father in 1901, at one moment of decision. His choices, as he saw them, were "Business, politics, public service for the South," and "I can't help but feel that the Southern matter is the biggest, and would give me the greatest opportunity for good work."[9]

Not only must Baldwin's interest in black education be placed in the wider context of his other Progressive commitments, but it is also important to recognize that his understanding of black education

7. Baldwin's two years' experience with the Southern Railway is the basis, apparently, for James Anderson's claim: "Baldwin went South as an agent of Northeastern capital to take charge of the region's railroads." Anderson, "Northern Foundations," 373. See also Eric Anderson, "William H. Baldwin, Jr.," *American National Biography.*

8. Brooks, *An American Citizen,* 118–23.

9. William H. Baldwin, Jr., to William H. Baldwin, September 16, 1901, in William H. Baldwin [III] Papers.

changed in important ways, as he was tutored by Booker T. Washington. His public and private comments between 1898 and 1905 show a remarkable development—a change over time that might be called "the education of a philanthropist." For Baldwin, this education entailed a shift from simple enthusiasm for the "industrial training" of ignorant southern blacks to a more complex understanding of the relationship of whites and blacks in America. By the end of his life, he believed American race relations were in a state of crisis. Facing a situation urgently demanding action, he became increasingly impatient with the excessive caution and repeated self-deceptions of his fellow philanthropists. His close association with Washington seemed to alter his outlook, forcing him to consider the viewpoints of blacks themselves—not just the ideas of their white patrons. He moved, the evidence suggests, beyond a businessman's enlightened self-interest to a genuine vision of commonweal.

Typical of his early statements was his 1899 declaration: "Except in the rarest of instances, I am bitterly opposed to the so-called higher education of the Negroes." Over the next several years, Baldwin came to understand that even Booker T. Washington's system of "practical education" required cooperation and support from black colleges and their graduates. When Baldwin died, Atlanta University president Horace Bumstead praised him for changing his mind. "It was no secret," he wrote, that Baldwin had once been "outspoken" in opposition to Atlanta University and similar institutions, stating his objections with "absolute frankness" and "vigor." "But he proved to be a candid man and open to conviction, and further investigation into the character and results of our work brought about a change in his attitude."[10]

Early in his career as a philanthropist, Baldwin declared confidently, "The present problem of Negro education is a problem of organization—of work not theory." Speaking to the American Social Science Association in 1899, he saw the duty of white men in straightforward terms: to "concentrate money and effort in the work of Hampton and Tuskegee," establish "other Tuskegees," and "build

10. We have been unable to discover the source for Baldwin's frequently quoted 1899 statement. Fosdick, who has been cited by many scholars, incorrectly gives the source as *The Southern Workman*, August 1899. See Fosdick et al., *Adventure in Giving*, 342n21. *The Bulletin of Atlanta University* 151 (January 1905): 1.

up a secondary system under the general control and supervision of Hampton and Tuskegee." What was needed was "a general education board" that would influence individual northern donors by identifying southern black schools worthy of aid. "The approval of an educational board, properly organized, will be in itself a warrant to those who may contribute that their gifts will be expended properly."[11]

In the same speech he made several comments about the "potential economic value of the negro population" that have been repeatedly quoted by historians. The Negro "is best fitted to perform the heavy labor in the Southern states," declared Baldwin. "He will willingly fill the more menial positions," working for lower wages than either native whites or immigrants. "This will permit the Southern white laborer to perform the more expert labor," he explained, "and to leave the fields, the mines, and the simpler trades for the negro." These facts showed the folly of the idea of deporting the South's black population, according to Baldwin.[12]

Such statements certainly support Louis R. Harlan's judgment that "on occasion" Baldwin "went beyond BTW's accommodationism in his attempt to placate the white South," and are the best illustration of the assertion that Baldwin's "public utterances had a decidedly racist tone."[13] Still, the speech deserves to be judged as a whole, not on the basis of one paragraph.

11. William H. Baldwin, Jr., "The Present Problem of Negro Education," 399–404. This speech is a revised version of the remarks Baldwin made at the 1899 Capon Springs Conference. According to a footnote in the *Proceedings of the Second Capon Springs Conference for Christian Education in the South* (1899), Baldwin's speech entitled "The Present Problem of Negro Education, Industrial Education" was "from notes written out" after the Capon Springs meeting "for the American Social Science Association, at Saratoga, September 5, 1899." See *Proceedings*, 67n.

12. Harlan, *Separate and Unequal*, 78; Weiss, *The National Urban League*, 37; James D. Anderson, "Northern Philanthropy and the Training of the Black Leadership: Fisk University, A Case Study, 1915–1930," 100; Anderson, *The Education of Blacks in the South*, 82; Lewis, *W. E. B. Du Bois*, 270. On the basis of this speech, Rockefeller's most recent biographer dismisses Baldwin as "baldly racist," unlike the Rockefellers. Ron Chernow, *Titan: The Life of John D. Rockefeller, Sr.*, 485. Baldwin, "Present Problem of Negro Education," 401–2.

13. *The Booker T. Washington Papers*, vol. 3, 530n. Washington made a somewhat similar comment in 1911: "Persons who knew him only slightly, after hearing him express himself on the race question, gained the impression that he was not in full sympathy with the deepest aspirations of the Negro people. But this impression was mistaken." *My Larger Education*, 18.

It must be noted that several of Baldwin's most offensive statements were copied from Washington himself. One can imagine the harried railroad executive preparing his speech with *Black-Belt Diamonds*, a collection of "gems" from Washington's speeches, open beside him. The comparison of "the Negro" with a child "who craves the superficial, the ornamental, the signs of progress rather than the reality" is slightly garbled copy of a statement made by the principal of Tuskegee. "The negro and the mule is the only combination so far to grow cotton" is a close paraphrase of a stale witticism in one of Washington's speeches. The claim that the evil of lynching "indicates progress," since "No progress is made without friction" also came, almost word for word, from Washington.[14]

Baldwin's accommodating pronouncements were mixed with other statements that some white southerners were certain to dislike intensely. There was "no possible justification" for lynching, he said, adding that mob violence was caused by "the dense ignorance of so many of the whites." The crop lien system was creating "a new form of slavery" in many parts of the South, he said at another point in the speech, though he saw no "immediate solution" for this "pathetic condition." Even attempts to placate the white South could backfire on an unwary accommodator. Speaking of "the social question," Baldwin declared that "social recognition, for this generation at least, is denied; properly so, naturally so." He added, in words that Washington could certainly endorse, "Any attempt to force it merely complicates the situation and injures the cause of the black man." Though modern readers are offended by any claim that segregation was proper or "natural," a contemporary southern critic cited the phrase "for this generation at least" as evidence that Baldwin had no principled objection to the goal of "social equality," but merely recognized that it was "impossible" for the time being.[15]

Washington's friend T. Thomas Fortune, the outspoken and erratic black journalist, was in the audience when Baldwin spoke. In a letter

14. "It is with an ignorant race as it is with a child: it craves at first the superficial, the ornamental signs of progress rather than the reality," wrote Washington. See *The Future of the American Negro* in *The Booker T. Washington Papers*, vol. 5, 312. Washington, *Black-Belt Diamonds: Gems from the Speeches, Addresses, and Talks to Students of Booker T. Washington*, ed. Victoria Earle Matthews, 113, 72.

15. Baldwin, "Present Problem of Negro Education," 402; *Proceedings of the Second Capon Springs Conference*, 70–71; *Southern Education: Whither?* For a copy of this pamphlet, see GEB Papers, Box 262, Bishop Warren Candler file, Rockefeller Archive Center.

Class of 1896, St. Paul's School, Lawrenceville, Virginia. Russell Memorial Library, St. Paul's College.

to Washington he expressed his surprise at the *"low tone of disparagement of the race developed by the discussion"* that followed Baldwin's address. He had in mind, no doubt, a comment from a conference participant that "the millions and millions of dollars furnished by Northern philanthropists and capitalists for the higher education of the southern negro are wasted and worse than wasted"—indeed, had "produced more crime than good." Given the floor "by courtesy of the Association, to speak for his race," Fortune strongly challenged this claim, as well as Baldwin's assertion that the "army of white teachers" who came south during Reconstruction had operated upon a false theory of education. "I do not consider that education as false, for the simple reason that it was necessary," declared Fortune. The Yankee schoolmarms deserved credit for bringing "morality and New England ideas of thrift into the black homes of the South."[16]

16. T. Thomas Fortune to Washington, September 5, 1899, in *The Booker T. Washington Papers*, vol. 5, 195; *Journal of Social Science* 37 (1899): 52–68. The "false point of view" that Baldwin condemned was the idea that southern blacks might "learn to live from the

Writing to Washington, Fortune added a comment that seemed to be aimed at Baldwin: "It is a pity" that our friends have "*to give away so much in discussion to gain so little.* I give away nothing." Washington's response was revealing. "I am sorry that you were so disturbed by Mr. Baldwin's address," he wrote. "He is a person that will bear educating," he declared, adding that Fortune should write to Baldwin, who would "appreciate" his frank disagreement. Although no letter of Fortune to Baldwin has been preserved, over the next six years Washington himself sought to continue Baldwin's education in philanthropy.[17]

In this speech and other public statements about education, Baldwin made a direct appeal to the self-interest of his fellow businessmen. Though such appeals could be interpreted as merely crude exploitation, his motivation was actually more complex. Indeed, since he was self-consciously "selling" a program of reform to skeptical nonreformers, one might argue that talk of self-interest was a tactic, a rhetorical tool that disguised and made palatable his profound idealism. For example, when Baldwin wrote to the organizer of a "Southern Industrial Convention," arguing that world market pressures would someday force white southerners to accept "the negro in the various arts and trades of the South" (despite the opposition of white labor unions), was his real concern promoting southern competitiveness or undermining suspicions about black education?[18] In any case, he used similar arguments whether he was promoting education in general or black education in particular.

His interest in education, he said, was not "due to a sentimental enthusiasm." In fact, he had discovered that many of his associates in educational reform were "hard-headed practical men of great business affairs," who had an obvious interest in "transforming the ignorant

---

fruits of a literary education," not, as David Lewis suggests, social equality. See Lewis, *W. E. B. Du Bois*, 241.

17. T. Thomas Fortune to Washington, September 5, 1899; Washington to Fortune, September 11, 1905, in *The Booker T. Washington Papers*, vol. 5, 195, 203. Fortune and Baldwin had earlier had a conversation in Baldwin's office, a discussion which "disturbed" Baldwin. "I don't think you want a Garrison or a Phillips to stir up the question of negro rights," Baldwin wrote afterward. Baldwin to Washington, November 27, 1898; cf. Baldwin to Washington, December 4, 1898, both in Washington Papers.

18. Baldwin to Newcomb Frierson Thompson, April 15, 1900, in *The Booker T. Washington Papers*, vol. 5, 482.

child into a productive consumer." But the support of Baldwin and other businessmen for education could not be separated from larger issues. In a 1902 speech to the Richmond Education Association, he maintained that "the kind of educational work to which we have directed our notice is essential to the preservation of our form of government." Practical businessmen supported this educational work "because they believe that the final uplift and survival of civilization demands it, and they believe that it is good business because the desire for better things follows education."

Rather than promising that education would preserve the status quo or create meek workers (of any color), Baldwin recognized the inherent connection between education and discontent: "The wrong kind of education may, and often does, produce poor results and discontented minds. Let us remember, however, that there are two kinds of discontent. The one is based on dissatisfaction with one's condition without means of bettering it. The other is that healthy discontent that is the first sign of progress—it is the right kind of education in process of fermentation." He added, in words that do not fit the stereotype of a Tuskegee man: "It is our problem to create a discontent, but at the same time to equip the individual with the necessary tools to improve his condition."[19]

At first, Baldwin took for granted the main outlines of the black educational system of circa 1900—a system dominated by thousands of individual donors. The schools these unincorporated philanthropists supported were more or less private, broadly Protestant, increasingly black operated, and oriented toward "character-building." Before he became the first chairman of the General Education Board in 1902, Baldwin's vision was limited to extending and rationalizing what was already in place.

Baldwin's first biographer missed the extent of development in his thought, as well as Washington's role in the change. According to John Graham Brooks, Baldwin was a straightforward, enthusiastic disciple of Edgar Gardner Murphy, an influential southern white "moderate" who campaigned for educational reform and against child labor. "With no man North or South was Baldwin in greater agreement," asserted Brooks. Murphy's book *Problems of the Present South* (1904) was for Baldwin "a kind of standard of right opinion" on the Negro question.

19. Baldwin, "Why a Businessman Should Be Interested in Public Education."

"No one has declared Baldwin's hope and thought with truer touch" than Murphy, stated Brooks.[20]

The personal papers of Baldwin and his associates present a more complicated picture. In the last two years of his life, Baldwin was, in fact, increasingly at odds with Murphy. At the same time, Murphy had growing reservations about Washington and Tuskegee.

Baldwin was initially impressed with Murphy, an eloquent Episcopal priest who represented the "best South" so central to the ideas of racial harmony advocated by Booker T. Washington. A Murphy speech at Tuskegee brought him to the attention of Baldwin, who, along with his fellow trustee Robert Ogden, arranged for him to deliver a major address in the North, speaking to a Philadelphia audience on March 8, 1900, on the theme "The White Man and the Negro at the South." For his part, Murphy read Baldwin's speech to the American Social Science Association and told the philanthropic northerner that he was "one of us."[21]

Murphy would become so effective at presenting a plausible case for the white South, both in his speeches and his essays (*Problems of the Present South* and *The Basis of Ascendancy*, published in 1910), that one historian has described him as "in effect the ambassador of Conservative Southern white civilization to the intellectual North." According to another scholar, Bruce Clayton, Murphy's writings "constitute the most imposing intellectual apology for White Supremacy in Southern literature."[22] This "moderate" defense of the southern racial order eventually raised questions in Baldwin's mind.

Indications of Baldwin's shifting attitude toward southern education and "justice for the negro" begin to appear in the summer of 1903, after he had extensive discussions with Washington. "I have had some very interesting meetings with Mr. Washington during the last month," he wrote to Buttrick. He saw "the whole country" as becoming "stirred up" over southern race relations. After "enough friction" had been created, Baldwin predicted, people would see that "the

20. Brooks, An American Citizen, 230, 231, 240.

21. Ralph Luker, A Southern Tradition in Theology and Social Criticism, 1830–1930, 319; William H. Baldwin, Jr., to Booker T. Washington, January 28, 1900, in Washington Papers.

22. Williamson, The Crucible of Race, 331; Bruce Clayton, The Savage Ideal: Intolerance and Intellectual Leadership in the South, 1890–1914, 195.

problem, so called" was a national matter and recognize "that aid must be given at once if we are to keep the peace." Aware that he was talking "heresy," Baldwin suggested that federal spending on education might be required: "If the Southern States separately cannot see the value of justice for the negro as well as education, and if, further, as I believe, the Southern States are not able to educate the negro except after a long period of time, I am inclined to think that it will pay to educate him through the assistance of the National government."[23]

In a letter to his onetime mentor, Charles Francis Adams, Baldwin explained the nature of the crisis in race relations as he saw it. "Race hatred," he wrote, was "gathering fast," growing in response to black progress. "Do not for a moment doubt that the friction that is being aroused is due largely to jealousy and to fear on the part of the ignorant white people that the negro will get on top." He anticipated a "vicious period" ahead with "a very large portion" of the North and West sharing "in the race hatred," although he hoped that justice would prevail in the end.[24]

At the summer meeting of the Southern Education Board at Lake George, New York, Baldwin repeatedly raised the question, "What has been done for the negro?" He gave a talk at the opening session of the three-day conference that, he wrote to Washington, "was based on my meeting with you Tuesday." Baldwin began by telling his colleagues of Washington's "anxiety and sense of responsibility . . . in view of the increasingly strained relationship between the two races in certain parts of the country." Showing "my true color from beginning to end," Baldwin wrote that he had made himself "the representative of negro justice." "I talked right out plainly about all the things that one seldom talks [about] with Southern men. . . . You know what I said without my attempting to repeat it," he wrote in a confidential letter to the Tuskegee educator. At a later session Baldwin threatened to resign from both the General Education Board and the SEB if doubts from "the negro race" about the boards' commitment to black education could not be dispelled. "In short, I turned loose on the whole situation, and although Mr. Peabody and Mr. Ogden did not

23. Baldwin to Wallace Buttrick, July 13, 1903, in GEB Papers, Box 305.
24. Baldwin to Charles Francis Adams, August 1, 1903, in Washington Papers.

agree with me, I have certainly set them all to thinking. . . . It was a very intense time."[25]

Baldwin's letters were usually short, often cryptic, and it is not easy to reconstruct precisely how he "turned loose on the whole situation." Unlike some of his colleagues, he clearly viewed America's race relations as demanding urgent action. In a letter to Buttrick he complained that "many of our friends" were motivated by "personal ambition" and prone to indulge a "spirit of self-glorification." Some method must be adopted, he said, "by which the negroes will feel that we are at least in sympathy with them." Buttrick told Washington that Baldwin had "brought matters to a head in the best talk I have ever heard him make. The whole discussion made a profound impact on our Southern friends."[26]

This view was more optimistic than Baldwin's; he doubted that the SEB had the capacity to "seize upon the larger questions that underlie our work." "The things that are on your mind and mine," he wrote to Washington, "are larger, broader, and need more courageous treatment than the Southern Education Board can possibly give." As far as Baldwin was concerned, America's racial crisis was getting worse: " . . . the problem is running ahead of us, and . . . we have got to go into the field to meet it." Writing to Buttrick a few days later, he chose a grimmer metaphor. The SEB was "merely an incident to the great undertow that is drawing us all in. I prefer to fortify myself against this undertow. I am not going to be drawn under. Nor am I going to stand on the beach and merely watch it."[27]

One southern member of the SEB was surprised by Baldwin's criticisms, having assumed that both northern and southern educational crusaders were united in the tactical decision "that for the first two years we would not emphasize the *negro* too much." A year earlier, commented Charles W. Dabney, Baldwin and Washington had agreed with the principle "that the *white man must be educated first.*" Now there were "many indications of a change of point of view, at least, on the part of most of our Northern friends," who had been "re-excited"

25. Baldwin to Washington, August 10, 1903, in *The Booker T. Washington Papers*, vol. 7, 259–61.

26. Baldwin to Buttrick, August 17, 1903, in GEB Papers, Box 305; Buttrick to Washington, August 18, 1903, in GEB Papers, Box 722.

27. Baldwin to Washington, August 19, 1903, in *The Booker T. Washington Papers*, vol. 7, 270. Baldwin to Buttrick, August 23, 1903, in GEB Papers, Box 305.

by "recent events" to consider "how they can help maintain [Negroes] against the white aggressors." The meetings were harmonious, though the "Southern men" felt "intense anxiety" about some of the things they had heard.[28]

"Recent events" certainly had created a sense of crisis in 1903. Not only had federal authorities made arrests in shocking peonage cases in Alabama, Florida, and Georgia, but also the summer was marred by several incidents of horrific mob violence, including the burning at the stake of a black man in Wilmington, Delaware, cheered on by a crowd of five thousand, and an attempted lynching in Evansville, Indiana, that was only prevented when local militia and sheriff's deputies opened fire on the mob, killing and wounding thirty. The principal of an American Missionary Association industrial school in Louisiana was murdered by shotgun-wielding ambushers in August 1903, and his successor was driven away a few months later. In addition to all this, James K. Vardaman's election as governor of Mississippi gave a frightening demonstration of the political appeal of unrestrained Negrophobia, even in a state where blacks had been disfranchised and thoroughly isolated. "The majority of white people in Mississippi oppose Negro education of any character," observed Washington in dismay.[29]

28. Charles W. Dabney to Charles L. Coon, August 27, 1903, in Southern Education Board Papers, Dabney Collection, Southern Historical Collection; Harlan, The Wizard of Tuskegee, 190–91. In fact, Washington had strongly repudiated the idea "that the white man should be educated first." In a letter to the president of Berea College, Washington declared, "There is but one interpretation to be put on such a statement, and that is that the education of the Negro must be stopped while the education of the white man goes forward." Washington to William Goodell Frost, February 11, 1903, in The Booker T. Washington Papers, vol. 7, 68–69. At the Lake George meeting, Baldwin had "called Dr. Dabney down" for neglecting Negro education in the SEB's Monthly Bulletin. At the same time Baldwin praised Murphy as "a man of true courage" and Edwin A. Alderman, president of Tulane, as "simply great." Baldwin to Washington, August 10, 1903, in The Booker T. Washington Papers, vol. 7, 260.

29. Luker, The Social Gospel, 217–23; Washington to Oswald Garrison Villard, August 31, 1903, in The Booker T. Washington Papers, vol. 7, 273. Baldwin tried to reassure Washington after Vardaman's victory, affirming that Vardaman and his supporters were "about twenty years too late" to succeed in eliminating black education. "The same spirit that met the situation thirty-five years ago will meet this situation just as soon as the issue is clearly defined," he predicted with poor prophetic accuracy. "Certainly the Southern Education Board will be heard." Baldwin to Washington, September 2, 1903, in The Papers of Booker T. Washington, vol. 7, 276.

Baldwin's new attitude on race relations manifested itself in a variety of ways. When Tuskegee students conducted a three-day strike in protest of a new schedule—a "rebellion," Washington called it— Baldwin responded: "My first impression was, that I was mighty glad to see a body of negroes had the courage to revolt against conditions which they thought were unjust." Based on his experience with railroad workers, he was confident that "some little thing" has grown into a bigger grievance and "some fault some where on the part of the teachers" had probably caused the student protest.[30]

Baldwin's changing understanding of racial issues led to quiet conflict with Edgar Gardner Murphy, fast becoming the leading voice of southern white "moderation." Though the available sources are tantalizingly incomplete, it is clear that the two men had important differences in 1903 and 1904, and that these differences were tied to their assessment of the Wizard of Tuskegee. Washington, who felt that members of the GEB and SEB had chosen "to drift out of touch with the colored people engaged in education in the South," used Baldwin to communicate his views to the philanthropists.[31] At the same time, Murphy became privately critical of Washington.

An indication of the gap between Baldwin and Murphy can be seen in their contrasting reactions to Carl Schurz's article "Can the South Solve the Negro Problem?" published in the January 1904 issue of *McClure's Magazine*. Based on experience going back to his report to President Johnson in 1865, the veteran reformer emphatically rejected the idea that white southerners "know best how to deal with the negro." He reminded his readers of previous "grievous mistakes" made by the white majority, including the notion that slavery was a blessing, the decision to seek southern independence in a "reckless war," and the postwar claim that blacks could not survive as free workers. He questioned whether disfranchisement of blacks was in the long-term self-interest of southern whites, blaming unreasoning "race-antagonism" rather than any legitimate fear of ignorant voters for suffrage restriction. "With many of the Southern whites," he

30. Washington to Baldwin, October 20, 1903; Baldwin to Washington, October 23, 1903, in *The Booker T. Washington Papers*, vol. 7, 298–300, 309. On the background of the student strike, "the only serious defiance of the school's authority in Washington's lifetime," see Harlan, *The Wizard of Tuskegee*, 145–48.

31. Washington to Baldwin, January 22, 1904, in *The Booker T. Washington Papers*, vol. 7, 409.

observed, "a well-educated colored voter is as objectionable as an ignorant one." Using ideas that resembled the proslavery arguments of the past, racial fanatics such as Vardaman were distracting the public from "the true problem" with such impossible schemes as Negro deportation and repeal of the fourteenth and fifteenth amendments. The real choice was clear: would the Negro be reduced to "a permanent condition of serfdom" or would there be "a movement in the direction of recognizing him as a citizen in the true sense of the term"?

Schurz did not advocate any "drastic" new legislation to deal with racial problems, nor did he deny that "the most essential work will have to done in and by the South itself." Still, he called upon enlightened white southerners "to banish the preposterous bugbear of 'social equality'" with its attendant "hysterics." With the right sort of appeals, "high-minded" southerners could lead even many of the most prejudiced whites to see "that white ignorance and lawlessness are just as bad as black ignorance and lawlessness; . . . that neither white nor black can override the rights of the other without endangering his own; and that the negro question can finally be settled so as to stay settled only on the basis of the fundamental law of the land as it stands, by fair observance of that law and not by any tricky circumvention of it."[32]

Washington immediately pointed out the article to Baldwin and dictated a personal note to Schurz, praising his essay as "the strongest and most statesmanlike word that has been said on the South and the Negro for a long number of years" and expressing his hope that it would be read widely by southern whites. Baldwin arranged a lunch meeting with Schurz and several philanthropists a few weeks later. Murphy had read the article, was "very bitter" about it, and only reluctantly agreed to meet with the author. "It was another illustration of Murphy's sensitiveness and Southern blood," Baldwin wrote to Washington. "He said that the article would make the Alabama people 'hate the negroes,' where they had not before." Baldwin suppressed an urge to say that Schurz's article "ought to make the Alabama people hate themselves," fearing to stir up "bad blood" with his colleague.[33]

32. Carl Schurz, "Can the South Solve the Negro Problem?" 258–75.
33. Washington to Schurz, December 28, 1903, in *The Booker T. Washington Papers,* vol. 7, 381. Baldwin to Washington, January 18, 1904, in Washington Papers; Harlan, *The Wizard of Tuskegee,* 191.

Murphy's objection to the article was, no doubt, based on Schurz's view of racial prejudice as "unreasoning" and dangerous. Murphy distinguished between race hatred and "race antipathy," insisting that race antipathy was a "blessing," a positive "force, conservative of racial integrity, of social purity, of public good." The white South's fear of "social equality," he wrote in *Problems of the Present South,* was rooted in an important truth: "The total abandonment of the dogma of racial integrity at the South would mean a land—not white, nor part white and part black—but a land all black; with perhaps many of those reversions of the standards of political and social life which have been exhibited in Hayti and San Domingo." In words published shortly after Schurz's article, and perhaps designed as a direct response, Murphy condemned northern "journalism of moral petulancy" that "will insist upon reading 'pro-slavery' designs into the elementary and most imperative policies of the South, and will find 'hatred of the negro' in customs which have protected him from hatred and made possible his existence and happiness."[34]

Though both Washington and Baldwin respected Murphy and saw him as an ally in the battle to preserve Negro education, they knew he had limitations, and neither the white railroad executive nor the black educator made Murphy "the standard of right opinion" on racial matters. In fact, as early as 1904 Murphy was willing to blame Washington for "the growing estrangement between the best people of the South and the best negroes of the South," asserting that many white southerners sensed "a distinct change of emphasis, if not direction" in Washington's leadership. Writing to Ogden, Murphy claimed that Washington and Tuskegee were "intensely unpopular" with Alabama whites, partly the result of "the just resentment of the 'showiness' of so large an institution." Two years later Murphy wrote to George Foster Peabody, treasurer of the General Education Board, warning that race relations in Alabama were worse than ever before. "Our truest and best people are in despair; and they hold Washington and Tuskegee to be largely responsible. . . . I fear that unless there is a change in the spirit and attitude of Tuskegee the very existence of the institution is in peril."[35]

34. Luker, *The Social Gospel,* 285–86; Edgar Gardner Murphy, *Problems of the Present South,* 270–71, 278–79.

35. Murphy to Washington, October 14, 1904, in *The Booker T. Washington Papers,* vol. 7, 105n; Murphy to Robert C. Ogden, March 8, 1904, Special Correspondence,

Murphy left no record of his reaction to Baldwin's own distinct change of emphasis, which was clear enough by 1904. Writing to Robert Ogden, Baldwin declared early in 1904 that he planned to "stand more openly in the future than in the past" on "certain questions which I have raised." Ogden responded by reminding Baldwin how complicated southern conditions were: "The South is insane upon the Negro question. Not one Southern man in ten thousand approaches correct views. . . . We are doing great good but can destroy it in five minutes." He added, with uncharacteristic pessimism, "Some times I almost despair." Baldwin had heard such arguments before and was growing impatient with them. "I very much wish," he wrote to his pious, white-bearded colleague, "that you could explain to me how you feel that we can destroy in five minutes any great good that is being accomplished." Referring to unnamed southern educational crusaders, perhaps including Murphy, Baldwin wrote: "The principal criticism I have to make is the untruthfulness of many people, and the lack of courage in speaking what they know to be the truth."[36]

Baldwin protested a specific example of "evasion" a few weeks later. In an interview with a southern journalist, Murphy had sought to downplay the fact that Ogden and his guests would visit several black schools on their annual southern railroad excursion. "He names practically all the places that your party plan to visit except the colored schools," Baldwin commented in a letter to Ogden. "I do not believe anything is to be gained by this kind of evasion. It is much better to be perfectly frank and straightforward with the Southern people," he observed. Southerners will note that black schools have been visited, will expect northerners to have an interest in such schools, and "will have no respect or confidence in a Northern man who at this late date pretends to be interested in the white schools and not interested in Negro schools."

The most significant fact about this letter is that it is plagiarized. Baldwin had simply appropriated—almost verbatim—a letter Washington had written to him a month earlier and sent it over his own signature to Ogden. Washington knew that he had a remarkable rapport

---

in Robert C. Ogden Papers, Library of Congress; Murphy to George Foster Peabody, April 12, 1906, in General Education Board file, George Foster Peabody Papers, Library of Congress.

36. Baldwin to Ogden, February 25 and 28, 1904, Special Correspondence, in Ogden Papers; Ogden to Baldwin, February 26, 1904, in Ogden Letterbook, Ogden Papers.

with Baldwin and clearly used him to communicate his concerns to "the two boards and friends of southern education," though even he might have been surprised at the smoothness of the collaboration in this case![37]

By the summer of 1904 Baldwin was desperately ill, unable to participate in the philanthropic matters so important to him. His death on January 3, 1905, deprived Washington of his most important contact in the "Ogden movement." Though Ogden, Buttrick, and the others continued to treat him with great respect, the Tuskegee educator's practical influence on the policies of the northern philanthropists was significantly diminished after 1905.

Baldwin's successors showed little of his sense of urgency, preferring careful planning, even inaction, to the possibility of ill-conceived gifts. They decisively rejected the opportunity to federate Tuskegee-style independent industrial schools, as Baldwin had hoped to do, and evinced limited interest in promoting the Tuskegee imitators as the primary answer to black educational needs. Ignoring a good deal of Washington's advice, the GEB eventually endorsed the "policy of cooperating with the white people of the South in promoting Negro education," making the stimulation of government spending on public education the first priority of its programs for black education—with aid for private and denominational schools a distinctly secondary emphasis.[38]

Washington found creative ways around this disappointment by inspiring new philanthropists and new forms of philanthropy. Beginning in the year Baldwin died, he cultivated Anna T. Jeanes, a wealthy Quaker donor to Tuskegee. By 1907 she had endowed the Jeanes Fund, a foundation committed to improving black rural education and carefully separated from the General Education Board. Washington was chairman of the Jeanes Fund board of trustees. In 1911 Washington met Julius Rosenwald, the philanthropic Sears, Roebuck and Company executive who had been inspired by a recent reading of Brooks's 1910 biography of Baldwin.[39] After his election to the

37. Baldwin to Ogden, April 11, 1904, in Special Correspondence, Ogden Papers; Washington to Baldwin, March 12 and January 22, 1904, in *The Booker T. Washington Papers*, vol. 7, 467, 409.

38. Report of the Special Committee on the Education of the Negro, May 25, 1911, GEB Dockets, 1911–1913, vol. 2, 274–80, GEB Papers.

39. Harlan, *The Wizard of Tuskegee*, 194–96. Julius Rosenwald to Lessing Rosenwald, October 5, 1910, Julius Rosenwald to Mrs. William H. Baldwin, August 30 1912, in Julius Rosenwald Papers, University of Chicago.

Tuskegee board in the following year, Rosenwald worked closely with Washington, quickly adopting many of the Wizard's understandings of black education. In 1913 he began his famous program in support of buildings for Negro rural schools, a program that assisted the construction of more than five thousand public schools in the next twenty-five years. Washington was a major influence on this huge project—and Tuskegee Institute administered the gifts as long as he was alive.

At the time of his death, Baldwin was a profoundly influential man. "An Inspiring Career," pronounced the *New York Times* in an editorial. Noting his interest in good government, education, vice reform, labor relations, and housing for the poor, the *Times* predicted that Baldwin's "rich bequest of right action" would produce lasting results. "Year by year his influence and his good fame were increasing;" commented *Century Magazine*, "only a little past forty, it seemed that the future held for him twice the opportunities of his already beneficent and exemplary career." According to another editor, "there has never been in the history of the country a finer citizen in business, nor one who more strikingly united idealism of aim with practical sagacity and method than Mr. Baldwin." "He is of more importance in the solution of the race problem in the United States than any other man," said another admirer.[40]

Contrary to these eulogists' expectations, Baldwin's influence waned quickly. This is true despite the fact President Theodore Roosevelt and former President Grover Cleveland helped to raise $150,000 for a Baldwin Memorial Fund at Tuskegee. Even though his widow, Ruth Bowles Baldwin, played an important role in the founding of the National Urban League, inspired by the idea that she was continuing plans originated by her husband, his ideas had less long-term significance than might have been expected.

In the years after his death, the great foundations, led by his own General Education Board, carefully rethought their philosophy of philanthropy and came to envision major conceptual changes in black education. Within a decade of his death, his former colleagues no longer shared Baldwin's confidence that "the present problem of Negro education" was a "problem of organization—of work, not theory," that northern philanthropists ought to "build up a secondary school

40. *New York Times*, January 4, 1905; *Century Magazine*, "A Life of Service," 69 (March 1905): 800; *Outlook*, January 14, 1905, 115.

system under the general control and supervision of Hampton and Tuskegee." Some of the key figures in this process concluded that Baldwin's approach had been shallow or unwise. By 1907 Wallace Buttrick was writing to Robert Ogden: "I cannot help feeling that Mr. Baldwin's work was almost wholly spiritual and 'inspirational.'" He continued, in praise that was faint, if not patronizing: "I do not like that last word, but after all, it describes what Mr. Baldwin really was in the educational field. His enthusiasm attracted Mr. Rockefeller, Jr. and for a time Mr. Gates also. After a while what they regarded as his lack of method dulled their enthusiasm somewhat, but I am sure that they have never ceased to appreciate his fine spirit and great devotion."[41]

Washington, by contrast, continued to praise Baldwin in the highest terms. Writing in 1911, he described him as the "man from whom . . . I learned, perhaps, more than any other"—excluding, of course, "General Armstrong, my first teacher" (characteristically, Washington did not emphasize what he had taught Baldwin). "I never met any one who was more genuinely interested than Mr. Baldwin in the success of the Negro people," he wrote in My Larger Education. Intensifying his praise, he added that Baldwin "understood, as few men have, the Negro people, and . . . was in full sympathy with their ambition to rise to a position of usefulness as large and as honourable as that of any race." He offered one subtle, perceptive criticism of his friend—a criticism that some people might have applied to Washington himself. In his concern that black Americans should not "mistake the appearance for the real thing," Baldwin "sometimes seemed to go too far," observed Tuskegee's Great Accommodator.[42]

For the historian, Baldwin's career is a reminder of the ways in which philanthropy changed after the formation of the General Education Board in 1902. He should be remembered not only for the people and issues that he decisively influenced, but also for certain ideas that were ultimately rejected, and for a definition of the "present problem of Negro education" which failed to prevail.

41. Baldwin, "Present Problem of Negro Education," 403; Buttrick to Ogden, July 31, 1907, Special Correspondence, in Ogden Papers.
42. Washington, My Larger Education, 15, 17, 18.

4

The General Education Board's Choices

We . . . pointed out the danger that by keeping alive, largely by Northern money, a large number of inferior negro schools, we might be hindering the Southern communities from regarding negro education as their own responsibility.

—Jerome D. Greene[1]

At the founding of the General Education Board in 1902, a well-informed observer might have plausibly prophesied that Tuskegee and Hampton would dominate the future of black education. Since the new GEB was led by William H. Baldwin, Jr., the chairman of the Tuskegee board of trustees, it would have been reasonable to predict that Booker T. Washington and his black protégés would eventually mediate all northern educational philanthropy for the South.

What actually happened was very different. Within a decade of Washington's death in 1915, the Washington philosophy, Washington's network of influence ("the Tuskegee machine"), and Washington's school were no longer preeminent in African American educational philanthropy. Indeed, by 1930 Tuskegee and Hampton were moving away from industrial education as a radical challenge to conventional education and recasting their curriculum as little more than a cautious imitation of a standard American college.

Central to these developments was a series of choices by the General Education Board, as the philanthropic leaders who succeeded Baldwin assessed the options available to them. For the historian, the opportunities that the philanthropists could not imagine illuminate the choices they saw as obvious.

1. Jerome D. Greene to Wallace Buttrick, January 7, 1914, Box 353, GEB Papers.

"The General Education Board is not interested in almsgiving," declared Abraham Flexner in 1915. "It is interested in . . . framing and developing a long-headed policy which will take years and perhaps even successive generations."[2]

Flexner was speaking to twelve selected educators at a private conference on "Negro Education" convened in the Broadway offices of the Rockefeller Foundation. Although Hollis B. Frissell, principal of Hampton Institute (and a GEB trustee), presided over the meeting, he was only the nominal chairman. The real leader of the conference, the man who controlled the structure and tempo of the discussion, was Flexner, assistant secretary of the General Education Board. Already famous as the author of a Carnegie Foundation report on medical education and an influential volume on prostitution, he was shortly to write the seminal essay "A Modern School," describing the vision of "progressive education." A leader in the reform-minded Public Education Association, Flexner was also a member of New York City's board of education, a position he used, for a time, to advocate more efficient and more "practical" schooling that integrated work, study, and play.[3]

The other participants included some of the most important names in black education. The presidents or principals of three black schools attended: John Hope of Morehouse, Fayette McKenzie of Fisk, and Frissell. Foundation philanthropy was represented by James H. Dillard, the president of the Jeanes Foundation; Thomas Jesse Jones, the executive secretary of the Phelps-Stokes Fund; and W. T. B. Williams, the field agent of the Slater Fund. Former GEB staff member Bruce R. Payne, now president of the George Peabody College for Teachers, was a spokesman for contemporary educational theory. Four of the thirteen men attending the conference were full-time employees of the GEB. Unlike many other philanthropic discussions of black education, the Negro Education Conference was not restricted to white men. The

2. Conference of the General Education Board on Negro Education, November 29, 1915 (hereafter referred to as Negro Education Conference), 70, GEB Papers.

3. Fosdick et al., *Adventure in Giving*, 151–53; Abraham Flexner, *Prostitution in Europe*; Lawrence A. Cremin, *The Transformation of the School: Progressivism in American Education, 1876–1957*, 280–81; Steven C. Wheatley, *The Politics of Philanthropy: Abraham Flexner and Medical Education*; Diane Ravitch, *The Great School Wars: A History of the New York City Public Schools*, 212–14, 227.

three black participants were Hope, Williams, and R. R. Moton, soon to be elected principal of Tuskegee.[4]

Equally significant, perhaps, were those not invited to the conference. The four major Protestant missionary societies (the American Missionary Association, the Freedmen's Aid Society, the American Baptist Home Mission Society, and the Presbyterian Board of Missions for Freedmen) gave far more to black education than the GEB, but not a single missionary society was represented at the conference.[5] Nor was anyone at the conference authorized to speak for independent black denominations or for state and federal authorities.

Although the Rockefeller family's interest in Negro education had contributed decisively to the founding of the GEB in 1902, the board gave little money to black schools in the first dozen years of its operations. Fearing overextension, unwise spending, and the antagonism of white southerners, the board moved so cautiously that at the time of the 1915 conference some friends of black education suspected that the GEB was "indifferent, if not hostile," to blacks. At the Negro Education Conference, Bruce Payne described his reaction to the GEB's first published report, issued in 1914. "I was impressed with the fact that . . . the General Education Board . . . had not spent very much of its money on Negro education." The report, he said, had given him, as well as several of his teachers, a "bad impression." "It looked as if the General Education Board did not believe in Negro education. . . . Three or four of my men came to me. . . . they said, 'This board does not believe in Negro education. It gave Peabody College more money than they spent on almost all the South.'"[6]

In their observations, assertions, and leading questions, Flexner and his GEB associates at the conference revealed the choices they perceived for educational philanthropy. Some of the most important choices they regarded as utterly obvious. For example, the GEB men believed that the only effective way to educate the black masses was

---

4. The others attending the conference were E. C. Sage, an assistant secretary of the GEB; Wickliffe Rose, GEB trustee; Sidney Frissell, field agent of Hampton; and Jackson Davis, field agent of the GEB.

5. For the missionary societies' giving, see McPherson, *Abolitionist Legacy*, 147. By the 1920s, the Episcopal organization, the American Church Institute for Negroes (founded in 1906), would be a more significant supporter of black education than either the Baptist or Presbyterian missionary societies. See chapter 6.

6. *New York Evening Post*, July 13, 1914, Negro Education Conference, 180–82.

Officers and trustees of the General Education Board at Hotel Samoset, Rockland, Maine, July 8–10, 1915. Rockefeller Archive Center.

public education, supported by taxation. Board initiatives in the area of primary or secondary education must have as their ultimate goal the stimulation of government spending. "The only way of really maintaining the public school systems in any state is by taxation," declared Flexner. "Anything else is a temporary makeshift." Wickliffe Rose, GEB trustee (and director of the International Health Division of the Rockefeller Foundation), said: "It is perfect folly for us to think of these Boards as sources of funds for the maintenance of the public schools of the South. What we do therefore should be done with reference to stimulating the right activity on the part of the States and the Counties and the Communities, so far as funds are concerned."[7]

Flexner emphasized the problem of competition between private schools and the emerging public ones, suggesting that "public school development" might "be retarded or injured if these private schools are made more permanent." At another point he asked, "Is there

7. Negro Education Conference, 66, 184.

any danger . . . that these privately supported schools will tend to become too large, and to cover too much ground; be too expensive to maintain to warrant the public school authorities in taking them over?" Thomas Jesse Jones responded that "the danger of competition is rather remote." "Do you know any such things in your actual experience, aside from your imagination?" asked Payne, but Flexner persisted in his line of questioning. "Let us look ahead twenty-five years," he said. Would not the GEB's plan to build up public education be impeded "by a counter-development of the other [private] type of institution?"[8]

The primacy of public schools, as Flexner saw it, required the death of many black private schools, schools that were too "inefficient" or isolated or sectarian to contribute to educational progress. (All the more reason, of course, not to invite representatives of parochial education to the conference.) Flexner's ideas on this subject echoed the board's assumptions about private education in general, for it was an *idée fixe* of Frederick Gates and other leaders of the board that America would only have a true educational "system" after extensive educational consolidation. Eventually private secondary schools, with a few exceptions, would disappear. Private colleges had an important role to play, but most were located in the wrong places, with uncertain support and weak academic standards. Flexner applied the lessons of medical education to black colleges. Near the end of the Negro Education Conference, he tipped his hand in a leading question: "Dr. Hope, what would be the effect of selecting four or five Negro colleges and building them up, making them good, honest, sincere, effective colleges so far as they went, and letting the others alone, not to suppress them or consolidate them but just to make them 'sweat,' would that tend in the long run to so stigmatize the inferior institutions that they would give up, the way the poor medical institutions are giving up?"[9] Clearly Flexner came to the conference committed to such a policy.

It has often been suggested that the GEB made its choices for black education with the object of skillfully controlling the nation's black population, especially the leadership group. Some scholars connect

8. Ibid., 56–57, 61, 66–67, 69–70.
9. Fosdick et al., *Adventure in Giving*, 128–31; Frederick T. Gates to Wallace Buttrick, June 8, 1909, Box 716, GEB Papers; Negro Education Conference, 161–62.

the GEB with the specific goals and needs of American industry.[10] Though promoters of black education did, on occasion, defend their activities in the language of economic self-interest (enlightened or otherwise), by 1915 the businessmen were no longer in charge. At the Negro Education Conference neither John D. Rockefeller, Jr., nor his father put in an appearance—nor did anyone play the role of Robert C. Ogden or William H. Baldwin, Jr. The philanthropic bureaucrats had taken over, and the rationale for GEB activities was expressed in the rhetoric of educational and social reform. For better *and* worse, black education per se was a secondary concern, justifiable only in the context of broader goals. Men such as Flexner saw important implications for all education in black educational experiments. At the same time, they had little sense of a crisis in race relations that required urgent, even desperate, action. But if they were unimpassioned, they also (for similar reasons) showed no interest in developing a distinctive, permanent caste education for black Americans.[11]

These themes were present in the 1915 conference. Referring to a current educational debate in New York City,[12] Flexner observed: "The effort of those who think they are progressive in education is to modify the existing curriculum, which is a traditional curriculum for white children, very much in the direction of what is perhaps proposed in the South as especially fitting for colored children." Others joined Flexner in criticism of all conventional education, for either whites or blacks. Harvard and Yale "and all those places" had entrance examinations that were "all off; all off!" They needed the advice of progressive reformers as much as the worst-managed black denominational "college." "If I had my way," said James H. Dillard, "Harvard and Yale would never have any more money." The South was particularly cursed by misplaced classicism in its colleges and high schools. Wickliffe Rose reported that he told one state superintendent:

10. This is a central theme of James D. Anderson's *The Education of Blacks in the South*. See also Donald Spivey, *Schooling for the New Slavery: Black Industrial Education, 1865–1915*.

11. See Steven C. Wheatley's perceptive observation on early-twentieth-century foundations: "It was the bureaucrats and not the plutocrats who did the decisive managing. . . . To be sure these philanthropic managers were obliged to drape their programs in mantles acceptable to the philanthropists, but the rubrics of Progressive reform were more than broad enough to accommodate their designs." *The Politics of Philanthropy*, x-xi.

12. See Ravitch, *The Great School Wars*, 189–218.

"I believe that if we go at this right, we will get a school for the colored people more quickly than for our own people, and it will *help get the right kind of [secondary] school for white people* when they see what it is." Bruce Payne said that he would be "mighty pleased" if white city schools cut out "sixty or seventy per cent of the work they are doing" to make room for "some of these industrial subjects." No one contradicted Thomas Jesse Jones's assertion: "There is no effort to make a caste education . . . it is simply a general movement in education."[13]

The three black educators offered several practical criticisms of the philanthropists' agenda. Though none of the three had any philosophical objection to a curriculum that combined "working with the hands" with intellectual training, each man offered cautious warnings about current practices in black education. John Hope affirmed his support of industrial education, noting that he had sent his own son to a private school when he realized that the Atlanta public schools offered no industrial education. "I believe in the modern sort of education," he said. "As I say, I took my own boy out in order that he might get it." At the same time, he warned his colleagues that black teachers feared "a different kind of education for negroes," especially when industrial subjects completely replaced academic courses in primary and secondary education.[14]

Moton and Williams repeatedly challenged the sufficiency of the current Hampton curriculum as a tool for training black leaders, and urged that the program be updated in light of recent educational progress. Industrial training was only one part of Hampton's mission, argued Williams: "We are trying to train men who not only will be skilled with their hands, but men who can lead in their communities, and unless you give them certain intellectual powers, no skill with their hands is going to enable them to lead." Hampton was not preparing people who could administer schools or serve as school supervisors. "I do not think Hampton is doing quite enough to perpetuate its own ideas of industrial education," asserted Moton, who was on the verge of leaving Hampton for Tuskegee. "We fit people for the positions

13. Negro Education Conference, 17, 131, 87, 20–23, 100 (emphasis added).
14. Ibid., 15–19. James Anderson misconstrues Hope's comment on "modern education," quoting it as a comment on college curriculum and an *attack* on industrial education. Hope in fact used "modern education" as a synonym for "industrial education." *The Education of Blacks in the South*, 259.

John Hope. Moorland-Spingarn Research
Center, Howard University Archives.

of smallest influence"—that is, primary school teachers. "I do not
want Hampton a college," Moton said, but graduates of Hampton and
Tuskegee needed another year of training "along the lines they are
doing now."[15]

In a discussion of higher "academic institutions for Negroes," Hope
cautiously challenged the idea that there were too many black colleges,
many of which should be dismantled: "When we realize how big a
population we are going to have . . . , it is a serious question in my
mind whether we ought to think about getting rid of those schools." In
addition, Hope—a devout Baptist—reminded his fellow educators of

15. Negro Education Conference, 110–13, 115–19, 122–26, 134–41. By 1920, under
the leadership of a new principal, Hampton had begun the transition to a collegiate
curriculum—a change opposed by Moton, the school's only black trustee. See Raymond
Wolters, *The New Negro on Campus: Black College Rebellions of the 1920s*, 232–34.

the power of "the denominational element" in the black community, often the motive power behind black self-help. If colleges sponsored by the northern missionary societies were closed, he asked, "what would happen?" The answer, he argued, was clear: "The Negroes would say, 'We are going to educate our children in our own schools,' and they would start another college, and we would be worse off than we are now. That is exactly what would happen in Georgia, if we should do away with Morehouse College and Spelman Seminary. . . . The Negro Baptists of Georgia would start a Baptist College of their own."[16]

None of the three black educators disagreed with Flexner's claim that much of the work done at black colleges was "pretentious," irrelevant, and "above the heads of the students for whom it was meant." Noting that he had "observed something very much like it in the colleges for white boys," Flexner wondered if black colleges would be willing to "cut away absolutely from the kind of standards they have taken over from white institutions[,] *where the work is not done either.*" Significantly, he thought it was "more important to concern ourselves about the Negro boys than the white boys" because doing so would offer "a better chance to accomplish something."[17]

The conference helped clarify the board's rationale for aid to black education, but did not produce any dramatic increase in spending, thanks to the GEB's theory of philanthropy. Ignoring inconvenient contrary views expressed at the conference, the board's ad hoc "Committee on Negro Education" (Frissell, Rose, Flexner, and E. C. Sage) issued a report in January 1916 that was full of arguments for continued caution. "The field of Negro education is almost without limit," stated the report, "the very magnitude of the work offering a temptation to spread out unwisely." Since the board possessed "at best only restricted funds," the wisest course in black education was to follow the same methods the GEB had successfully applied "in other fields." That is, the GEB might "through demonstration, work out salient methods,

16. Negro Education Conference, 150–60. "I think I had a chance to say some things that might not have been said by others there," Hope told a friend. Leroy Davis, A *Clashing of the Soul: John Hope and the Dilemma of African American Leadership and Black Higher Education in the Early Twentieth Century,* 211.
    17. Ibid., 162–68, emphasis added.

Robert Russa Moton.
Moorland-Spingarn Research Center,
Howard University Archives.

the widest development of which must be dependent upon public funds." Though the GEB policy was predicated on building up strong public schools, the report recognized the need for some support for private schools—"a few of the really valuable schools"—especially since private schools educated most of the teachers employed in public systems. "Candor compels us to admit," declared the report, "that many decades will elapse before Negro education is adequately provided through taxation."[18]

Certain familiar assumptions were reiterated in the report. Many black private secondary schools were "weak and superfluous," and the money spent on them "more or less unwisely expended." There were "too many Negro colleges and universities," creating a climate of educational "chaos," in which poorly equipped, grandiose institutions blurred the distinction between real and imitation. "The Board cannot be the main prop of any one school," for to do so would be to

18. "Negro Education," January 24, 1916, 1–3, Box 329, GEB Papers.

ignore the necessity of local support and local interest in a school's success.[19]

The report gave lukewarm support for advanced education (observing that "The Negro is determined to have some opportunity for higher education") and recognized a need for black physicians "in the South." "The Negro physician . . . is needed and is likely to be more and more needed," noted the committee, clearly assuming an intensifying racial separation in the South.[20]

Seeking to offer a broad justification for black educational philanthropy, the report asserted: "The type of education that these schools are working out has a significance far beyond the needs of the Negro race." Writing in the midst of World War I, Flexner and associates saw important reasons for "greater activity . . . at this time," as the world was experiencing a clear illustration of "the disastrous consequences of social prejudice and misunderstanding."[21]

The "greater activity" anticipated by the report did not take place until the mid-1920s. Then in an eight-year period (1924 to 1931) the GEB appropriated nearly $25 million for black education, or about three times the total spending of the previous two decades. The bulk of the increased aid went to private colleges and secondary schools, not public institutions. This striking burst of educational spending represented nearly 40 percent of the GEB's entire effort for black education from 1902 to 1960.[22]

What accounts for the huge increase in GEB appropriations for black education? At first glance, the board appears to have reversed the policies followed under Wallace Buttrick, principal executive officer from 1902 to 1923. From 1923 to 1928 the GEB was led by Wickliffe Rose, the first southerner to head the foundation. Perhaps the spending bulge of the late twenties was simply the result of new leadership. As noted in chapter 2, W. E. B. Du Bois perceived a distinct shift in GEB policies as "the more liberal element among young Southerners became members of the board."[23]

The board conducted another major review of black educational policy in 1922. Another special committee, made up of Rose, Dillard,

19. Ibid., 4, 5, 6.
20. Ibid., 5.
21. Ibid., 5, 6.
22. See appendix.
23. Meyer Weinberg, ed., *W. E. B. Du Bois: A Reader*, 92.

and new trustee Raymond B. Fosdick, prepared a memorandum on the GEB and Negro education, paying particular attention to the question: "What is the theory or principle underlying the Board's policies?"[24] If the GEB suddenly perceived new options in the 1920s, this document should reveal them.

There was, however, no radical departure, no sweeping change proposed in the document produced by Rose, Dillard, and Fosdick. The memorandum presented a somewhat stronger defense of higher education for blacks than earlier policy statements, although this was largely a matter of nuance and tone. The statement repudiated caste education, but similar statements had been made before, though less emphatically or directly.

According to the 1922 statement, "a clear answer" had been obtained to the question of the theory behind the GEB's policies. This answer was so balanced and subtle that it might well have served as a public statement instead of a private working position. It is worth quoting in full:

The Board's interest is neither sentimental nor merely humanitarian; it is practical. The Negro race is numerous and widely scattered; it is with us to stay. The Negro is the neighbor of the white; he is a citizen; in some states he votes; almost everywhere his civic and political position improves, as he becomes better educated. Economically, he is an increasingly important productive factor. Steadily, since the abolition of slavery he has developed race pride. More and more he wants his own leaders. Aside from any concern which may on humanitarian grounds be felt for the Negro for his own sake, it is clear that the welfare of the South, not to say the whole country—its prosperity, its sanitation, its morale—is affected by the condition of the Negro race.[25]

Except for the comments about education improving African Americans' civic and political position, and the reference to "race pride," the statement could have been issued as educational propaganda aimed at white southern taxpayers. In its invocation of the "practical," it was a good illustration of a strategy which sought to make education neutral, nonpartisan—a lowest-common-denominator platform upon which humanitarians and men of affairs could unite, ignoring questions of racial equality.

24. "Report to General Education Board Special Meeting at Gedney Farms Hotel, October 12–14, 1922," section 6, p. 24, Box 331, GEB Papers.
25. Ibid., 24–25.

Wallace Buttrick and James Hardy Dillard. Rockefeller Archive Center.

But the rest of the 1922 report suggests the inherent contradictions of the apolitical approach, for *it* could never have been endorsed by the white South's political and educational leaders. In essence, "the theory or principle underlying the Board's policies" was profoundly controversial: "the Negro must be educated for the same reasons that other races need to be educated and trained." The report unequivocally repudiated the assumptions central to southern white support of black education. "Once started, Negro education cannot logically be stopped at any arbitrarily determined level. The Negro cannot be educated 'for his place' any more than the white man could be educated for his place; for in this modern world no man and no race will accept the place which some other man or some other race selects for him." Blacks share with whites, the committee declared, those aspirations that make a deferential social order impossible in modern conditions.[26]

26. According to Fosdick, Buttrick "used to tell a story" about a conversation he had with Theodore Roosevelt, with the moral that "there is no place to stop" in Negro

Such statements sound startling if one assumes that earlier policies sought black "education for servitude," but the authors did not intend to recast board policies. "As a general proposition . . . ," affirmed the committee, "we believe that the Board's attitude and policy have been sound."[27] In fact, the thrust of the report was to justify and recapitulate a series of assumptions the GEB had used from the beginning.

Like all previous GEB policy reviews, the report emphasized the primary role of state schools and the need to stimulate "public interest and public support." The speed of educational development depended, according to the committee, not on the wishes of "outside organizations," but rather on "the proper response from the public." Because "public school facilities for Negroes lag and will long lag behind those for whites," private secondary schools would be necessary for some time to come, though their function could be expected to adjust to "progress in public education." Probably a very few of the strongest schools should be given some sort of endowment, while gradually diminishing aid would be extended to a few others in order "to keep their operations within their assured income," and, perhaps, hasten their "absorption into the public school system." Likewise, the South would need "a few strong independent colleges" for blacks because no public colleges could be counted on to provide "academic education," although the "Southern public" did show "a growing sense of the responsibility for higher education of Negroes in so far as teacher-training, agriculture and the mechanic arts are concerned." The board also needed to support black medical education, another area neglected by the white South.[28]

In short, it is difficult to make the case that the board started spending more money on black education because it had developed a new rationale for its activity. Wickliffe Rose, in addition, was hardly

---

education, since industrial education required teachers trained in normal schools, which in turn required instructors trained in colleges and universities. Fosdick et al., *Adventure in Giving*, 188. "Report to GEB Special Meeting," 25. The GEB's first published report made a similar point about the aspirations of blacks and whites, though in more cautious language. Arguing that "the higher education of the Negro ought not to be neglected," the report stated: "The reasoning followed in dealing with secondary schools and colleges for whites is equally valid for Negroes." *The General Education Board: An Account of Its Activities, 1902–1914*, 203–4.

27. "Report to GEB Special Meeting," 26.
28. Ibid., 26–29.

the person to make a sharp break with previous policy formulations. He was the only man to serve on each of the three major reviews of black education in 1911, 1916, and 1922. He strongly supported the original decision (1911) that "The General Education Board can best aid Negro education in the South by cooperating with State and local authorities in building up a system of public schools for the training of Negro children that live on the farm."[29]

If the large expenditures of 1925–1931 were not the result of a change in philosophy and cannot plausibly be tied to Rose's new leadership, then perhaps the GEB was reacting to a new threat, a perception that racial order was challenged in some particularly dangerous way. In other words, the spending bulge may have been a response to a new mood among blacks, an effort to contain the assertiveness of the New Negro with the "right" sort of education.

There is a certain superficial plausibility to this explanation. Evidence for it, however, does not exist. The GEB records for this period do not suggest that foundation officers perceived a frightening crisis in human relations. The document with the fullest discussion of race relations, Jackson Davis's paper, "Recent Developments in Negro Schools and Colleges," seems to offer qualified approval of the new mood among blacks, even as it deprecates an "alarmist note" among whites: "One notices," Jackson wrote, "a buoyant, confident, militant note in Negro poetry and the press. Resistance to all forms of enforced segregation is almost as outspoken in the South as in the North. In the South, the Negro is more impatient, more aggressive, less inclined to conciliate prejudice and opposition."[30]

There is a simpler explanation for the GEB's dramatically increased spending. The southern educational revival, in which state educational spending increased sixteenfold between 1900 and 1925, took a long time reaching voteless blacks. Black public high schools, for example, were rare until the 1920s. Then in years of relative prosperity, after long and careful promotional activity by the GEB and other foundations, scores of new black public high schools were created and

29. "Report of Special Committee on the Education of the Negro," GEB Dockets, 1910–1913, vol. 2, May 25, 1911, p. 274; Rose to Buttrick, April 11, 1911, Box 353; both in GEB Papers.

30. Jackson Davis, "Recent Developments in Negro Schools and Colleges," 5, Box 315, GEB Papers. For another comment on "the rapid growth of race consciousness of the Negro group," see Annual Report of the General Education Board, 1928–1929, 33–34.

black secondary enrollment increased dramatically. The number of black public high schools in the former Confederate states jumped from 21 in 1915 to 143 in 1925. Between 1920 and 1925 Negro secondary enrollment in southern public schools increased 600 percent. By 1930, according to Horace Mann Bond's statistics, ten southern states enrolled 79,000 black secondary students—nine times as many as in 1920. College enrollments showed a similar increase, jumping from 1,643 in 1916 to more than 13,000 in 1927.[31]

With soaring enrollments and increased public commitment to black education, it was difficult to meet the demand for teachers. In 1927, Jackson Davis estimated that 1,000 to 1,200 new teaching positions had "been created annually in the Negro schools for the past ten years." Adding annual turnover in the teaching force—resignations, retirements, and the like—a GEB report estimated that 8,000 new teachers were needed annually.[32] Quite simply, teacher training, which had been a major focus of GEB planning from the beginning, propelled the spending bulge of the 1920s.

From the GEB's perspective, the policy established in 1911, and adumbrated from the beginning, had paid off. The process had been slow, but then the philanthropic theorists had always believed their strategy would require years of careful preparation. (Flexner had even envisioned "successive generations" for his "long-headed" policy to work.) When circumstances changed, when the white public began to show the "proper response," the philanthropists demonstrated their flexibility and made the adjustments their game plan had anticipated.

It is possible to imagine a variety of hypothetical options for a philanthropy founded in 1902 and interested in black education. The GEB—or an organization like it—could have courted confrontation with the white South, directly pursuing the Reconstruction agenda of equal political and "civil" rights and "schools for all." In theory, such a philanthropic enterprise could have made open alliance with defense and protest groups or even encouraged the migration of blacks out of the South. Though such a program can be imagined,

31. Horace Mann Bond, *The Education of the Negro in the American Social Order*, 206–7; Davis, "Recent Developments," 2–3. Cf., Bullock, A *History of Negro Education in the South*; Anderson, *The Education of Blacks in the South*, 197–204.

32. Davis, "Recent Developments," 8–9; *Annual Report of the General Education Board, 1928–1929*, 28.

it was, considering the current assumptions on race and politics, highly unlikely in the years between 1902 and 1930. And the GEB rejected from the start the most plausible radical strategy for 1902— concentrating all its resources exclusively on black education.[33]

Given the conditions of the early-twentieth-century South, as well as the Rockefellers' decision to focus on "general education," the real-world choices for the GEB were relatively straightforward. In simplest terms, the board could either support the existing structures of black education or seek to create something more worthy of support. In choosing the policy of supporting, or stimulating, public education, the board chose, of course, the second option. As a result, large-scale aid for black education was postponed for nearly two decades.

There were powerful arguments for the decision to place primary emphasis on tax-supported, state education. "This is the agency upon which all modern states depend for training the masses in the arts of civilization," stated the 1911 report of the special committee on Negro education. "It is the only educational agency yet devised that is at all equal to a task of such enormous proportions." Even at its most niggardly and irresponsible, the state generated far more revenue for black education than the private groups working for the same cause. As part of the GEB review of 1911, Buttrick carefully checked the statistics of philanthropy. He found that all nine major foundations and missionary societies gave just under $1 million to black schools in 1909–1910. In the same fiscal year, Hampton and Tuskegee raised about $890,000 in contributions from separate sources. By contrast, fourteen states and the District of Columbia spent approximately $6 million on Negro education.[34] Clearly, voluntary philanthropy could never effectively compete with state-mandated, coerced "philanthropy," however illiberal.

If, as a matter of dollars and cents, the public strategy was rational, it overlooked key political facts. As long as most blacks could not vote, public schools would be totally controlled by southern whites and schools for blacks were bound to be inferior. From a political standpoint, there was something to be said for the ragged arrangements of 1902, built on uncoordinated fund-raising and thousands of individual donors, since the education sponsored thereby was independent,

33. Fosdick et al., *Adventure in Giving*, 3–9.
34. Exhibit B, GEB Dockets, 1910–1913, vol. 2, 254–59, GEB Papers.

to a degree, of the wishes of white southerners. Resourceful black leaders and specific groups of donors, either northern whites or denominationally motivated southern blacks, offered significant alternative influences on Negro schooling. Even the crafty accommodations of Booker T. Washington and his imitators allowed for more in the way of black management and black representation than a virtually all-white state bureau of education cautiously subsidized by progressive northern agencies.

Instead of cooperating "with the white people of the South in making efficient the public school funds," the GEB in 1902 (or 1911 or 1915, for that matter) might have simply supported the educational structures already in place. If the board had chosen this option, there were three realistic alternatives for aiding African American education. The first was to make large donations through the major missionary societies (as the board later did with the Jeanes and Slater Funds). The missionary societies, it is important to note, were still the major support for black colleges and secondary schools. In the first decade of the board's operation, the four primary missionary societies spent more than $11 million on black schools enrolling some ten thousand college and high school students.[35]

Although the Rockefeller family had long supported church schools, and Gates and Buttrick, the key leaders of the GEB in its early years, were former Baptist ministers, with Buttrick a former officer of the American Baptist Home Mission Society, this alternative was most unlikely. The GEB had been founded upon assumptions quite different from the principles of the missionary societies.[36] As Buttrick, Gates, and their associates thought through a rationale for GEB experiments in education, they saw themselves as new philanthropists, seeking efficient and scientific solutions to the root causes of social problems,

35. Even before the formation of the GEB, an officer of the American Baptist Home Mission Society was proposing that Rockefeller consider "placing in the hands of the ABHMS a lump endowment sum." Anderson, *The Education of Blacks in the South*, 251. McPherson, *Abolitionist Legacy*, 146–47.

36. Fosdick et al., *Adventure in Giving*, 13–17. See Buttrick's long letter to Gates, December 21, 1903, on an aid request from the American Baptist Home Missionary Society. Buttrick contrasts the Baptist point of view with that of the GEB, which was concerned about "the general educational needs of the colored people, regardless of denominational convictions or affiliations." He added that "intense denominationalism" among blacks (and all southerners) could be an obstacle to public school growth. Box 260, GEB Papers.

rather than as sentimental givers who responded to mere symptoms or sought sectarian goals.

The missionary educators, for their part, were more likely than other northerners to be skeptical about the educational revival associated with the GEB and SEB. The neoabolitionist journal the *Independent*, which probably represented the attitudes of the leaders of the American Missionary Association, had both praise and criticism for the Southern Education Board. The *Independent* condemned the SEB in 1902 for promoting the "muddled nonsense" that "we must educate the whites, to teach the negroes to work, who already do most of the work," but in the following year defended Robert Ogden from attacks by the *Manufacturers' Record* and stated that the SEB's influence "will be widely felt for good." Harlan Paul Douglass, Congregational clergyman and AMA leader, thought the Ogden movement had elevated "one-sidedness into a theory."[37]

The next generation of foundation leaders after Buttrick and Gates were even less likely to support direct funding of the missionary societies. Indeed, in some cases they were hostile to religious organizations and missionary motivation. Abraham Flexner, for example, privately regarded organized, institutional religion as "a parasitic growth." Edwin Embree, president of the Rosenwald Fund, was reputed to be contemptuous of the Christian churches.[38]

Alternatively, the GEB could have bypassed the northern missionary societies, choosing instead to work directly with selected southern black schools, including both institutions supported by northern agencies and by southern black denominations. This option is discussed in early GEB reports and officers' correspondence. A 1903 report from Wallace Buttrick, for example, envisioned cooperation with "approved" private schools "for at least a generation." In the following year he visited three Texas schools sponsored by the American Baptist Home Mission Society and came away "stirred up" with the possibilities. Riding the Iron Mountain Railway ("bet. Texarkana and Little Rock"), Buttrick dispatched an enthusiastic missive to Gates.

37. Luker, *The Social Gospel*, 151–53, 302–10; *Independent*, April 24, 1902, April 9, 23, and 30, 1903; H. Paul Douglass, fragment of a draft of chapter 9, *Christian Reconstruction*, in Beam-Douglass Collection, Amistad Research Center.

38. Abraham Flexner to Wallace Buttrick, January 22, 1926, Box 304, GEB Papers; Robert W. Patton to Bishop H. J. Mikell, December 6, 1938, in American Church Institute for Negroes Papers, Archives of the Episcopal Church, Austin, Texas.

"All the work of the Home Mission Society suffers from lack—utter lack—of expert supervision," he wrote. The "haphazardness" of "the work of all the H. M. schools," with two or three exceptions, he found "exceedingly painful." "Why should $100,000 a year be given to 20 or more schools throughout the Southern States and each school left to pursue its own way without a definite and comprehensive plan and purpose, without expert inspection, without authoritative supervision and without constant study of changing conditions and possibilities!" Armed with "growing knowledge of the situation," Buttrick was confident about the future of these schools if they could be "Hamptonized" and appropriately supervised. Slipping into the cadence of a Pauline epistle, he wrote: "What then? Kill the schools? No. They represent too much moral earnestness, too much organized effort, too much genuine aspiration." The remedy, he argued, was for the GEB to adopt a policy that pushed them in the right direction: "Do not give them a dollar unless they accept supervision, do genuine work, and hold to a course of study in which there is orderly progress from the elementary to the secondary."[39]

The most significant proposal for direct GEB support of denominational schools came in a 1907 report on Negro colleges written by W. T. B. Williams. Though Williams's report has been described as "consistent with the philanthropists' interests" and dismissed as an "attempt to reduce dramatically the opportunities for black students,"[40] it was in fact a diplomatically worded challenge, even a rebuke of sorts, along with a creative proposal for future funding. Noting that colleges for African Americans had "received little or no assistance from the General Education Board," Williams warned Buttrick that many black people interpreted this neglect "of the patent needs of the Negro colleges" as "a criticism of their work"—though, of course, the GEB had not ("in all probability") intended any negative judgments. Despite "the common opinion that there are too many Negro colleges," Williams noted that very little college work was being done in black schools adorned with the title "university" or "college." Quoting

39. Buttrick Report, June 12, 1903, Box 304, GEB Papers. In a review of North Carolina, Buttrick concluded, by contrast, that "private schools for negroes" were "sufficiently numerous" and should not be "further promoted" by the GEB. See Wallace Buttrick, "The Educational Condition and Needs of North Carolina," 25, Box 304, GEB Papers. Buttrick to F. T. Gates, October 14, 1904, Box 716, GEB Papers.
40. Anderson, *The Education of Blacks in the South*, 255.

extensively from Du Bois's paper "The College-Bred Negro," Williams argued that college training was especially important for the creation of race leaders. He made a cautious case for something very like the GEB policy that eventually emerged, identifying Richmond, Atlanta, Nashville, and New Orleans as "well located" for development as centers of black collegiate education. He thought "three or four" of the twelve schools specifically mentioned in his report could be effectively upgraded with GEB aid. "There is an appreciable increase in the number of students desiring to take a college course," he noted— without any suggestion that such aspirations ought to be discouraged.[41]

Williams closed his twelve-page report to Buttrick with an appeal for a "special case": Atlanta Baptist College, as Morehouse College for men was known before 1913. This school, "one of the most efficient and deserving" of the black schools, had the strong support of Negro Baptists in Georgia and neighboring states, who were proud of their school and "keenly appreciative of the recent appointment of a colored man [John Hope] as its president." After praising the curriculum, teaching force, and "firm discipline" of Atlanta Baptist, Williams pointed out the special need of the college: a $40,000 building "for recitation purposes and chapel exercises." He urged the GEB to "seize the present opportunity" to aid an exemplary school "at the critical moment."[42] Morehouse College did eventually receive large gifts from the GEB, but not until the 1920s, after the expansion of public secondary education for blacks and in conjunction with larger phil-anthropic plans to promote cooperation among the black colleges of Atlanta.

The third and most obvious option for the GEB would have been to aid the little Tuskegees, those independent industrial schools es-tablished across the South in imitation of Booker T. Washington's educational work. Such a course had been favored by Baldwin, who had called as early as 1899 for the organization of "a general education board, by which effective work may be accomplished throughout the South," a board that would influence individual donors by identifying southern Negro schools worthy of aid by northerners who wanted their gifts to be "expended properly." As he saw it, the duty of white men was to "concentrate money and effort in the work of Hampton

41. W. T. B. Williams to Wallace Buttrick, May 22, 1907, Box 200, GEB Papers.
42. Ibid.

and Tuskegee," "establish other Tuskegees," and build up "a secondary system under the general control and supervision of Hampton and Tuskegee, that their influence may be far-reaching."[43]

But when the GEB had the opportunity to promote a consortium of little Tuskegees, it decisively rejected the possibility. In 1913 a group of the stronger, better-known independent industrial schools, including Snow Hill, Manassas, Utica, Fort Valley, and Kowaliga, organized as the Association of Negro Rural and Industrial Schools and sought foundation aid for a program of standardizing curriculum and accounting practices, eliminating "unworthy" schools, and coordinating overlapping and competing fund-raising programs. This organization had the strong support of NAACP board member Oswald Garrison Villard, who persistently (though unsuccessfully) pressured the GEB through John D. Rockefeller, Jr., to support the association or at least show sympathetic concern for its goals. "Everywhere these privately built up industrial schools are the ones that are developing teachers for the colored people," wrote Villard, adding that "the financial distress of these schools" was "very great," with at least fifteen "on the verge of collapse." Surely, Villard thought, the GEB would be interested in the efforts of these "fine young colored principals."

Demonstrating the decisive influence of the GEB staff, Buttrick advised against financial aid or even significant moral support. He wrote to Rockefeller in opposition to Villard's appeal, arguing that the program of supporting a network of state and local supervisors and agents in the public schools promised to be far more effective. Since the private schools were "almost entirely dependent for their support on funds solicited by individuals in the north," their future was precarious, and Buttrick could only hope that eventually some of these schools would be "taken over by state authorities."

"I do not wonder," he conceded, "that Mr. Villard is impatient over apparently slow progress of the work now being done by the General Education Board, but I believe that we have adopted the better method and that in twenty-five years from now vastly more will have been accomplished than would be possible under the policy of supporting private schools."[44]

43. Baldwin, "Present Problems of Negro Education," 399–404.
44. Jerome Greene to Wallace Buttrick, January 7, 1914; Wallace Buttrick to Jerome Greene, January 9, 1919; Oswald Garrison Villard to John D. Rockefeller, Jr., January 26,

Buttrick did not bother to mention what once would have been a decisive argument: Booker T. Washington was opposed to the idea. Suspicious of an organization that was sponsored by a founder of the National Association for the Advancement of Colored People and, indeed, convened its first meeting at the NAACP headquarters, Washington refused to attend this conference of little Tuskegees, and only reluctantly sent a Tuskegee representative to the second annual conference.[45] But by 1914 not even Washington's wholehearted support for the independent industrial schools would have deflected the philanthropists from their plans.

When the Negro Education Conference convened in 1915, two weeks after Washington's death, the GEB's most important choices had already been made. Neither enhanced missionary education nor more Tuskegees were part of the "long-headed" long-term answer sought by Flexner and Buttrick.

1914; all in Box 353, GEB Papers. Oswald Garrison Villard to Buttrick, February 1913, Buttrick to John D. Rockefeller, Jr., February 5, 1914, in Box 203, GEB Papers.

45. Harlan, *The Wizard of Tuskegee*, 435–36. Washington condemned the association as a "paper organization" that duplicated functions already being performed by Thomas Jesse Jones's investigation of Negro education. In addition, he believed that several of the schools in the organization were "totally unworthy." Washington to Alfred T. White, June 1, 1915, in *The Booker T. Washington Papers*, vol. 13, 314–15.

5

The Founding of the American Church Institute for Negroes, 1906–1914

The [American Church] Institute offers to those who are anxious to advance in an effective way the cause of Christ and of education among the negroes an opportunity to use in that work a corporation competent to do in its field what the General [Education] Board does in its larger field.

—George Foster Peabody[1]

To make Episcopalians is not the first purpose of our schools. . . . It is rather to contribute our share in preparing the rising generation of Negroes to discover themselves and their possibilities, to find their real and necessary place in our civic and industrial life, and to make their racial contribution to the moral safety and progress of our Christian civilization.

—George Alexander McGuire[2]

One way to understand the powerful influence of the General Education Board is to examine in detail the smaller philanthropies that imitated the richly endowed foundation and sought to secure its support. The GEB could plan carefully, both in private meetings and public reports, issue persuasive propaganda, and use its gifts to prod educational innovation in a favored direction, but, in the end, it could not simply order people to do its bidding. As the recommendations of the GEB trickled through the layers of the southern educational

1. *The Pacific Churchman*, April 15, 1907, in George Foster Peabody Papers, Library of Congress.
2. "Things Done and to Be Done," *Spirit of Missions* 76 (December 1911): 1020–21.

system, other philanthropists and educators had to decide how to respond to the initiatives of faraway experts.

In 1906 a new philanthropic agency entered the field of African American education. Founded by prominent white Episcopalians, the American Church Institute for Negroes soon became a significant supporter of selected black denominational schools. Though historians have neglected the ACIN,[3] it is an excellent case study in northern philanthropy for black schools, an illustration of the gradual taming of "dangerous donations." On a small scale, the early history of the ACIN shows the ideas and practices that transformed northern philanthropy in the early twentieth century. By virtue of being born late, the ACIN was shaped decisively by the secular foundations, especially the General Education Board, rather than by the long-established Protestant missionary societies. At the same time, the institute was strongly affected by southern white efforts to control the rhetoric and tactics of outside benevolence. Here also the experience of the ACIN has wider relevance.

The American Church Institute for Negroes began with a straightforward and challenging task: finding a way to improve the quality of Episcopal schools for southern blacks. Though the denomination had been engaged in this form of outreach since the end of the Civil War, the mission to black America was not thriving in 1906. From 1865 to 1904 the Episcopal Church's ministry to southern blacks had been directed by an agency called variously "The Protestant Episcopal Freedmen's Commission to Colored People," the "Commission of Home Missions to Colored People," the "Commission on Colored Work," and the "Commission on Negro Work." In 1904, however, the commission was "pronounced . . . a comparative failure" and dissolved.[4]

Subsequently, the Episcopal Church's National Board of Missions, to which the agency had reported, appointed a committee "on the work among colored people" to devise more effective forms of ministry. One of the ideas that emerged from this committee was the decision to form the ACIN.

Those instrumental in establishing the ACIN also were convinced their church's work among "colored people" had been done so poorly

---

3. For an exception, see Enck, "The Burden Borne," 348–55.
4. Robert W. Patton, *An Inspiring Record in Negro Education*, 4; Harold T. Lewis, *Yet with a Steady Beat: The African American Struggle for Recognition in the Episcopal Church*, 48, 125.

that it constituted a shame and embarrassment to "the rich Episcopal Church."[5] Believing that affluent whites in the Episcopal Church had a moral and social responsibility to do better, they envisioned the ACIN as a catalyst for establishing a system of strategically located church schools that would provide blacks high-quality industrial education, teacher training, and, for a select group of black men, preparation for the Episcopal ministry. They were certain such institutions had tremendous potential for helping to solve the South's and ultimately the nation's black-white racial problems.

Motivated by these goals, the founders of the ACIN sought to shape it into the Episcopal Church's "central agency" for the funding and direction of its black schools. Some of the founders were experienced educational missionaries, having been involved in the campaigns of the Southern Education Board (SEB); all were familiar with and admired the work of the General Education Board. George Foster Peabody, perhaps the most influential of the ACIN founders, was a "charter member" of the SEB, a trustee of the GEB, and treasurer of both the SEB and GEB. He also sat on the boards of the University of Georgia and four black schools—Hampton and Tuskegee Institutes, the Penn School, and Fort Valley Normal and Industrial Institute. A successful investment banker with holdings in railroads, public utilities, and mining enterprises, Peabody retired from business in 1906 at the age of fifty-four to devote himself to his philanthropic interests. A leading figure in the Progressive wing of the Democratic Party, in 1904 he served as his party's national treasurer.[6]

In one of its earliest appeals to Episcopal Church members for money, the board of the ACIN described the agency as a smaller version of the GEB—"a conspicuous illustration of the demand of this day for centralized, responsible, and efficient conduct of philanthropic activity." Just as the GEB was "a logical and necessary expression" of current philanthropic practice, so the ACIN would use similar corporate methods "to do in its field what the General Board does in its larger field."[7]

5. George Foster Peabody to Mr. Ketcham, May 17, 1922, in Peabody Papers.

6. Louise Ware, *George Foster Peabody, Banker, Philanthropist, Publicist*, viii, 47–56, 70–85, 114, 123, 132, 102–3, 159; Fosdick et al., *Adventure in Giving*, 1, 19–20, 63–64, 65, 78, 89.

7. *The Pacific Churchman* 43, no. 18 (April 15, 1907), Peabody Papers.

George Foster Peabody. Special Collections, Lucy Scribner Library, Skidmore College.

As a further assurance that the ACIN was no organization of naive idealists acting solely on altruistic impulse, potential donors were assured that "the board is acquainted with the educational situation in the South, and in entire harmony with those approved ideas and methods for the education of the negro which are now accepted by all expert students and workers in the field of education." The exact meaning of this statement was made clearer in the next paragraph, which described "the Institute's ideals of education" as "thoroughly practical," rooted in three fundamental assumptions: "the necessity of thorough-going industrial training of negro boys and girls"; recognition "that the economic future of the negro must be largely upon the land, where the difficulties which now confront him and retard his progress are fewer in number and less pronounced in effect"; and the belief that blacks must be supplied "competent leaders" of their race, "trained for every responsibility entailed by an efficient economic, intellectual, moral, and religious leadership." The ACIN appeal sought funds from church members to "secure in its schools such manifold and complete training inspired by the spirit of Christ."[8]

Although George Foster Peabody played an important role in launching the ACIN and was a significant figure in sustaining and expanding its work, he neither originated the idea nor was he the only person of influence involved in its creation. The idea came from David Hummell Greer, a native of Virginia who was Episcopal bishop of New York, then the largest and wealthiest diocese in the Episcopal Church. During several years as a member of his denomination's national Board of Missions, Greer chaired the committee "on the work among colored people." Over a period of time, this involvement convinced him the Episcopal Church, by failing to establish strong, well-supported black schools in the South, had fallen shamefully behind those other white churches and secular agencies who were significantly involved in addressing the race problem in that region. It also distressed him that "great [educational] institutions" for southern blacks, such as Hampton and Tuskegee Institutes, "founded in the South outside of our own Church," were "very generously supported by our Church people, while our own schools were left in poverty to struggle for their existence." As chairman of the committee of the Board of Missions commissioned to study this problem, Greer

8. Ibid.

shaped the tone and content of the report. Certain that "the growth of the Episcopal Church among the negroes meant good for them and for the country," Greer and his allies used the report to obtain the board's approval in May 1906 to create a new agency—"a small autonomous body of twelve churchmen"—that he hoped would carry on an effective educational ministry among southern blacks, insuring that gifts from wealthy Episcopalians would be "administered by men who understood the problems involved." The new agency, "though authorized by the [Episcopal] Church . . . had no share in the general income"; from the beginning it "had to solicit from individuals the means for . . . existence."[9]

At the same time Greer was forging ahead with his efforts to revitalize the work of the Episcopal Church among African Americans, a group of black Episcopalians offered their advice regarding how "colored work" should be reorganized. In a unanimous resolution, the Conference of Church Workers among Colored People (CCWCP) requested the Board of Missions to appoint a "colored priest" to the denomination's national staff in order to direct "the work among colored people in gathering information and statistics for the benefit of the church-at-large, and making such visitations in the field as might stimulate, arouse, and help the missionaries there employed." The CCWCP, an organization whose membership included the leading black Episcopal clergy and laity, had been founded in 1882, largely at the initiative of black Episcopal clergyman Alexander Crummell. At the time the CCWCP sent its resolution to the Board of Missions,

9. Harold Martin, "Outlasting Marble and Brass": The History of the Church Pension Fund, 103–4. The Board of Missions assumed that the ACIN would quickly receive a sizable endowment from its founders and their friends. Viewing the ACIN as a unique body, the Board of Missions continued to appropriate funds for other forms of ministry to African Americans, including schools that were not affiliated with the ACIN. Charles Lewis Slattery, David Hummell Greer, Eighth Bishop of New York, 205, 207–8, 212–14. Greer to Hunter, January 8, 1906, in Howard Chandler Robbins Papers, The General Theological Seminary. "Committee of Reference of the [Episcopal Church's] National Council, "Report on the American Church Institute For Negroes," April 28, 1948, 3–4, ACIN Papers. Tollie L. Caution, "The Protestant Episcopal Church: Policies and Rationale upon which Support of Its Negro Colleges Is Predicated," 277. William Wilson Manross stresses that the creation of the ACIN was "approved by the [Episcopal Church's national] Board of Missions, though not specifically authorized by General Convention." See Manross, A History of the Episcopal Church, 338. [Robert W. Patton], "American Church Institute for Negroes," Spirit of Missions 101 (July 1936): 336. Patton, An Inspiring Record, 10–11.

there was not and had never been an African American, clergy or lay, on the Episcopal Church's national staff. In 1900 the Episcopal Church listed 742,569 communicants (confirmed members, twelve years or older). Of that number, in 1903 approximately 15,000, or slightly under 2 percent, were estimated to be African American.[10] Bishop Greer and the other members of the Board of Missions—all whites—did not act on the CCWCP request.

Greer's perspective on the Episcopal Church and southern black schools was greatly influenced by Peabody, also a transplanted souther-ner.[11] Both men were ardent admirers of Samuel Chapman Armstrong, founder of Hampton Institute, and were proud of their membership on Hampton's board of trustees. Greer also believed strongly that Thomas Dudley Underwood, the Episcopal bishop of Kentucky who preceded him as chair of his denomination's Committee on Colored Work, had understood rightly the dangers posed by worsening black-white relations in the South. In the 1880s and 1890s Dudley lamented the increasing separation between the races that had come about with the end of slavery, arguing that for blacks the result would be "degradation and decay." This prospect held great peril for the white South, which had to live alongside and interact with blacks. The "hope" and "salvation" of the Negroes, Dudley insisted, would come from "association" with and "guidance" by "Southern white men of good will."[12]

Greer was convinced the Episcopal Church's schools for Negroes, if adequately funded and correctly organized, could be used to "train [the black] mind and soul and body for Christian citizenship," thus reduc-

10. George Freeman Bragg, History of the Afro-American Group of the Episcopal Church, 161. [Harold T. Lewis], "Whose Service Is Perfect Freedom." The Episcopal [Church's] Commission for Black Ministries, 2; Lewis, Yet with a Steady Beat, 137–39; J. Carleton Hayden, "Different Names but the Same Agenda: Precursors to the Union of Black Episcopalians," 2–3; George Freeman Bragg, Afro-American Church Work and Workers, 5. Lewis, in Yet with a Steady Beat, uses "CCWACP" as the acronym for Conference of Church Workers among Colored People; in this volume the acronym for this organization is CCWCP. Robert Prichard, A History of the Episcopal Church, 229; Willard B. Gatewood, Aristocrats of Color: The Black Elite, 1880–1920, 276.

11. See Peabody's memorandum [undated, circa 1906] on the initial steps for organi-zation of the ACIN, which was probably drafted for the benefit of Greer and Samuel H. Bishop, the first ACIN director, in ACIN Papers.

12. Thomas Underwood Dudley, "How Shall We Help the Negro?" 273–80. For a perceptive analysis of Dudley see Ralph E. Luker, The Social Gospel, 23–24.

ing, perhaps even eliminating, the dangers to which Dudley pointed. Put another way, Greer hoped these educational institutions could produce black men and women who would be exponents of white culture and religion, and servants of the practical needs of their people as teachers, farmers, artisans, ministers, and nurses. Such people would be dependable allies of "Southern white Christians," who, in good times and bad, could turn to graduates of black Episcopal schools as brokering agents between two separate and unequal racial communities.[13]

Once the Board of Missions gave authorization to establish the ACIN, Greer and Peabody moved into a dynamic partnership to launch the new organization. They quickly gathered around them a formidable group of fellow Episcopalians as the initial board of trustees, including William Lawrence, the affluent and widely influential Episcopal bishop of Massachusetts; Nicholas Murray Butler, the equally influential president of Columbia University, a major figure in American educational reform and former president of the Industrial Education Association; Alfred Thayer Mahan, strategist and military historian; the prominent banker Robert C. Pruyn of Albany; and New York laywer Francis Lynde Stetson, known as banking tycoon J. P. Morgan's "attorney general." The remaining board seats went to Episcopal bishops and rectors whose dioceses or parishes gave them access to rich potential donors. Almost as a matter of course, this handpicked board elected Greer its president and Peabody its treasurer. The twelve persons who composed the first ACIN board were white and male; though four were southern born, all, with one exception, resided in the Northeast. There would be no variation from this pattern until 1909, when James Hardy Dillard, a white Episcopalian from Virginia who was president of the Jeanes Fund, was elected. From that time on whites resident in the South were consistently members of the board and, in 1914, a white southerner was appointed director of the ACIN. Even though two African Americans, Alexander Crummell and Henry B. Delaney, Archdeacon for Colored Work in the Diocese of North Carolina, had been members of the Board of Missions' Committee on Colored Work, no black would be elected to the ACIN board until 1945.[14]

13. Slattery, *Greer*, 205–7.
14. Ibid; "The Triennial Report of the Board of Missions," *Journal of the General Convention. Richmond. October 2–19, 1907* (New York: The General Convention, 1907), 445. On the board of trustees, see Lawrence's autobiography, *Memories of a Happy Life.*

Steps to secure a legal charter and selection of a director were among the earliest matters of business to concern the ACIN board. Greer and Francis Lynde Stetson, legal adviser to the diocese of New York, were authorized to have the institute incorporated in Virginia, presumably as a statement that the South would be its field of operation. A month later, on the recommendation of Bishop Greer, Samuel Henry Bishop was chosen the first director of the institute.[15]

Bishop, a forty-three-year-old white Episcopal priest, was a graduate of the University of Vermont in his native state and of New York City's Union Theological Seminary. After leaving Union, he lived for a time in New Orleans and studied at Columbia University, the University of Berlin, and Oxford University. His experience included work in white parishes in New York City, New Jersey, and Colorado, where he headed a congregation at the time of his ACIN appointment. As a student and after ordination to the priesthood, he had devoted "much time and thought to the study of the science of philanthropy in connection with the organization of modern charities," particularly with regard to "religious and educational activity in the South." From 1899 to 1905 he was assistant editor of the journal *Charities: A Weekly Review of Local and General Philanthropy* and assistant secretary of the Brooklyn Bureau of Charities. Trained both as social worker and clergyman, Bishop believed that "the first duty incumbent upon a charity worker is to create the conditions of ready communication between the applicant and himself, a bond of sympathy or revelation; so that the applicant as a living person with his mental and moral characteristics is clearly

The significance of Butler's public career is discussed in Ravitch, *The Great School Wars*, 184–86 and Albert Marrin, *Nicholas Murray Butler*, 23, 13–52. For Mahan see W. D. Puleston, *Mahan: The Life and Work of Captain Alfred Thayer Mahan*, U.S.N. Cecil D. Halliburton, *A History of St. Augustine's College, 1867–1937*, 28. For Stetson, see Ron Chernow, *The House of Morgan*, 73–75, 150. The four southern-born trustees were Greer, Peabody, Ernest M. Stires, rector of New York City's St. Thomas Church, and Richard Pardee Williams, rector of Trinity Church and Archdeacon of the Diocese of Washington, D.C. Minutes, Board of Trustees, American Church Institute for Negroes, April 20, 1909, ACIN Papers. Bragg, *History of the Afro-American Group*, 163; Trustee Minutes, ACIN, September 24, 1945, ACIN Papers.

15. Trustee Minutes, February 12 and March 30, 1906, ACIN Papers; Slattery, *Greer*, 214. From 1906 to Bishop's death in 1914 he was titled variously as "Agent of the [ACIN] Board," "General Agent of the [ACIN] Board," or "Special Representative of the [ACIN] Board." From 1914 until 1921, when the ACIN board formally termed its executive officer "Director," Robert W. Patton, Bishop's successor, also used these various titles. Trustee Minutes, November 13, 1906, February 11, 1921, ACIN Papers.

Samuel H. Bishop, circa 1906. Virginia Theological Seminary.

conceived, his problem apprehended, and some method of solution suggested."[16]

16. *Charities* was an influential voice in the Progressive-era social justice movement. See Walter I. Trattner, *From Poor Law to Welfare State: A History of Social Welfare in America*, 75–93, 206. Samuel H. Bishop, "The Psychology of Charity Organization Work," 2. See also Samuel H. Bishop, "A New Movement in Charity," 446–47.

Greer, who had known Bishop as a priest of his diocese, believed him the right man to direct the ACIN and arranged for George Foster Peabody to meet him. Bishop's appointment became a certainty after his interview with Peabody, who concluded that Samuel Bishop "had . . . been raised up at this very time to be the active agent in developing the work of the Institute." After Bishop accepted the ACIN directorship, Peabody bombarded him with advice on the best ways to carry out his work, most of which Bishop took to heart.[17]

An eloquent, well-read man, Bishop sought to understand and respect the beliefs and feelings of the blacks and whites he encountered in his new job. In 1907 he introduced himself and the ACIN to W. E. B. Du Bois by letter. After Du Bois responded, Bishop wrote again, telling him, "I heard . . . that you are an Episcopalian," and sharing his hope that the institute would be instrumental in ensuring "the [Episcopal] church" did not lag "behind science in recognizing the manhood of the Negro." The priest concluded by inviting Du Bois "to be on the watch for any intellectual or moral contribution you can make to our work."[18] "My family," Du Bois replied,

> represents five generations in the Episcopal Church. . . . I have however no particular affection for the Church. I think its record on the Negro problem has been simply shameful and while I am looking forward with interest to the work which the Church Institute proposes to do yet I confess I have many misgivings. The fact of the matter is that so far as the Negro problem is concerned the southern branch of the Church is a moral dead weight and the northern branch of the Church never has had the moral courage to stand against it and I doubt if it has now. . . . it is certain that the Church has always been behind science and the fact

17. For biographical sketches of Samuel Henry Bishop see Charles Ripley Gillett, ed., *Alumni Catalogue of Union Theological Seminary in the City of New York, 1836–1926* (New York: Association of the Alumni, 1926), 325; *Who's Who In America: A Biographical Dictionary of Notable Living Men and Women of the United States* (Chicago: A. N. Marquis and Company, 1912), vol. 7, 176 and vol. 8 (1914–1915), 200, as well as his obituaries in the *New York Times*, June 1, 1914; in *Crisis* (8 [July 1914]: 127); and in *The Churchman*, June 6, 1914. George Foster Peabody to David Hummell Greer, April 12, 1906, in Peabody Papers. [Samuel H. Bishop] [First Report] "To Board of Directors, n.d. [circa fall 1906], ACIN Papers. For examples of Peabody's directives see George Foster Peabody to Samuel H. Bishop, February 26, 1906; Peabody to Bishop, March 16, 1906; Peabody to Bishop, April 11, 1906; all in Peabody Papers.

18. Bishop to Du Bois, April 16, 1907, Herbert Aptheker, ed., *The Correspondence of W. E. B. Du Bois*, vol. 1, 130–31.

of the matter is, they have been behind most every thing else, certainly behind other churches in recognizing human manhood and Christian equality.[19]

Out of these initial exchanges a friendship grew, and when the National Association for the Advancement of Colored People was founded in 1909, the ACIN director became a member. Two years later, he was a prominent and active figure in events that led to the founding of the National Urban League and served as a member of its first executive committee.[20]

Du Bois, whose conversation and writings influenced Bishop's thinking on black-white race relations, assessed the Episcopal minister as "a delicate and sensitive man . . . who felt painfully and deeply the tragedy of the American Negro, and who also knew by inti-mate contact and association the peculiar mental processes of [white] Southerners and Northerners on the subject."[21] At other times, with disappointment, Du Bois also saw him as a person willing to com-promise on issues crucial to the well-being of the African American community, sometimes by necessity, at other times by choice.

Du Bois was probably unaware of just how far Bishop strayed from the views of some southern Episcopal leaders. Among paternalist white clergy, the ideas of Du Bois and Washington were not the sole options. Certain influential voices insisted, in fact, that both men were wrong, that "the place to begin the negro's education" was "neither in the intellect, as Burghart Du Bois has contended, nor in the hand as Booker Washington is contending," but in the black man's "weak point"—his "moral nature." As the *Southern Churchman* put it: "No work that Hampton or Tuskegee can do is going to be permanently useful until the work of such schools as St. Paul's and St. Augustine's has been done first." Bishop would find it difficult to gain the confidence of men who thought this way.[22]

19. Du Bois to Bishop, May 1, 1907, ibid., 131. Some southern white Episcopalians were willing to admit that the church had a "wretched record" in ministering to blacks. See the following pieces in the *Southern Churchman*: "Church Work among Colored People," June 4, 1904; "The American Church Institute for Negroes," June 4, 1910, October 19, 1912.

20. Guichard Parris and Lester Brooks, *Blacks in the City: A History of the National Urban League*, 33, 358, 509; Weiss, *The National Urban League*, 44, 45.

21. [W. E. B. Du Bois], "Samuel Henry Bishop," 127.

22. *Southern Churchman*, June 4, 1904, October 28, 1905.

Bishop immediately began a series of visits to Episcopal schools for blacks, ostensibly to conduct "a thorough survey of the educational system of the South, and a second [survey], equally thorough, of the work of the [Episcopal] Church in educating the Negroes." The data gathered by the newly hired director on his tours of inspection, and his interpretation of what he had seen and heard was, not surprisingly, in complete accord with the views of Greer and Peabody. Bishop's report was used as the justification for the ACIN board's decision in regard to one of its earliest and most difficult major policy decisions: how to respond to the "many little parochial schools in the South [that] applied for affiliation with the Institute." These institutions, poorly supported by local Episcopal parishes and dioceses and desperate for funds, were often the only schools offering primary education for blacks in their area. Announcement of the formation of the ACIN stimulated hope by those who kept them alive that the ACIN would be a source of financial support. But this was not the direction in which Greer, Peabody, and Bishop wished to go. Using Bishop's report as the rationale, Greer made it clear to the board that the purpose of the ACIN was "not the establishment and support of parochial schools and primary education, for which he hoped the southern states would in time make ample provision, but the training of ministers, teachers, nurses, professional men and women . . . [and] provision for vocational education."[23]

Initially, only three institutions were accepted for affiliation. Each one was chosen, as Bishop said—using language characteristic of Progressive educators—"to create typical examples of correlation and development." The three were St. Augustine's Normal and Collegiate Institute in Raleigh, North Carolina, established in 1868; the Bishop Payne Divinity School (BPDS), a seminary for black candidates for the Episcopal ministry founded in 1878 in Petersburg, Virginia; and St. Paul's Normal and Industrial School in Lawrenceville, Virginia, which opened its doors in 1888.[24] This early decision by the ACIN board created ill feeling toward the institute in those dioceses where the "many little parochial schools" were located and sustained by black and white supporters.

23. George Foster Peabody to David Hummell Greer, April 12, 1906, with enclosure, in Peabody Papers. Slattery, *Greer*, 214–15.

24. On the changing names of the Bishop Payne Divinity School, see Odell Greenleaf Harris, *The Bishop Payne Divinity School: A History*, 2, 4, 9.

Greer, Peabody, and Bishop predicted that from the institutions affiliated with the ACIN would come "clergymen at Petersburg, farmers and mechanics at Lawrenceville, teachers and nurses at Raleigh." The institutions were envisioned as the nucleus of a black Episcopal educational system to which similar schools would be added in other strategic parts of the South. Theodore Du Bose Bratton, the Episcopal bishop of Mississippi, spoke for many other southern white Episcopalians when he interpreted these early actions as assurances that soon the ACIN would "come to the relief of every Southern diocese by developing in each at least one Industrial High School for the Christian training of teachers and leaders of the Negro race."[25] What Bishop and the ACIN actually achieved was less grand, however. Between 1906 and 1914 Bishop persuaded the board of trustees to add four small normal and industrial schools: in 1910, St. Mary's Industrial School, Vicksburg, Mississippi; St. Mark's Industrial School, Birmingham, Alabama; St. Athanasius Industrial School, Brunswick, Georgia; and, in 1914, St. Paul's Industrial School, Atlanta, Georgia. Bishop also began the practice of listing St. Agnes Hospital Training School for Nurses, founded in 1896 and for much of its history an affiliate of St. Augustine's School, as a separate institution.

In the fall of 1906 Greer, Peabody, and Bishop led a party of ACIN trustees on a tour of the initial three schools chosen for affiliation with the ACIN. This excursion in George Foster Peabody's "private railroad car" imitated Robert C. Ogden's luxurious annual southern tours for white "leading citizens" of the North whom he wanted to draw into his campaigns to stimulate public and private support for education in the South. This trip confirmed the trustees' perception of the institute as, in Peabody's words, similar to "a holding company in the public utility field." With this as their guide, the ACIN trustees in subsequent meetings in New York City quickly agreed the institute's major work would be to assist its affiliated schools by undertaking certain responsibilities no individual school could do as well for itself. These were identified as direction of "fundraising campaigns"; securing "grants . . . from educational and other charitable foundations";

25. [Samuel H. Bishop], "Plan for the Organization of the Educational Work among the Colored People of the South by the Protestant Episcopal Church," n.d., in Peabody Papers. Bratton, *Wanted Leaders! A Study of Negro Development*, 155–58. Patton, *An Inspiring Record*, 6.

management of the schools' investments; and aiding them "in meeting [financial] emergencies." In addition the board committed itself to promote "sound educational procedures," curricula "based on Christian character," and upgrading of "substandard facilities."[26]

Greer and Peabody, with support from Bishop, played the major role in making these early decisions. They also brought the board to the consensus that effective Episcopal schools for southern blacks did not alienate their students from their place of origin or make them antagonistic toward the South's segregated social order. Rather, they made their greatest contribution, as schools and Christian institutions, when they sent their graduates back "to their native [racial] communities as ministers, teachers, nurses, or social workers, in order that they might work toward the goal of betterment of local conditions." To the ACIN trustees this meant the graduates functioned as agents of progress and social peace, by promoting harmonious relations between black and white southerners without challenging a segregated social order.[27]

During his early tenure as director of the ACIN, Samuel Bishop traveled extensively in the South to visit the institute schools, attend meetings of the schools' boards of trustees (on which he sat as an ex officio member), and counsel with southern bishops, both those in whose diocese an ACIN school was located and those who hoped soon to have one. His chief concern on these visits was to begin the process of shaping St. Augustine's and St. Paul's into institutional models of the strategically located industrial education and normal schools for blacks the ACIN board hoped to place throughout the South.[28]

Of the three, St. Augustine's was the healthiest because it had no outstanding debt. Yet it lacked the money to improve the quality of its faculty, retain its best teachers, and make crucial improvements in its plant. Bishop also felt the school suffered from the requirement that its "teachers should be colored and members of the Episcopal Church." Regarding these restrictions, he reported to the ACIN trustees: "I seriously doubt whether competent colored teachers belonging to our church can be found for an institution of academic grade." At the same

26. Halliburton, St. Augustine's, 29. For Ogden, see chapter 2. Caution, "Protestant Episcopal Church," 277–78.
27. Ibid.
28. [Bishop], [First Report], ACIN Papers.

time he thought it inadvisable to create an integrated faculty because of the tensions it might create among teachers. Next to its need for additional funds, Bishop's greatest concern for St. Augustine's was its lack of an agricultural education program. While acknowledging that it met an indispensable need by functioning as the black "academic" Episcopal school, an "enlargement" of the curriculum was imperative. "Whatever may be the character of the student body and whatever may be their intellectual and professional aims, they should have some training in agriculture; for they must lead an agricultural people, and they must have sympathy with and first-hand knowledge of the life of their people." Bishop anticipated no difficulties in working with the school's white principal to move "St. Aug's" in the direction he thought best.[29]

The ACIN director's early visits to Lawrenceville, Virginia, where St. Paul's was located, left him hopeful about the potential of that institution as a first-rate industrial school, but conscious of the many obstacles to this goal. St. Paul's had unpaid debts; its revenues needed to be increased; and in order to develop a serious industrial education program, major sums were required for an expansion of its plant, the purchase of equipment for shop courses, and salary increases to keep qualified teachers, who, lacking contracts, had to await the principal's decision whether to rehire them or not at the beginning of each academic year. Over time Bishop would come to believe the most formidable of those obstacles was James Solomon Russell, the black Episcopal priest who had founded the institution. Russell was principal of the school and Archdeacon for Colored Work in the Diocese of Southern Virginia. Bishop's dealings with Russell, difficult from the start, left him convinced that Russell was a shrewd, manipulative, frequently disingenuous person. As Bishop pushed for changes that challenged Russell's control of St. Paul's, the black clergyman became one of his most troublesome opponents.[30]

Initially, Bishop judged everything to be fine at the Bishop Payne Divinity School, the Episcopal Church's theological school for African

29. Ibid., 7–8.
30. "Draft of [the Report on] St. Paul's Situation," 1911, Joseph B. Cheshire Papers, #146, Southern Historical Collection. (This document is a preliminary draft of the Phelps-Stokes Fund assessment of St. Paul's School done at the request of the ACIN board.) [Bishop], [First Report], 4–5.

Americans, all of whose administrators and faculty were white. The school had been created after the Civil War because of the general policy of segregation in the denomination's major seminaries where white candidates for ministry were educated. Leading black Episcopal clergy and laity, however, both individually and through the Conference of Church Workers among Colored People, quickly disabused him of any belief they were satisfied with the school. In 1907 the CCWCP sent the General Convention of the Episcopal Church a unanimous resolution expressing the hope "that the day is not far distant when . . . the Theological Seminary founded for the [Negro] race may offer advanced training as good as that of any seminary in the land." In addition to rating the quality of the theological education provided at Payne as substandard, the CCWCP, with the support of Henry Yates Satterlee, the white Episcopal bishop of Washington, D.C., began a campaign to reopen King Theological Hall, a divinity school for black Episcopalians that had been established in 1889 and closed sixteen years later.[31]

Under the terms of an 1889 agreement between the Protestant Episcopal Church and Howard University, King Hall was an affiliated unit of Howard University's theological department, though funded and administered by the Episcopal Church. While the Episcopal divinity school had its own administrative and classroom building adjacent to the Howard campus, its students had access to Howard's classes and facilities. During the sixteen years of its existence, King Hall was headed by a "warden," William Victor Tunnell, a black Episcopal priest who was also a professor in Howard University's department of English.[32] Situated on the campus of the best institution of higher education for African Americans in the United States and part of the vibrant black community in Washington, D.C., King Hall exposed its students to some of the leading black scholars, teachers, preachers, and politicians of their race, including Alexander Crummell, who during the first nine years of the school's existence was rector of St. Luke's Episcopal Church in the District of Columbia.

31. [Bishop], [First Report], 4. Bragg, History of the Afro-American Group, 163.

32. Rayford W. Logan, Howard University: The First Hundred Years, 1867–1967, 84, 97, 119, 128; Bragg, History of the Afro-American Group, 163, 178; "131. The King Theological Hall. (For Colored students)," Inventory of Church Archives in the District of Columbia (Washington, D.C.: District of Columbia Historical Records Survey, 1940), 285–87.

The seminary was a setting almost guaranteed to produce Episcopal clergy committed to racial equality and who aspired to be members of the "talented tenth."

King Hall's closing in 1905, a consequence of the Board of Missions' decision to discontinue its appropriation for the divinity school, had been criticized by many black Episcopal clergy and laity as well as by Bishop Henry Yates Satterlee, who had been a lecturer at the school. The stated reason for failure to renew the appropriation was decline in student numbers. But Satterlee, in a circular letter to the bishops of the Episcopal Church, charged that "most of the Southern bishops . . . believe . . . the whole atmosphere of Washington [D.C.] is harmful to the negro race, and that every Candidate for Holy Orders educated here must necessarily imbibe ideas regarding social and political equality of the negro and white races." That was why, Satterlee charged, the southern bishops refused to allow their black ministerial candidates to study at King Hall, preferring to send them to Bishop Payne Divinity School in Petersburg, Virginia. "The aim of King Hall," he continued, was "to root" in its students the "New Testament ideal" that " 'in Christ Jesus' " there " 'can be neither bond nor free.' " This scriptural insight had been the solution "of all the political and social difficulties with which the Church has had to contend." And it had special relevance in regard to how "colored People" should be educated and treated, for they "are different today from what they were thirty years ago." According to Satterlee, "Those mulattoes who are one-half or three-fourths white, may be classed as 'negroes,' but, as a matter of fact they have one-half or three-fourths of the brain power and moral force of the white race, and they are bound to make the most out of their opportunities of life, intellectually and morally." If the Episcopal Church, Satterlee concluded, "is to keep in touch with the best and most progressive of the negro people. . . . it must not bring up its colored clergy in the position of tutelage."[33]

33. During the time the seminary was open, "approximately 12 students a year attended and were in residence." When King Hall was closed, its library, of "about 2,000 volumes," was given to the Bishop Payne Divinity School, and the property sold to Howard University, which converted the former main building of the hall into its "musical conservatory." The income "from the funds held by the trustees of King Hall" was used to provide "scholarships . . . to colored students studying for the ministry of the Episcopal Church; principally to those attending the Bishop Payne Divinity School." "131. King Theological Hall," *Inventory*, 285–86. Charles H. Brent, *A Master Builder: Being the Life*

Criticisms of Bishop Payne Divinity School and calls for reestablishment of King Hall moved Samuel Bishop to open a discussion with the leading black Episcopal clergy and laity on these questions. One of his points of contact with them was the annual meeting of the CCWCP. At the 1908 CCWCP meeting in Brooklyn, Bishop shared his plan to reopen King Hall as a training center for "catechists" or lay missionaries. This scheme was Bishop's compromise proposal to placate blacks who wanted to revive King Hall and not offend southern bishops opposed to any training center for black clergy other than the one they controlled at Petersburg. Upon presenting his scheme to the CCWCP delegates, he "was pretty seriously attacked and the Institute through me." For Bishop this was a learning experience in listening to members of the group to whom he and other white Episcopalians sought to minister. "Lay it down in your heart," he wrote a close white friend, "however much you may doubt the efficiency of the best colored men, you mustn't [sic] doubt their discernment. You cannot fool them a bit. What they want is becoming clear to them, and that conference of Colored Church Workers is a body with which we have got to reckon and whose legitimate aspirations . . . we must realize."[34]

The opposition was so intense to his plan for King Hall that Bishop came away convinced "the idea would be perfectly futile, would not win students, and would be a waste of money." After the Brooklyn meeting it was clear to him "that what these colored people want . . . is the kind of seminary that Union [Theological Seminary in New York City] or [the Episcopal Theological School at Harvard University in] Cambridge is, doing the same kind of work and manned by colored men." Chastened, Bishop abandoned the attempt to revive King Hall in any form. What he had done, however, was add to the doubts in the minds of southern bishops about him and convince the CCWCP he was manipulable, while lacking the force and influence to work his will on the powerful whites who controlled the ACIN.[35]

---

and Letters of Henry Yates Satterlee, First Bishop of Washington [D.C.], 339–40. Satterlee's use of the terms "colored people" and "mulattoes" rather than "Negroes" reflected the fact that large numbers of African Americans in the Episcopal Church were visibly of mixed race. Like many other whites and blacks at this time, he used the term "Negro" only to describe those African Americans he assumed to be unmixed racially.

34. Samuel H. Bishop to Richard Pardee Williams, September 1908, ACIN Papers.
35. Samuel H. Bishop to W. P. Thirkield, September 26, 1908, ACIN Papers.

One of the first issues to which Bishop and the other officers of the ACIN had to respond in 1906 was the distrust of white Episcopalians in the South. Five years later Bishop would recall: "The Institute met at the very start a great deal of prejudice, misunderstanding, and some hostility." Southern Episcopal bishops were angered that, with the exception of Richard Pardee Williams, a priest of the Diocese of Washington, D.C., no white resident of the South served on the ACIN board. And in the minds of these critics, Pardee barely counted. The bishops rightly considered the District of Columbia unrepresentative of typical black-white relations in the South; and they discounted Pardee because he was a defender of the assertive, educated African Americans who dominated black Episcopal parishes in the District, a good number of them connected with Howard University.[36]

When Charles E. Woodcock, bishop of Kentucky, wrote to Bishop, demanding an explanation for the paucity of whites resident in the South on the ACIN board, the director defended the institute with the explanation that, for convenience's sake, it was important that board members live near New York City, where most meetings would take place. Appealing to Woodcock's southern sensibilities, Bishop asserted that "for the present" responsibility for southern black education should rest on northerners, since they must accept blame for the "twelve dismal and awful years of reconstruction experiments," as well as for the mostly "ill-advised" educational philanthropy of "earlier years," mistakenly based on "an assumption of [the North's] superior wisdom and morality which was most painful for the south to endure." Less diplomatically, the ACIN director reminded the bishop of Kentucky that "the North is enormously rich and can afford now to do its duty, and ought to do it more efficiently in that it has learned how to do it more wisely and graciously." Counseling patience, "later on," he assured Woodcock, "it will I think become necessary that the South be represented on the board."[37] Bishop's responses to Woodcock and other southern bishops who felt that white Episcopalians from their dioceses had to be participants in the development and implementation of ACIN policies did not still criticism of the institute. To the contrary, his actions and words during the eight years of

36. Bishop, "Report to the Executive Committee," Trustee Minutes, January 14, 1911, ACIN Papers. Brent, *Satterlee*, 341.
37. Samuel H. Bishop to Charles E. Woodcock, August 8, 1906, ACIN Papers.

his directorship added to their concerns, convincing many southern bishops the Vermonter held some of the same Yankee attitudes of "superior wisdom and morality" that had made black education so problematic to southern whites since the end of the Civil War.

When Bishop Greer, attempting to assuage the criticism of southern white Episcopalians, proposed that Thomas Nelson Page, a native of Virginia, be elected a trustee of the ACIN, Bishop resisted the suggestion strenuously.[38] A novelist, essayist, lawyer, and diplomat, Page was one of the most prominent apologists for the white southern point of view on race relations in the late nineteenth and early twentieth century. His novels and essays consistently disparaged the ability of blacks to be responsible participants in politics and frequently characterized blacks as more "beast" than human. He faintly condemned lynching but hastened to explain it as an expression of whites' "determination to put an end to the ravishing of their women by an inferior race"— even though his own statistics proved that neither rape nor alleged rape was the cause of the majority of black lynchings.[39]

In response to Greer's assertion that Page's presence on the ACIN board would stimulate contributions from wealthy Episcopalians, North and South, Bishop countered:

> To my mind the necessity that the Episcopal Church stands for righteous ideas is much more important than that it get money. I am not half so much interested in the material projects of the Institute as in the attempt to commit the church to the divine principle of generous justice . . . the church must not be behind science in the recognition of what is distinctively a Christian principle, namely that God created of one blood all nations of men for to dwell upon the face of the whole earth. That proposition is rapidly becoming an accepted fact of anthropology and ethnology, and Mr. Page is "away out of the lines" of that accepted fact.[40]

Moving beyond the issue of Page's fitness for service on the ACIN board, Bishop gave Greer a lecture on the common humanity of blacks and whites, asserting that "the Negro has contributed to European civilization both blood and ideas" and that "industrial initiative up

---

38. Bishop to Greer, April 13, 1907, in Peabody Papers.
39. Thomas Nelson Page, *The Old South: Essays Social and Political*; Page, *Red Rock: A Chronicle of Reconstruction*, 356–58, 582; Page, *The Negro: The Southerner's Problem*, 80, 91, 100, 163, 247–48.
40. Bishop to Greer, April 13, 1907, ACIN Papers.

to the point of a good deal of skill was manifested by the Negro long before it was manifested by any other people." Assuring Greer that he did not "believe in radical and boisterous preaching of ideas that antagonize southern white people," Bishop insisted that "when it comes to a crucial matter like the doctrine of manhood, with all that involves, as lying at the basis of any possible divine work to be done by the Institute, it means to me all the moral seriousness I have." Returning to the subject of Page's suitability as an ACIN trustee, Bishop concluded: "In short, The Institute has got to stand, if men who are both intelligent and good are to give it sympathy and support, upon the fundamental proposition that the Negro is a man, and that proposition Mr. Page essentially denies." Page was not invited to be a trustee of the American Church Institute for Negroes.[41]

From the time Bishop became ACIN executive director until his death in 1914, he prevented whites who did not believe in the ability of African Americans to benefit from academic, industrial, and Christian education from becoming prominent figures in the work of the ACIN; he also sought to change their minds. When Joseph Blunt Cheshire, the conservative bishop of North Carolina, asked him for "material on the higher education of the Negro," Bishop recommended Du Bois's study, *The College-Bred Negro*, commenting that African Americans' "use of higher education" since emancipation constituted "an extraordinary tribute to the moral earnestness and mental spirit of educated Negroes." Typically, he expanded on this theme, telling Cheshire that the "Negro teachers of the South" needed more than "primary, grammar, and industrial schools" to be "adequately educated."[42] He then proceeded to challenge the widely held opinion among white southerners

> that the Yankee teacher who went South immediately after the [Civil] war started wrong in beginning [the education of the former slaves] with Latin and Greek rather than with the training of the hands to work. As a matter of fact the Yankee teacher was not to blame, because that was all we knew about education anyway. . . . the Yankee teacher was but expressing the universal idea and practicing the general method of American education.[43]

41. Ibid.
42. Bishop to Cheshire, October 25, 1913, ACIN Papers.
43. Ibid.

Because Bishop and his staunch ally George Foster Peabody believed the majority of southern Episcopal bishops and laity were hostile to a comprehensive range of black education, they blocked the election of most white southerners as ACIN trustees. Richard Pardee Williams of the District of Columbia and James Hardy Dillard of Virginia were exceptions because they were believed to hold enlightened views of black potential. When pressed on the question of why a church agency whose work was centered in the South had such a paucity of southern trustees, Bishop sometimes offered the dubious excuse that "Southern bishops . . . are unable to spend the time and money necessary to attendance at bi-monthly board meetings."[44] In a frank comment on this matter to a Boston friend who was also a philanthropist, Peabody pointed to the trustees of St. Paul's School in "southside" Virginia, who did

> not expect much of negroes and are quite content to let crude and inefficient conditions continue. It is necessary that anyone who tries to improve conditions shall believe in the negro's capability both moral and intellectual. I have personally for that reason opposed naming of certain prominent southerners as trustees of the Institute and have insisted that we should have a general agent who was profoundly convinced of the capability of the negro as has been demonstrated at Hampton and many other schools.[45]

Bishop's articles on racial issues added to the doubts and discomforts conservative white southerners felt about him. His writings usually contained some of the standard racist rhetoric of his day, but just as frequently he pointed to virtues, strengths, and achievements of blacks. In "Romance of the Negro," a 1910 piece intended to generate renewed interest in educational mission work among African Americans, Bishop made a number of controversial statements. He noted that "the black race alone among the so-called inferior peoples has been able to stand and to increase in the presence of the stronger race." He praised Negroes as the first race to have "evinced industrial ambition in the use of the products of the earth for commercial purposes." He pointed to Negroes' mixture of African, Caucasian, and Native American blood and their assimilation of Western culture as making them "a sort of crucible in which God is working out by

44. Bishop to Henry L. Phillips, November 11, 1911, ACIN Papers.
45. Peabody to Ida Mason, March 26, 1912, in Peabody Papers.

experiment the problem of the adjustment of races." In "The Negro and the Church," another article written the same year, he explained the withdrawal of most African Americans from the Episcopal Church immediately after the Civil War as due, in part, to the ways in which the denomination "made the Negroes uncomfortable . . . evinced a decided inertia and indifference to their religious condition. . . . [and] refused them the right of self-government."[46]

Perhaps Bishop's most controversial article, "The Church and the City Negro," appeared in 1911. Written while he and other Progressives, black and white, were working to establish the Urban League, the article used some of the same arguments and statistics employed to justify creation of this new social service agency. As a member of the NAACP and a friend of W. E. B. Du Bois, he may also have drawn on their conversations and Du Bois's highly regarded study, *The Philadelphia Negro: A Social Study*, in shaping this piece. Here Bishop expressed disagreement with Booker T. Washington's judgment that the problems of urban Negroes were due mainly to "inefficiency," asserting that the more fundamental reasons were the lack of "practical educational opportunities for Negro youth in the South," which stimulated them to migrate North, and "antidemocratic forces at work in the city," including black exclusion from the labor movement, intense job competition that favored white immigrants, racism, and segregation. To counter these "antidemocratic forces" he called on "Church people" to work to eliminate "racial arrogance" and to "secure for the Negro absolute fairness and absolute freedom of opportunity."[47]

The appearance of this article provoked an angry response from Robert Beverly, a prominent white Virginia layman, who accused Bishop of denying the necessity for segregation of the races. Beverly found particularly outrageous Bishop's statement that "segregation of all classes of Negroes, good and bad, in crowded quarters . . . tends to destroy that social differentiation and righteous aristocracy of excellence which are the motive forces in the progress of a race or of a group."[48] In his response Bishop equivocated, protesting the charge was unfair—"I do profoundly believe in social segregation—

46. Bishop, "Romance of the Negro," 204–5. Bishop, "The Negro and the Church," 437–41.
47. Bishop, "The Church and the City Negro," 297–99.
48. Ibid., 298.

believe in it not only for the safety of the white man, but for the good of the Negro." Although Bishop's defensive and contradictory reply was clearly intended to conciliate Beverly, he refused to concede the necessity for permanent racial segregation.

> The Negro people in this country must for any time we can now foresee be a distinct racial group. . . . What the future may mean neither you nor I nor anyone else can determine. Of course if two races are to live within one political organization, there must be an intimate moral, intellectual, and religious relationship between the races and to some extent a social relationship. . . . I do not believe, as I think no right-minded man believes, in an enforced ghetto either for Jew or for Negro, but [in] the measure of segregation which protects the white race from degradation and enables the Negro to develop his own racial as well as personal sufficiency.

This reply cannot have satisfied Beverly's or other conservative whites' doubts about Bishop's soundness on the race issue, especially since his unorthodox views continued to be reflected in his subsequent published writings.[49]

Implementation of the ACIN founders' vision for Episcopal black education rested on the ability of Bishop and his collaborators to raise significant sums of money. In an attempt to do this, Peabody, in concert with Greer and Bishop, drafted an appeal in 1907 to members of the Episcopal Church for two hundred thousand dollars. The appeal, though publicized in a variety of ways, including printed notices in Episcopal Church publications, yielded small return. Peabody then encouraged the ACIN board to submit an application to the Rockefeller-funded GEB for "such appropriation as the Board may deem it expedient or possible to give," promising to use his friendship with the Rockefellers and his position as treasurer of the General Education Board to ensure the request received serious consideration. Peabody may have also felt certain that the ACIN would receive a significant sum from the GEB because of the grants it had made to the Southern Education Board, "a sister organization," which Peabody had started with a thirty-thousand-dollar gift. He viewed the ACIN

---

49. Samuel H. Bishop to Robert Beverly, May 24, 1911, ACIN Papers. Beverly continued to object to Bishop's ideas. See his letter to the editor in the *Southern Churchman*, November 2, 1912. See also Bishop, "In Topsy-Turvy Land," 127–29, and Bishop, "The Struggle," 244–46.

as another sister organization to the GEB, one with the potential to have an even greater effect than the SEB. But the officers of GEB, though interested in supporting southern black schools, had made a policy decision not to fund the denominational agencies that managed them. Consequently, they rejected the ACIN application.[50]

At the same time as the officers of the ACIN continued efforts to secure substantial grants from the General Education Board, they constantly sought to raise funds within their denomination. Indeed, Greer, Peabody, and Bishop took it for granted that once the institute was established, it would either be the recipient of sizable regular appropriations from the national Episcopal Church, presumably through the Board of Missions, or of major gifts from wealthy Episcopalians, or both, they hoped. These three and other supporters of the ACIN understood that only by securing substantial sums of money could their hopes be realized for the ACIN to exercise a role in southern black education similar to that of the General Education Board. As became quickly apparent, money was not forthcoming in sizable amounts from any quarter. The Board of Missions, which had sanctioned the creation of the institute, was extremely resistant to doing much more than using the ACIN as the occasional instrument for the distribution and oversight of the same relatively small sums it had appropriated prior to 1906 for the support of black Episcopal schools. And though some Episcopalians of means responded to ACIN appeals, none offered even a small percentage of the $43 million John D. Rockefeller, Sr., had by 1907 put at the disposal of the General Education Board.[51]

Since he bore special responsibility for fund-raising, Bishop was probably the first to realize fully how handicapped the ACIN's fund-raising activities were by the widespread belief that its founders and their affluent friends would endow it generously. Throughout his tenure as ACIN director, he lamented that the Board of Missions had "organized the Institute under a misconception," supposing it "was to be financed by two or three men who never intended to."

50. Two hundred thousand dollars is first stated as the goal in George Foster Peabody to David Hummell Greer, April 12, 1906, ACIN Papers. For an example of the appeal notice, see *The Pacific Churchman* [Diocese of California], April 15, 1907, 14. Samuel H. Bishop to Wallace Buttrick, December 21, 1907, ACIN Papers. Fosdick et al., *Adventure in Giving*, 19–20. For a discussion of the GEB's willingness to fund specific ACIN schools but not the institute, see chapter 6.

51. Fosdick et al., *Adventure in Giving*, 327; Ware, *Peabody*, 105.

The names most frequently mentioned were George Foster Peabody, who was mistakenly assumed to be the possessor of vast wealth; Episcopal Bishop William Lawrence of Massachusetts, who had a sizable personal fortune and was amazingly successful at inducing affluent Episcopalians to support charitable causes; and J. P. Morgan, the financial titan whose generous gifts to the Episcopal Church were legendary. Peabody, the only one of the three who would have given large sums to the ACIN, had, "at the peak of his business career," a net worth between "three and four million"; the other two were not interested.[52]

Faced with this situation, Bishop sought the assistance of David Greer and George Foster Peabody in his efforts to increase appropriations from the Church Missions Board and persuade rich members of the Episcopal Church to contribute to the institute directly. Greer, as the highly regarded bishop of his denomination's wealthiest diocese, was well situated to undertake some aggressive fund-raising for the ACIN. And his leading role in establishing the institute and drawing Bishop into it gave every expectation he would. Yet this failed to happen, for at least three reasons: Greer too expected Peabody to make major gifts or solicit them from his friends the Rockefellers as personal contributions or grants from the General Education Board; criticisms of the institute by southern Episcopalians dampened his enthusiasm; and he was distracted by his leadership of a "nationwide appeal . . . for millions of dollars" to build a cathedral in his diocese.[53]

By 1908 the failure of the ACIN to attract major funds for its work was raising questions about the institute's ability to continue to pay the director's salary. To force this issue to the trustees' attention, Bishop

---

52. Samuel H. Bishop to Phillip M. Rhinelander, December 23, 1913, ACIN Papers. Ware, *Peabody*, 133–34. Ware gives specific estimates of Peabody's gifts to the University of Georgia and Skidmore College, but offers only the general comment "that his gifts to the schools for Negroes . . . flowed in a steady stream." See Ware, *Peabody*, 131, 136–37, 191. On Lawrence, see *Memories of a Happy Life*, chapters 16, 21, 25, 28, and 29; Martin, *"Outlasting Marble and Brass,"* 81–105. For information on J. P. Morgan's gifts to the Episcopal Church see ibid., 55, 59–60, 65, 86, 154.

53. Robert Patton, who in 1914 succeeded Samuel Bishop as ACIN director, attributed the institute's difficulties in raising money from 1906–1914 to "the San Francisco earthquake, the famines in China and Russia, the financial depression beginning in 1907, [and] a nationwide appeal led by Bishop Greer for millions for the building of the Cathedral of St. John The Divine." All these, he believed, "militated against the Institute appeal for $100,000 a year and additional sums for endowment." Patton, *An Inspiring Record*, 13.

informed the secretary of the board: "I have a call to the University of Vermont (my college) and am seriously considering it." He also made it clear he wished to continue with the institute. "I have not been very successful as a money getter," he admitted, "but . . . it is not entirely my fault." Much of the difficulty he attributed to "a very unfortunate financial history due to the series of events from the San Francisco [earthquake] disaster to the [financial] panic [beginning in 1907]." But the greatest difficulty was the lethargy of the ACIN board. "If I stay," he demanded, "the Board has got to 'brace up' and help me get money." These comments were meant to be shared.[54]

News of Bishop's job offer from Vermont produced a letter of praise for his work from A. B. Hunter, the principal of St. Augustine's School in North Carolina. In his response Greer acknowledged that the ACIN director "has proved himself to be a most invaluable man, especially in placing the Institute upon a good and well organized basis," and expressed the "hope that some satisfactory arrangement can be made to keep him." Aware Hunter's letter was meant also to goad him to greater exertion, Greer added apologetically:

> If I had more leisure to give to the matter[,] I could devote myself to the task of raising money [for the ACIN]; but unfortunately my time is so preempted with Diocesan duties, which have recently been much increased, that I am not able to devote much time to raising funds for the Institute. But I am going to have a talk with Mr. Bishop . . . and hope that we may devise some plan whereby the work of the Institute can be made more appealing to the conscience and pocketbook of American churchmen.[55]

Greer found funds for Bishop's salary, but neither he nor any of the other ACIN trustees made the funding and endowment needs of the institute a major priority. As Bishop continued to demand a response to this problem in 1909 and 1910, his entreaties irritated ACIN trustee Francis Lynde Stetson, the Bishop of New York's legal adviser, who observed at a board meeting that the establishment of the ACIN had been "premature," for it lacked endowment, foundation grants, or regular appropriations from the Missions Board of the Episcopal Church. The clear implication was that the ACIN needed to be

54. S. H. Bishop to R. P. Williams, September 25, 1908, ACIN Papers.
55. David H. Greer to A. B. Hunter, October 3, 1908, in Howard Chandler Robbins Papers, The General Theological Seminary, New York City.

jettisoned. Accelerating his efforts to increase ACIN funds, Bishop lobbied members of the Missions Board with the argument that "40 or 50% of the money expended for the Negroes in the past has been either wasted or used so inefficiently as to be practically wasted," but that now, in the institute, the Episcopal Church possessed an agency doing effective work in the field of black education; and if supplied with adequate funds, it could do a larger and even more effective job. Shrewdly, he enlisted the aid of George Foster Peabody in pressuring Greer, a member of the Board of Missions, to exert himself to secure a minimum grant of three hundred thousand dollars for the ACIN, by insisting at budget meetings that "this negro work" is "the very first obligation of our church."[56]

When the Missions Board failed to provide the three hundred thousand dollars, in 1910 the ACIN submitted a second grant application to the GEB, this time for one hundred thousand dollars "to be used for the development of normal and agricultural work in the schools connected with the Institute." Bishop assured the ACIN board "there is considerable reason for hoping that some amount will be granted[,] either in bulk sum for buildings, or an annual grant for a certain period of years." At the same time he continued to challenge the institute trustees to become better fund-raisers, as it was likely that "any [GEB] grant will be conditional on the [Episcopal] Church's raising a like amount or perhaps double the amount."[57] Conscious of the GEB's policy of providing monies to schools rather than to denominations and religious agencies with which schools were affiliated, the ACIN application included this pledge of allegiance to the GEB agenda:

> The Institute appeals to your Board not because it is a church institution, but because it is trying to do on behalf of the Protestant Episcopal Church in the United States of America the kind of work that is being done by Hampton and Tuskegee Institutes and by the General and Southern Education Boards. That is to say, it is aiming to send forth well trained teachers to stimulate the moral and economic life of the Negro people, to increase taxation for school purposes and the extension of the public school term, to promote teachers' conferences and school extension

56. Samuel H. Bishop to Francis Lynde Stetson, May 12, 1909; Bishop to Arthur Selden Lloyd, April 18, 1910; both in ACIN Papers. George Foster Peabody to David H. Greer, June 16, 1910, in Peabody Papers.

57. Bishop, "Report to Executive Committee," Trustee Minutes, January 14, 1911, ACIN Papers.

societies in our schools and in public school communities, and in brief to work for the economic, social, and moral as well as the religious uplift of the Negro people.[58]

After a preliminary review of the ACIN grant request, the GEB asked the institute to revise and resubmit it, a responsibility which fell to Samuel Bishop. In the original application Bishop had requested a lump sum of $100,000; this time he carefully itemized the projected uses of the amount requested—$53,000 for classrooms and dormitories at St. Augustine's and St. Paul's, plus slightly more than $10,000 to cover anticipated deficits in the two schools' operating budgets. And he reduced the overall request by $27,000, a reduction almost certainly explained by the last paragraph of Bishop's letter, in which, with obvious embarrassment, he asked the officers of the GEB to "allow me to correct an intimation made in a previous letter, that the Institute proposed to hold some part of the grant of your Board as an endowment." To further buttress credibility, he listed the ACIN's annual appropriation to its schools as just under $17,000 per year from 1906 to 1911, plus an additional $30,000 in individual gifts to the schools from members of the Episcopal Church. To counteract rumors of negative attitudes toward the ACIN by white Episcopalians in the South, Bishop attached a "circular . . . signed by all the bishops of southern dioceses" endorsing the institute, a sign of "the active sympathy" and "financial support" of the "white citizens."[59]

The GEB must have rejected this application. Less than two months later Bishop told Leighton Parks, rector of one of the Episcopal Church's wealthiest parishes in New York City, that the ACIN was "in horrible distress for money, and I have not been able to reach the rich though I am responsible for the raising of funds." Responding to

58. Samuel H. Bishop to General Board of Education [sic], August 27, 1910; Samuel H. Bishop to General Board of Education [sic], August 27, 1910; Samuel H. Bishop to General Board of Education [sic], November 29, 1910; all in ACIN Papers. Privately, George Foster Peabody wrote to Wallace Buttrick, director of the GEB, urging that the ACIN application be given every consideration and suggesting that the GEB give the institute "a certain sum each year . . . for the next five years . . . dependent . . . upon the amounts contributed by the [Episcopal] church" to the work of the ACIN. Buttrick's reply was noncommittal. See George Foster Peabody to Wallace Buttrick, June 13, 1910; Wallace Buttrick to George Foster Peabody, June 24, 1910; both in Peabody Papers.

59. Samuel H. Bishop to the General Education Board, January 25, 1911, in Peabody Papers. Despite Bishop's statement, at least one southern bishop, Charles Minnigerode Beckwith of Alabama, did not sign. See below.

rumors Parks had heard of antagonistic relations between the ACIN and southern Episcopalians, Bishop assured Parks that the "Institute had made local boards consisting of Southern white men responsible for the management of the various schools with which it is connected, thus engaging the responsible interest of southern white men."[60]

Late in 1911 Bishop explained to a fellow Episcopal cleric that "the giving of money by quite considerable foundations and by moneyed persons has been refused the Institute on the score of no southern representation [on the ACIN Board]." Bishop refuted this charge, pointing to trustees James Hardy Dillard, whom he described as "the wisest and most important southern educator," and William C. Rives, a member of a distinguished Virginia family. He continued to argue that Greer, Peabody, and Stires should also be considered southerners even though they resided in the North. "But," he admitted, "this representation is not satisfactory to the southern bishops or to the foundations I have in mind."[61]

It was certainly not satisfactory to Charles Minnigerode Beckwith, bishop of Alabama, who beginning in 1910 was an inveterate critic of the ACIN, refusing to even join with other southern bishops in the courtesy gesture of signing an endorsement of the agency. Seeking to mollify Beckwith and other southern critics of the institute without giving them seats on the ACIN board, in 1911 Bishop persuaded the institute trustees to authorize establishment of an ACIN advisory council whose membership consisted largely of southern white bishops. Once established, the advisory council, to which Bishop turned for advice and counsel on difficult and controversial matters, began to play a significant role in defusing tensions between the officers of the ACIN and southern leaders of the Episcopal Church.[62]

60. Samuel H. Bishop to Leighton Parks, March 10, 1911, ACIN Papers.

61. Samuel H. Bishop to Henry L. Phillips, November 11, 1911, ACIN Papers. For information on Dillard, see Benjamin Brawley, *Dr. Dillard of the Jeanes Fund*. William C. Rives and his wife were members of Calvary Episcopal Church in New York City. See Brent, *Satterlee*, 103.

62. Samuel H. Bishop to George Foster Peabody, June 16, 1910, in Peabody Papers. Samuel H. Bishop to Joseph Blunt Cheshire, October 31, 1911, in Cheshire Papers. Representative of the role of the Advisory Council is the part it played in resolving tensions between St. Paul's School and the ACIN from 1911–1912. See Joseph B. Cheshire to David H. Greer, February 22, 1912, in Cheshire Papers; "Opinion of the [Advisory] Council," appendix document in Samuel H. Bishop, "Report to the ACIN Board," September 1912, in Peabody Papers.

These southern whites might have been less amenable if they had known that at the same time Bishop launched the advisory council, he was attempting to persuade Henry L. Phillips of Philadelphia, the black Episcopal priest who was president of the Conference of Church Workers among Colored People, to become the first African American trustee of the ACIN. Bishop appealed to Phillips on the ground "that the colored constituency of our Church should be represented on the governing body of the Institute," assuring him he was uniquely qualified to integrate the ACIN board. Phillips refused the invitation, responding that it would create a conflict with his role as a trustee of St. Paul's School.[63] The real reason for Phillips's refusal was probably his unwillingness publicly to align himself with the ACIN, an organization under suspicion in the black Episcopal community, and with Bishop, who was at the time engaged in a furious struggle with James Solomon Russell, Phillips's friend and fellow black Episcopal cleric, over control of St. Paul's School.

Bishop's failure to persuade Phillips to join the ACIN board caused him to seek another way to secure support and participation from the African American community. This was an important concern to him because of his growing belief that blacks should have some share in shaping the policies and administration of the institute, and his hope that greater black involvement might generate contributions for the institute, especially increased giving for its schools from black Episcopal parishes. In pursuing these goals, Bishop had to counter the hostility of leading black Episcopal clergy who demanded that the denomination seek converts among black Americans. They opposed any plan that used the ACIN merely as a device to deal with a general social problem that threatened whites. In June 1911, he persuaded the ACIN trustees to appoint George Alexander McGuire, an African American Episcopal priest, as field agent.[64] McGuire, a talented man who had built flourishing black Episcopal parishes in

63. Samuel H. Bishop to Henry L. Phillips, November 11, 1911, ACIN Papers. Phillips was rector of the Church of the Crucifixion, a large and influential black parish, and Archdeacon for Colored Work in the Diocese of Pennsylvania. For a history of his life and ministry see "Henry Laird Phillips Wanted Cannibals", 10, 28.

64. Trustee Minutes, June 17, 1911, ACIN Papers. George Freeman Bragg, one of the most prominent of the black Episcopal clergy, frequently raised the issue of proselytization and questioned ACIN policy. For representative examples, see his letters to the editor in the *Southern Churchman*, March 25, 1911, and January 16, 1926.

Cincinnati; Richmond; Philadelphia; Cambridge, Massachusetts; and in Arkansas, where for four years he had been Archdeacon for Colored Work, was an unflinching enemy of racism in his denomination. One of the major goals of his ministerial career was to implement Alexander Crummell's vision of blacks in the Episcopal Church functioning as educated and progressive Christian leaders of their race.

With this appointment, McGuire became the first black staff officer of the ACIN. For two years he traveled throughout the country as Bishop's lieutenant, inspecting institute schools and attempting, with little success, to raise funds in black and white Episcopal parishes. By 1913, disgusted and "discouraged by the status of Negro Episcopalians" in their church, he resigned, returning to his native home, Antigua in the West Indies. In 1919 he left the denomination, certain that the Episcopal Church would never nurture or tolerate the presence of a cadre of articulate, educated blacks able to function as leaders of their race. Shortly after, he became chaplain-general of Marcus Garvey's Universal Negro Improvement Association, and, with the support of a small group of equally disgruntled black Episcopalians, founded the African Orthodox Church, eventually becoming its first bishop.[65] Thereafter, in his speeches, sermons, and writings, he denounced whites as

> the most avaricious of races. Not content with Europe, they took part of Asia and Africa. They came over here and took America from the red man, and because they would not work for them, they brought members of our race from Africa. They call us the white man's burden, and I hope that the burden will keep him down until we get back to our homeland. . . . We must go as missionaries among the whites and teach them the everlasting brotherhood of man.[66]

The next few years saw little improvement in the institute's financial resources. Episcopal Church giving to the agency remained small and the foundations, while willing to make grants to some of the schools under the care of the ACIN, had no interest in transferring major sums

65. J. Carleton Hayden, "George Alexander McGuire," in Rayford Logan and Michael R. Winston eds., *Dictionary of American Negro Biography*, 416–17; Lewis, *Yet with a Steady Beat*, 100–106. Cf. McGuire, "Things Done and to Be Done," 1020–21.

66. Randall K. Burkett, *Black Redemption: Churchmen Speak For The Garvey Movement*, 161. For two excellent biographical sketches of McGuire's life, see ibid., 157–80; and Gavin White, "Patriarch McGuire and the Episcopal Church," 151–80.

to a denominational supervisory agency whose parent body was able to raise millions of dollars for other major projects. The officers of the GEB may well have felt that if Episcopalians wanted the ACIN to be a foundation, it was their job to endow or fund it, rather than begging secular agencies to put their monies at its disposal. By 1912 Bishop Greer had grown weary of the seemingly hopeless responsibilities of trying to raise an endowment for the institute or to secure a regular appropriation from the Board of Missions for it. He also wanted to be relieved from the embarrassment of association with an agency that lacked the resources to do its work properly. When Samuel Bishop learned that Greer was considering relieving him as ACIN director, "dropping the whole administrational [sic] and supervisory work of the Institute, and simply employing" McGuire "to make [financial] appeals for funds," he implored George Foster Peabody, James Hardy Dillard, and his other allies on the Trustee Board, including Ernest Stires, rector of St. Thomas Church, New York City; Hamilton Wright Mabie, author and editor of *Outlook*; and Robert C. Pruyn, the Albany banker, to help him prevent this. Working in concert with Bishop, these men were successful in pressuring Greer to change his mind. Bishop was certain that Beverly Dandridge Tucker, bishop coadjutor of southern Virginia, had been instrumental in convincing Greer to consider dismantling or reducing the scope of the institute, and that Tucker's efforts to that end were almost certainly abetted by James Solomon Russell of St. Paul's.[67]

As Bishop sought to push St. Paul's toward improvement, he clashed repeatedly with Russell, who in Bishop's opinion made impossible even the limited industrial education of which the school was then capable by using the "industrial department" to do "contract work" for local white businesses and farmers. Despite its outstanding debts and inadequate revenues, contract work was so profitable that the St. Paul's board of trustees paid taxes on the earnings. Russell's percentage of profit from this income made it "unnecessary for him to collect his salary" as principal of St. Paul's. To the dismay of Bishop and the ACIN trustees, the board of trustees (dominated by whites from Brunswick County in which the school was located) not only sanctioned Russell's style of management but also defended him from criticism. Countering

---

67. Bishop to George Foster Peabody, May 3, 1912; Bishop to Peabody, May 11, 1912; both in Peabody Papers.

these assurances, Bishop charged that Russell was exploiting St. Paul's School and its students for financial gain and discrediting industrial education. By 1908 Bishop had become so disgusted with Russell that he was telling Episcopal supporters of southern black education: "Up to this point St. Paul's has not been an industrial school at all. There has been almost no educational value in the industrial training, but it has been mainly a business enterprise exploiting student labor to the extent of driving students out of the trades."[68]

Over the next two years Bishop sharpened his public criticism of Russell as an administrator in comments to the board of trustees of his school and in communications to the two Episcopal bishops in southern Virginia, one of whom, Coadjutor Bishop Tucker, served on the St. Paul's board of trustees. He also urged the school's major contributors to withhold their gifts until changes were made in the administration and curriculum of the institution. Soon Bishop and Russell were engaged in open battle for control of St. Paul's. Despite Bishop's best efforts, Russell retained the support of the black and white members of his trustee board. In March 1912, Russell launched one of his strongest counterattacks, when he persuaded the school's trustees to pass what Bishop characterized as "a rather violent memorial," stating the director of the institute had "attempted to render the government of the principal and the board unnecessary." This memorial was sent to the ACIN trustees and the Board of Missions, chaired by Arthur Selden Lloyd, former bishop coadjutor of Virginia.[69]

It was this communication and a series of informal conversations between Greer and Tucker of southern Virginia that caused Greer to consider whether Samuel Bishop should be relieved of his position and the ACIN dissolved or restructured. Tucker was certainly only one of a number of southern white Episcopalians who encouraged

68. [Bishop,] [First Report], 4–5 and Samuel H. Bishop, "Confidential Report [on] St. Paul's School, [1906], 1–5, ACIN Papers. The Board of Trustees of the St. Paul's Normal and Industrial School to the President and Members of the Board of the American Church Institute for Negroes, [January 1912], in Cheshire Papers. Samuel H. Bishop to David Hummell Greer, April 4, 1907; Samuel H. Bishop to William C. Doane, February 17, 1908; both in ACIN Papers.

69. Henrietta Gardiner to George Foster Peabody, April 27, 1911, in Peabody Papers. The Board of Trustees of St. Paul's Normal and Industrial School to the President and Members of the Board of the American Church Institute for Negroes, [January 1912], in Cheshire Papers. Samuel H. Bishop to George Foster Peabody, February 10, 1912, in Peabody Papers.

Booker T. Washington visiting St. Paul's. James Solomon Russell is second from left. Russell Memorial Library, St. Paul's College.

this notion in Greer's mind. Bishop, once again turning to George Foster Peabody for support, explained that "the whole situation at St. Paul's roots in the fact that Mr. Russell has succeeded in gaining Bishop Tucker's sympathy and support—an easy achievement because of Bishop Tucker's limited sense of what Negro education ought to be and his well known Virginia hostility to any outside criticism."[70] By his constant attacks on Russell, Bishop had created a formidable enemy; one shrewd enough to shape his responses and counterattacks in a way that encouraged southern white Episcopalians such as Tucker to come to Russell's aid and join him in using the conflict as an excuse for eliminating both Bishop and the ACIN.

Uncowed, Bishop secured the support of his largely white Southern Advisory Council and, with Peabody working to ensure that the

70. Samuel H. Bishop to George Foster Peabody, March 5, 1912, in Peabody Papers.

ACIN board did not desert him, held his ground. With equal firmness he told the two bishops in southern Virginia who had been working against him that it was "their business either to get in touch with [the] Institute and me and see if we cannot work the thing out, or to withdraw [St. Paul's School from the Institute] and publish a statement [of explanation] to the Church." By this time Bishop was convinced that Russell was a manipulative liar who was unethically enriching himself at the expense of St. Paul's School. "If I had half his astuteness," he confidentially shared with Peabody, "and knew a quarter of the methods by which he does certain things, I could became a multi-millionaire."[71]

Bishop's refusal to be intimidated produced a compromise. The Board of Missions and the ACIN hired the Phelps-Stokes Fund, an educational foundation, to do an assessment of St. Paul's School and prepare a report on their findings. The report, presented to the ACIN board in March 1914, declared the "criticisms made by Samuel H. Bishop in the past on St. Paul's School are absolutely justifiable and that the suggestions he now makes are necessary to the welfare of the school and the honor and usefulness of the [Episcopal] Church." The report cited a number of problems at the school, including a bookkeeping system that made it impossible to "clearly and absolutely" determine "whether or not the gross income of the school is honestly and efficiently used" and "centralization of power in the office of the business manager of the school [Russell's son-in-law] who is neither by experience, by insight, or by temperament competent to exercise so exclusive a control." While Russell was credited with having "founded . . . built" and maintained the school, the report noted that in recent years "the school was more maintenance to him than he to it, as he [and his family] largely lived upon school supplies." Perhaps the most damning assessment came from the report's criticism of the arrangement between Russell and the white governments of Brunswick County and Lawrenceville, whereby St. Paul's, "while paying taxes of $1,000 per year to the village and county" for profits realized from the contract work done by its students for whites, bore the responsibility of providing public education for black students "in Lawrenceville and the immediately outlying district."

71. Samuel H. Bishop to George Foster Peabody, September 17, 1912, in Peabody Papers.

As the report put it: "It is not too strong to say that the community of Lawrenceville is grafting upon the school at the rate of a thousand dollars a year, and that therefore its attitude toward the school cannot be dispassionate or be possessed of any particular moral value."[72]

The report recommended "appointment of a white man, preferably a southerner, as . . . treasurer of the school, who shall control and be responsible for the entire financial management;" "appointment of an assistant principal or dean . . . for the educational administration of the school," who shall report directly to the school's trustees; immediate institution of a revised system of bookkeeping supervised by the auditors used by Hampton and Tuskegee Institutes; no further expenditure of funds for expansion of the physical plant without "specific action" of the St. Paul's board; and elimination of contract work that involved "undue exploitation of student labor for the financial interest of the school." The Phelps-Stokes Report was a complete victory for Bishop, qualified only by the general agreement of all concerned that the changes recommended must take place with Russell remaining principal in name. It seemed certain that if he was removed the school would collapse. In a report to the ACIN board shortly before his unexpected death, Bishop savored his victory, assuring the institute trustees that it would not be difficult to find "the proper men for treasurer and . . . assistant principal."[73]

Through skillful lobbying and deployment of his friends on the ACIN board and the Board of Missions, Bishop kept the institute going and preserved his job as executive director during the years 1912–1914. The most constant of his allies continued to be George Foster Peabody, who believed as strongly as did Bishop in the value and importance of the institute. Stressing to Peabody how crucial his presence would be at a coming trustees' meeting, Bishop lamented: "Oh, if I only had some strong men to help me raise money, what a work I could do! But if you are not to be present at the Board meeting,

72. [Bishop], "The General Agent's Report to the Board," March 7, 1914, ACIN Papers.

73. "Draft of St. Paul's Situation" [Preliminary Draft of the Phelps-Stokes Report], [March 1914]; [Samuel H. Bishop], "The General Agent's Report to the Board," March 7, 1914, ACIN Papers. For the views of Russell's white defenders, see the laudatory articles on St. Paul's in the *Southern Churchman*, February 25, May 20, 1911; April 20, 1912; February 1, 1913.

I think the situation will be perfectly hopeless."[74] Along with Peabody, other allies who received similar communications were present and vigorous in their support.

Peabody, certain of the potential of the ACIN schools and confident about the extent of his influence in the denomination and philanthropic circles, also launched a special offensive in 1912. His efforts were concentrated on stimulating Greer and Arthur Selden Lloyd, the bishop who chaired the Board of Missions, to greater activity in support of the institute and Samuel Bishop. Peabody insisted that the national Episcopal Church was morally bound to assist "our [white] southern brethren" in "work for the negro," and that "three-quarters or nine-tenths of the effective missionary work of the Episcopal church among the negroes must be along the educational lines which the Church Institute comprehends . . . and in the ten to twenty schools which our [southern] bishops are ready to establish in cooperation with the Institute." To do this Peabody demanded that Greer and Lloyd ensure that the ACIN receive no less than three hundred thousand dollars from the Episcopal Church's national budget. Once the denomination made this commitment, Peabody assured Greer and Lloyd, then J. P. Morgan and others of his means would believe the Episcopal Church took the work of the ACIN seriously and be willing to add their support in the form of major gifts.[75]

In the fall of 1913 Bishop and Peabody persuaded Greer to cooperate with them in organizing a fund-raising service for the ACIN in the Cathedral of St. John the Divine while the Episcopal Church's General Convention was meeting in New York City. In addition to raising money, the event was also intended to acquaint the convention delegates with the work of the institute and encourage them to become active supporters. On the day of the service, October 20, 1913, "more than a thousand" African Americans, "some of them coming from Brooklyn and as far as the Oranges [in New Jersey]," attended. Many were alumni of black Episcopal schools; others, members of black Episcopal churches in New York City and the surrounding area, were drawn by the appeal of hearing the special choir for the

74. Bishop to Peabody, September 17, 1912, in Peabody Papers.
75. Peabody to Greer, May 7, 1912, in Peabody Papers. Two years earlier Peabody had asked Greer to exert himself to secure three hundred thousand dollars from the Board of Missions for the ACIN. Peabody to Greer, June 16, 1910, in Peabody Papers.

service, composed of singers from the "colored parishes" of the New York Diocese. According to some attendees, the cathedral's white ushers, feeling that the sizable black presence created a problem of racial etiquette, allegedly solved it through the creation of a "jim crow" or segregated seating area in the back of the church for blacks. Supposedly, this was meant to minimize physical contact between the races, particularly for the benefit of Episcopalian segregationists from the South, and ensure that seats at the front were kept for whites. Rumors following the service that this had taken place produced outrage and hurt feelings among numbers of blacks and whites.

But for many present, the addresses delivered at the service were the ultimate insult. The main speakers were two southern white bishops, C. K. Nelson of Atlanta and Thomas F. Gailor of Tennessee, each of whom made a fervent appeal for gifts to the ACIN. Not to support black education, declared Bishop Nelson, would be to "share in the crime of the century." At the same time, both bishops "made the assertion that the 'negro problem' had come when the ballot had been given to the negro." Nelson advised blacks and those who sought to help them that "there are many things which the negro needs much more than a vote," including "a quickened and enlightened conscience such as can be imparted to him in no other way than by the religion of Christ." The heart of Gailor's address was the assertion that "southern states had spent $100,000,000 for negro education within the last forty years, and that the negro, by his progress, had justified all that had been done for him." Bishop Greer, who as president of the ACIN hosted the service in his cathedral, warned that "the negro would have to work out his own problem, and that it was the duty of the [Episcopal] Church to help him to become all that God had meant for him to become." No black clergy or laity active in the Episcopal Church or associated with the ACIN schools were invited to speak, something that also drew critical comment.[76]

What was said and done at the service outraged W. E. B. Du Bois, editor of the NAACP's *Crisis* magazine. In an editorial review of the event, titled "The Episcopal Church," he gave his anger free rein. "In the red blood guiltiness of the Christian church in America toward black folk," Du Bois opened,

76. *New York Times*, October 20, 1913; Henrietta Gardiner [Letter To The Editor], *Crisis* 7 (February 1914): 181; *Southern Churchman*, November 15, 1913.

the Episcopal church has undoubtedly larger share than any other group. It was the Episcopal Church that for 250 years made itself the center and bulwark of man stealing and chattel slavery. It was the Episcopal Church that deliberately closed its doors in the face of the praying slave; it was the Episcopal Church that refused after the [Civil] war to educate the freedmen, and is still refusing, and it is only on the rostrum of the Episcopal Church that such reactionary heathenism could find welcome expression as was uttered by the bishops of Georgia [Atlanta] and Tennessee.

Refuting "lies" told at the service, Du Bois dismissed as ridiculous the assertion that premature black voting was the root cause of the United States' race problem, for it was only "the ballot of reconstruction times that kept the freedmen from reenslavement." The statement that millions had been spent by the South to educate the Negro he denounced as a "venerable lie . . . paraded again to salve the conscience of the guilty South." Nelson's use of Du Bois's research on southern blacks to support charges of rampant immorality among Negroes, and to designate immorality a particular trait of "most [non-Episcopal] Negro preachers," he denounced as "deliberate falsification." It is not the American Negro who stands in "unusual need of moral training," Du Bois thundered, "but the American white man. . . . especially the white man of the South," who is "a thief and a libertine to a greater extent than the Negro ever was or ever will be." Accepting as fact accounts of the segregated seating at the cathedral service, Du Bois condemned it as yet another insult to "the emancipated and risen race whom the [Episcopal] Church for two centuries had insulted and spit upon." Such behavior he characterized as typical of the "smug faced hypocrites who are making the Episcopal Church in America a hissing in the ears of righteous men." Why, Du Bois asked, were two southern whites such as Nelson and Gailor "thrust forward" to tell lies, while workers in the field of southern black education such as James Hardy Dillard, Samuel H. Bishop, and George Foster Peabody were left "in the background"?[77] Despite Bishop's hopes, the service at New

77. Du Bois was baptized in an Episcopal Church, which he attended occasionally as a child and youth. In adulthood, however, his "religious views were wholly decoupled from orthodox Christianity and from any notion of a personal deity." Lewis, *W. E. B. Du Bois*, 166. [Du Bois], "The Episcopal Church," 83–84. In its February 1914 issue *Crisis* carried a "Letter To The Editor" denying there had been segregated seating at the ACIN's

York's cathedral failed to produce either an increase in revenues for the ACIN or greater cohesion between black and white Episcopalians.

In the days following the service the race issue became a major focus of the General Convention when a resolution was introduced "to establish a [separate] racial missionary district for the negroes in the South." Many black Episcopalians and their white allies found the language used by both those opposed to and those in favor of the resolution insulting. During the convention an intense and acrimonious debate took place in the all-white House of Deputies, during which "Advocates of the plan predicted that the Protestant Episcopal Church would lose its negro communicants if a racial diocese were not established, while opponents of the measure said that the negro communicants, if permitted to form a separate diocese[,] would establish a separate and independent church." Because neither side could garner enough votes to win, the matter was tabled.[78] This debate between white church leaders, all of whom took the legitimacy of segregation for granted, offended Episcopalians who believed segregation inconsistent with genuine Christianity.

From 1912 on, desperate to improve the institute's income and its standing, both within and outside the Episcopal Church, Bishop began to pursue allies in new quarters. When he received notice of "a plan for certification" for schools for Negroes, "involving inspection, visitation, and report to givers," he wrote to the director of the project, Thomas Jesse Jones, a researcher at the United States Bureau of Education, introducing himself and explaining that he headed an organization which exercised that very role in relation to black Episcopal schools. Bishop proposed that the institute enter into partnership with Jones and his sponsoring agencies "to help standardize school and college work for Negroes and certify to the public the institutions that ought to be helped."[79] There is no record of Jones's interest in the offer, probably because he and a research team he had assembled

---

cathedral service. Du Bois refused to retract any part of his editorial. See A. G. Combs [Letter To The Editor], *Crisis* 7 (February 1914): 181.

78. *New York Times*, October 23, 1913. One of the responsibilities of the General Convention, the Episcopal Church's chief legislative body, was the drafting and approval of the denomination's budget for all its activities and agencies, including the Board of Missions.

79. Bishop to Jones, April 25, 1912, ACIN Papers.

were already deeply engaged in preparing an influential two-volume assessment of southern black education that would appear in 1917.

Persisting in his search for new partners, Bishop took the lead in developing a conversation between himself and his counterparts in the major Protestant denominations who were also responsible for overseeing and generating financial support for their religious communities' schools for blacks. He hoped these discussions would produce a mutually supportive ecumenical consortium of Protestant churches engaged in black educational mission work. His efforts began to bear fruit when the "secretaries of the home-mission boards of the larger religious bodies in the country" met in November 1913 for what was announced as the "first of a series of conferences with a view to co-operative effort in educational work for the Negro." This meeting in New York City produced an agreement that the denominations represented would work jointly to improve "universities, colleges and normal and industrial schools" for Negroes by producing a common statement of educational values; eliminate "fictitious and inefficient" educational institutions; maintain "a standard of financial and educational management" to which all the institutions must "conform"; discourage duplication of "work at extravagant cost in certain localities"; and foster and strengthen those institutions "which are doing honest and effective work." In his report to the ACIN board on these developments, Bishop gave himself major credit for this ecumenical initiative. What he had endured as director of the institute since 1906 made his need to claim the credit for activities that promised to bring him a measure of consistent support understandable. Perhaps Bishop hoped the consortium would eventually produce an interdenominationally funded religious foundation able to support church schools for blacks as the General Education Board did.[80]

In January 1914 Bishop presented to the executive committee of the ACIN board an invitation from the interdenominational consortium inviting the Episcopal Church to participate in a "campaign of religious bodies doing educational work for Negroes for the purpose of raising $2,000,000 from the Negroes themselves." Bishop almost certainly played a significant role in the decision of the consortium to issue the invitation to the affiliated denominations, though this

80. [Samuel H. Bishop], untitled and undated report to ACIN trustees beginning: "In November last the secretaries of the home-mission boards, etc.," ACIN Papers.

time, when reporting it to the ACIN trustees, he did not claim any credit. The executive committee received the communication and laid it aside for consideration by the full board. Whether this initiative would have been approved by the board is uncertain; and, if so, whether it would have ultimately strengthened the ACIN is unclear. Certainly, if approved, participation by the Episcopal Church in such a campaign would have been largely Bishop's responsibility. In May 1914, however, he entered St. Luke's Hospital in New York City for a "minor operation," during the course of which he died from a "brain hemorrhage."[81]

Although ACIN financial records are incomplete, it is possible to estimate institute spending on black education during the eight years of Bishop's leadership. According to a 1911 GEB document, the ACIN had spent $107,845.62 on Negro education in five years, including $39,643 for the current fiscal year. That same year, several other foundations made grants to black educational institutions in the following amounts: American Missionary Association, $211,000; General Education Board, $87,000; Jeanes Fund, $53,351; Slater Fund, $80,000.[82] While clearly not a "heavyweight" in southern black education, the ACIN was by 1910 a significant presence.

According to Bishop, direct appropriations from the institute averaged about $17,000 a year during the first four years of the ACIN's existence. Thus 1910–1911, with its nearly $40,000 in spending, was a very good year, as expenditures doubled from the earlier levels. If, as seems likely, the agency continued to generate income in the $39,000 range from 1912 to 1914, Bishop's final years, a reasonable total estimate of the institute's gifts to its affiliated schools from 1906 to 1914 would be roughly $264,000.[83]

81. Trustees Minutes, March 4, 1914, ACIN Papers. *New York Times*, June 1, 1914; "The Death of Mr. Bishop," *Spirit of Missions* 79 (February 1914): 472; [Du Bois], "Samuel Henry Bishop," 127; "Samuel Henry Bishop," *The Churchman*, June 6, 1914.

82. General Education Board Dockets, 1910–1913, vol. 2, 254–59, GEB Papers. "Contributions by Nine Northern Educational and Missionary Societies for the Education of Colored People, latest fiscal year. January 1911," GEB Papers, p. 1.

83. Samuel H. Bishop to the General Education Board, January 25, 1911, in Peabody Papers. This figure for the total of the ACIN's gifts is based on $108,000 for the first five years and a hypothetical figure of $39,000 as the amount distributed in the years 1911, 1912, 1913, and 1914.

Although the Board of Missions supplemented ACIN funds during Bishop's years, it provided its own direct grants to ACIN schools and to parish and diocesan schools for Negroes throughout the South that were not affiliated with the institute. Despite the ACIN's special commission to support and improve Episcopal schools for blacks, the Board of Missions, jealous of its prerogatives as the chief missionary agency of the Episcopal Church, refused to channel all gifts for black education through the institute. In 1913–1914, for example, St. Augustine's School received $4,400 from the ACIN and $13,017 from the Board of Missions. This arrangement subverted Bishop's authority, weakening his ability to push the heads and trustees of the schools for improvements in educational quality and administrative efficiency. St. Paul's School provides another illustration. In 1912–1913, as Bishop was challenging what he perceived as the backward, inefficient, and corrupt elements in James Solomon Russell's administration, the school received $18,173 from the Board of Missions, while the ACIN contributed only $5,011.[84]

With encouragement and assistance from George Foster Peabody, Bishop repeatedly sought funding for the ACIN's expansion and educational work from the GEB and other northern foundations. Initially, Peabody and Bishop believed the GEB might provide all or a portion of the seed money needed to attract major gifts from individual Episcopalians and others able to give millions, thus allowing the institute to develop into a Christian foundation equal to or greater in influence than the GEB. These hopes were frustrated when no major gifts came from individuals and the GEB persistently refused to channel aid through the ACIN. Once Bishop was convinced it was unlikely that any person would endow the institute on a scale approaching that of the General Education Board, he began to search for revenue through an attempt to enter into what he hoped would be a potentially income-producing partnership with Thomas Jesse Jones and the Phelps-Stokes Fund. When the overture produced nothing, he next sought to bring the institute into a consortium of Protestant denominational school agencies, hoping to launch a cooperative fund-raising effort in the African American community. After his death, nothing more was said of this possibility.

84. Thomas Jesse Jones, *Negro Education: A Study of the Private and Higher Schools for Colored People in the United States*, vol. 2, 444, 615.

Samuel H. Bishop was a man of idealism and "zeal," who, through the American Church Institute for Negroes, sought to use education and the Episcopal Church to improve the situation of southern blacks. In pursuing this goal, he believed that the blacks should play a part in shaping and implementing the goals of the institute. Everything about Bishop stamped him as a Yankee Progressive with a commitment to the "abolitionist legacy," traits that were evident to conservative southern whites and to blacks. Despite his best efforts, he failed as a fund-raiser and in his efforts to secure the trust and enthusiastic cooperation of white southerners. Yet even his opponents acknowledged that as "a constructive critic" of the underfunded and often poorly managed institute schools, he had "worked wonders in the improved standard of all the schools."[85]

85. Bratton, *Wanted*, 166; Patton, *An Inspiring Record*, 5; McPherson, *Abolitionist Legacy*, 3–10; Luker, *The Social Gospel*, 1–6.

6

The Triumph of the South
Robert W. Patton and the ACIN

There is a blind Samson in this land
Shorn of his strength and bound in bonds of steel
Who may, in some grim revel, raise his hand
And shake the pillars of this common-weal
Till the vast temple of our liberties
A shapeless mass of rubbish lies.[1]

—Spirit of Missions

They [southern Episcopalians] still refuse to permit any criticism of the
action of the white South toward Negroes and they are determined to
pretend that Southern civilization in its attitude toward black folk is the
best in the United States if not in the world.

—W. E. B. Du Bois[2]

F ive months after Samuel H. Bishop's sudden death, the trustees of
the ACIN invited Robert W. Patton, a forty-five-year-old white
Episcopal priest from Virginia, to serve as "special agent" for a period
of six months.[3] This initial appointment, presumably a trial period for
both Patton and the ACIN, developed into a twenty-six-year tenure
that would make Patton the longest-serving director of the institute.
A native southerner, he referred to his early years in Virginia as one
of his qualifications for heading the Episcopal Church's educational
work among blacks, recalling, "Before and during the war between the
States my mother, like many other devoted Churchwomen, conducted
a school for Negro youth on our plantation in Virginia. Born less than

1. Quoted in Isabel Carter, "American Church Institute for Negroes," 668.
2. W. E. B. Du Bois, "Wallace Battle, The Episcopal Church and Mississippi," 282.
3. Trustee Minutes, ACIN, October 21, 1914.

four years after the war, when a youth of about 10 years of age, following my mother's example, I conducted a little school for Negroes. Thus my service in the education of Negro youth began." Introducing a note of humor, he noted with mock modesty: "I was not very successful. My brightest scholar turned out to be one of the worst scamps in the entire country. But during those years I learned to be exceeding sorry for them and to love them, including my rascal, who could surpass Uncle Remus himself in his stories of Brer Rabbit, Brer Bear, and Brer Fox."[4]

Prior to accepting the institute post, Patton's ministerial experience included eight years as a successful parish rector, first in Virginia and then in Pennsylvania. This was followed by a very productive year as a fund-raiser and administrator for the Sewanee Province, which encompassed the dioceses in the southeast and part of the central South, and for the Southwest Province. This led to his appointment in 1906 to the staff of his denomination's national Board of Missions, with special responsibility for raising funds. Patton's rapport with the southern bishops and his contacts with wealthy Episcopalians, particularly those in the South, attracted the ACIN board to him. Entirely Virginia-educated, he had graduated from Randolph-Macon College, attended the University of Virginia Law School for a year, and earned his divinity degree at the Virginia Theological Seminary.[5]

One of the earliest statements of Patton's difference from his predecessor was his refusal to accept the ACIN directorship "unless it was understood that the [Episcopal] Church in the South is the principal in the case"; this, he told the board, was the only basis on which "I could hope to develop a successful policy." Once this condition was met, he took up his new work. Though constantly distracted by his other responsibilities as a church bureaucrat, Patton worked skillfully to build alliances with key church figures whom

4. Patton, An Inspiring Record, 3.

5. For the boundaries of the province of Sewanee and the province of the Southwest, see The Living Church Annual: A Cyclopedia and Almanac 1917 (Milwaukee: The Young Churchman Company, 1916), 99. "The New Secretary For Departments Four and Eight" ["Eight" was mistakenly substituted for Seven], Spirit of Missions 71 (August 1906): 674–765. In the early twentieth century, the term "department" was used interchangeably with "province." Stowe's Clerical Directory of the Protestant Episcopal Church in the United States of America. 1941 (New York: Church Hymnal Corporation, 1941), 220.

Robert W. Patton, early 1920s.
Virginia Theological Seminary.

Bishop frequently had antagonized. Under Patton the ACIN began to receive more consistent financial and political support from southern dioceses. In 1917 the ACIN board received "resolutions passed by the Synod [legislative body] of the Province of Sewanee, recommending the work of the Institute, and pledging its hearty support in every way." One of Patton's most effective moves was to build a political alliance with the southern bishops, particularly with Theodore Du Bose Bratton, bishop of Mississippi, and Thomas F. Gailor, bishop of Tennessee, both conservative and influential figures greatly interested in black educational ministry. As Patton explained to George Foster Peabody, with whom he established an uneasy and sometimes strained partnership: "The effectual way of getting Boards to vote intelligently is to get the thinking men on your side in advance of the meeting. . . . Our next move should be to back up Bishop Bratton and Bishop Gailor in their plans for Negroe [sic] Education. . . . for their plans are sound."

In 1921, long after Patton had settled into the directorship of the ACIN, he would recall: "It was ten or twelve years after the Institute was incorporated before . . . [it] received the kind of cooperation from Southern Dioceses which it is now getting." Persuading southern bishops to get their dioceses to pay the institute funds committed for black schools was accomplished only "by long years of patient, persistent effort, and never could have succeeded had it not been for my personal, affectionate relations to all of the Southern bishops through years of intimacy with them all, as a guest in their homes, and by helping them in other diocesan responsibilities." It is impossible to imagine Patton challenging Episcopalians, as his predecessor Samuel Bishop had, to eliminate "racial arrogance" and "secure for the Negro absolute fairness and absolute freedom of opportunity," or condemning segregation as a practice that "tends to destroy . . . the motive forces in the progress of a race or a group."[6]

In 1919 and 1920 the institute and its supporters were forced to adjust to major changes. Bishop David Hummell Greer, who in partnership with George Foster Peabody had created the institute, died in 1919. Though Greer's support had been erratic—at times nonexistent—from 1906 until his death he lent his prestige to the organization by serving as its president. He was succeeded by Bishop Arthur Selden Lloyd, president of the Episcopal Church's Board of Missions. Though Lloyd was an understandable choice, his election was almost certainly advocated, and perhaps arranged, by Patton, in the hope that Lloyd, by holding the presidency of both agencies, would facilitate the ACIN's ability to secure funds from the Board of Missions. Lloyd and Patton were longtime friends, dating back to the years when Lloyd had served as bishop in the diocese of Virginia. In 1920 the Episcopal Church reorganized the structure of its national bureaucracy, replacing the old Board of Missions with a new body called the National Council of the Episcopal Church.[7] The reorgani-

6. Robert W. Patton to G. M. Brydon, April 17, 1922; Trustee Minutes, December 11, 1917; Robert W. Patton to Frank W. Creighton, May 1, 1931, all in ACIN Papers. Patton to Peabody, May 8, 1918, in Peabody Papers. For Bishop, see chapter 5.

7. Greer's biographer believed he died disappointed "because the [Episcopal] church had not responded more generously to the [ACIN] appeal and opportunity." Slattery, *Greer*, 215. Trustee Minutes, September 24, 1919, ACIN Papers; A. C. Zabriskie, *Arthur Selden Lloyd*, 153–78, 247. David L. Holmes, *A Brief History of the Episcopal Church*, 145; Manross, *A History of the American Episcopal Church*, 351–52.

zation stimulated an intense debate about the continued existence of the American Church Institute for Negroes as an autonomous agency, with those opposed arguing that its work should be subsumed under the Missions Committee of the new National Council. One of the greatest demonstrations of Robert Patton's political skills and the strength of his friendship with leading clergy and laity was the survival of the ACIN, essentially unchanged.

Though Patton accepted permanent appointment as director of the institute in 1915, he did not curtail his work as a staff member of the Board of Missions or its successor the National Council. To the contrary, he greatly expanded these responsibilities when, in 1919, he became "Director of the Nation-Wide Campaign" (NWC), a massive effort to raise $28 million to fund the Episcopal Church's entire domestic and overseas missionary program, which did not conclude until 1925.[8] In 1940 Patton recalled:

> By 1914, when I was asked to take on the work of the Institute I hesitated a long time, fearing that having already much more than I could do in engagements all over the Church, accepting the work of the Institute might defeat the major purpose of mobilizing the mind of the whole Church for the Nation-Wide Campaign. It was finally agreed that I should go ahead with the major purpose, and take care of the Institute as a secondary aim. I was importuned to give up the Nation-Wide aim and give my whole time to the Institute. That would have been an unwise decision because had I done it the Institute schools, in the long run, would have lost much more than they could have gained.[9]

Thus while Patton was mastering the intricacies of his work for the ACIN, he also headed the Episcopal Church's national fundraising office, supervising departments for "Survey, Field, and also one on Spiritual Resources, Life, Service, and Stewardship." For practical purposes, this meant his time and energy for the institute was sharply limited until the Nation-Wide Campaign ended. He did ensure, however, "after a rather long, hard fight," that the ACIN was included

8. Lewis B. Franklin, "The Nation-Wide Campaign," 185; Zabriskie, Lloyd, 205–7; Manross, A History of the American Episcopal Church, 352–53; Robert W. Patton, "Report to the ACIN Board," December 13, 1927. Although the Nation-Wide Campaign was originally set to conclude in 1922, its failure to meet goals of roughly $9,333,000 each year during the triennium 1919 to 1922 forced its directors to extend it into the triennium 1922–1925, at the close of which it was declared over. See George Foster Peabody to Robert W. Patton, December 30, 1922, in Peabody Papers.

9. Patton, An Inspiring Record, 10–11.

as one of the Episcopal Church agencies designated a beneficiary of funds produced by the campaign. Despite the considerable time, money, and energy devoted to the Nation-Wide Campaign, "the drive was only moderately successful" because those running the campaign were unsuccessful in convincing enough potential donors that it was much more than an expedient for generating large sums of money for the Episcopal Church's national treasury. In the case of the ACIN, it generated only a modest increase in funds.[10]

When Patton spent time in the South working on the Nation-Wide Campaign, he usually scheduled visits to institute schools and drew southern diocesan officials into discussion on how to strengthen the present and future work of the ACIN. By 1920 these conversations, particularly those with Bishop Bratton of Mississippi and Bishop Gailor of Tennessee, had convinced him that "it was mistaken policy for the Institute to confine its efforts to maintaining simply the old schools taken over many years ago, and that its aim should be rather to establish a good High and Industrial School for Negroes in every diocese." This had been the ACIN's policy since 1906, but it had not been implemented because of lack of money. Patton also concurred with Gailor's contention that "on account of this lack of Church schools the colored people were tempted away from the [Episcopal] Church." Expansion in the number of institute schools promised to more effectively address the racial needs of the South and assuage the resentment of those dioceses that supported educational work among Negroes but received no ACIN funds. George Foster Peabody had long shared the same convictions and encouraged Patton to press the ACIN board to find the resources for expansion.[11]

Under Patton's leadership the number of institute schools rose slowly from the eight he inherited from Bishop. In 1916 the number dropped to seven when an industrial school in Atlanta, Georgia, was destroyed by fire and never rebuilt. The total rose to eight again when Fort Valley High and Industrial School in Fort Valley, Georgia, was

10. Ibid., 13, 10–11. Cf. Robert W. Patton to Edward S. Lines, April 20, 1920, in Peabody Papers. Patton's absorption with the Nation-Wide Campaign irritated George Foster Peabody. See Peabody to James Hardy Dillard, November 30, 1923, in Peabody Papers. Robert W. Patton to George Foster Peabody, January 31, 1920, in Peabody Papers. Manross, *A History of the American Episcopal Church*, 352.

11. Robert W. Patton to Edward S. Lines, April 20, 1920; Trustee Minutes, September 30, 1920; George Foster Peabody to Frances Farr, April 15, 1920, all in ACIN Papers.

added in 1919, largely as a result of George Foster Peabody's efforts. A year later the number of affiliated institutions reached nine with the addition of Gaudet Normal and Industrial School in New Orleans. When Okolona Industrial School in Okolona, Mississippi, joined the ACIN in 1921, the institute still claimed nine affiliates (St. Mary's, in Vicksburg, Mississippi, was probably dropped or closed when Okolona was accepted, for it was general policy to have only one ACIN school in a state). The affiliation of St. Mary's Industrial School in Columbia, South Carolina, and Hoffman-St. Mary's Industrial School in Keeling, Tennessee, in 1921 and 1922 made eleven. Sometime in the mid-1920s, St. Mary's in South Carolina was dropped or closed. In 1924 St. Athanasius School in Brunswick, Georgia, closed because of lack of support from the Episcopal Church in that diocese, reducing the number of ACIN schools to eight.[12] When Frederick Reese, the bishop of Georgia, implored George Foster Peabody to provide or secure emergency funds from northern Episcopalians to save it, Peabody demurred. "I am always regretful," he told Reese

> to send any word of disappointment to friends anywhere, particularly in the South, but I do confess that when I observe the rich whites in our Southern cities making abundant and luxurious provision for their own houses, grounds and roads, and no sewerage or paving very often in streets for Negroes, who so largely produce the wealth they flaunt, I am, as a Southern man, grievously distressed at their interpretation of the message of the Christ.[13]

The addition in 1924 of the Voorhees Industrial School of Denmark, South Carolina, in which Peabody played a crucial role, brought the

12. When Patton became director in 1914, the eight ACIN schools were St. Augustine's Normal and Collegiate Institute; Bishop Payne Divinity School; St. Paul's Normal and Industrial School; St. Agnes Hospital Training School; St. Mary's Industrial School, Vicksburg, Mississippi; St. Mark's Industrial School, Birmingham, Alabama; St. Athanasius Industrial School, Brunswick, Georgia; and St. Paul's Industrial School, Atlanta, Georgia. Bratton, *Wanted*, 167. J. Carleton Hayden, "The Episcopal Church and Black Education," 33; Patton, *An Inspiring Record*, 13. Peabody's role in drawing the Fort Valley School into the ACIN is borne out in the extensive correspondence in his papers regarding the school, beginning in 1906; see also Ware, *Peabody*, 115–16. In 1936 the name of Hoffman–St. Mary's School was changed to Gailor Industrial School to honor Bishop Gailor of Tennessee, recently deceased. Frederick F. Reese to George Foster Peabody, July 2, 1925, in Peabody Papers.

13. George Foster Peabody to Frederick F. Reese, June 22, 1926, in Peabody Papers.

total back to nine.[14] Despite the appeal of southern bishops for an ACIN-supported normal and industrial school for Negroes in each of their twenty-one dioceses and the endorsement of this goal by the ACIN board, with enthusiastic support from both Patton and Peabody, expansion was slow and the goal of a school in every southern diocese would never be realized.

The appearance in 1917 of Thomas Jesse Jones's two-volume study, *Negro Education: A Study of the Private and Higher Schools for Colored People in the United States*, forced Patton and the trustees of the institute to grapple with a negative assessment of the ACIN schools and the agency's oversight of them. The report declared it "evident that the white members of the Episcopal Church have not given serious consideration to the colored schools of their church. The church has contributed a small proportion of its wealth, but the number and condition of the schools indicate a lack of interest in the work."[15]

Throughout the 1920s, Patton pushed the institute trustees to support his efforts to address the problems pointed out by Jones's report. One of the earliest steps in this direction was the trustees' approval of a resolution in the fall of 1917 "that the treasurer of the Institute should write to the school Principals and to the Presidents of the School Boards, and suggest the adoption of the special form of Annual Financial Statement as recommended by Dr. Jones." Four years after the appearance of Jones's study, Patton reported to the trustees that "a prominent official of the General Education Board" had recently assured him "the management of the Institute schools had improved materially during the past few years." By 1927 the director was so confident that the criticisms of the Jones Report had been addressed, he included the following statement in his annual report to the board: "We [the Institute] are now recognized by the great educational agencies as being one of the most important, if not the most important, body, potentially, in training Christian leadership of the Negro."[16] Though the ACIN's financial support of its schools had

14. Robert J. Blanton, *The Story of Voorhees College from 1897 to 1982*, 115; Ware, *Peabody*, 116n.
15. Jones, *Negro Education*, vol. 1, 146–48.
16. Trustee Minutes, October 2, 1917, December 9, 1920; "Director's Report to the ACIN Trustees," February 26, 1927, all in ACIN Papers.

increased since 1917 and the quality of its oversight improved by 1927, Patton was guilty of overstatement.

In 1922 the national office of the Episcopal Church published a book by Theodore Du Bose Bratton, the bishop of Mississippi, entitled *Wanted Leaders! A Study of Negro Development*. This public relations piece presented the history and current work of the ACIN in glowing terms. Appearing at the height of the Nation-Wide Campaign, its immediate purpose was to increase the number and amount of pledges to the NWC that would go to support the institute and its schools. Patton was certainly consulted in the preparation of the work; he may very well have ghostwritten parts. In any case, *Wanted* was a clear statement of what white Episcopalians in the South wanted the institute and its schools to do for them. The book had two major themes: the familiar call for an institute-sponsored Episcopal normal and industrial school in every southern diocese, and a vision of ACIN schools as places where the Episcopal Church would help create the emerging southern black elite for the South's segregated social order. Bratton made a special appeal for increased financial support for the segregated Bishop Payne Divinity School for Negroes, which he described as maintaining "the same standard" as the Episcopal Church's divinity schools for whites. This was said despite the school's poor physical condition, inadequate financial resources, lax standards of admission, and great difficulty in recruiting students.[17]

Early in the 1920s the ACIN began to respond to critical comments about its failure to bring any of its normal and industrial schools to collegiate level. Many of these criticisms came from African Americans—students, their parents, teachers, and contributors. The criticisms were a call for change; an appeal that institute schools be given the financial, physical, and human resources to permit them

17. Bratton, *Wanted*, 157, 171–72, 161. Patton anticipated Bratton's appeal for Bishop Payne Divinity School in an article he wrote early in the year Bratton's book appeared. He beseeched white Episcopalians not to let the institution "languish for lack of a sum of money so relatively small that one is ashamed to confess that Churchmen withhold it." Patton, "Objectives of the Centennial Offering, I. The Bishop Payne Divinity School," 26. Odell Greenleaf Harris, *It Can Be Done: The Autobiography of a Black Priest*, 23–24, 37, 40–42. Cf. Harris, *The Bishop Payne Divinity School: A History*, 11. The ACIN trustees discussed the problems of BPDS in 1917, including a suggestion that "the course of training might be enlarged or changed so as to admit of training the young men for different forms of Social Service Work, as well as for the Priesthood." See Trustee Minutes, October 2, 1917, ACIN Papers.

Thomas Jesse Jones, 1937. William R. and Norma B. Harvey Library, Hampton University.

to offer a higher level of academic and professional education. At a trustees meeting in March 1922 there was discussion of pressures from black Episcopalians and from many of the southern bishops to make St. Augustine's in Raleigh "the Negro College for the Episcopal Church," to which Bishop Gailor offered the assurance that if this were done "it would be of great help in the future training of colored men in the ministry of the Church." The implication of Gailor's comment was that many of the BPDS students lacked a college degree, or were poorly prepared for divinity school, or both. By 1924 the ACIN trustees had decided, as George Foster Peabody put it in a fund-raising letter, that eventually St. Augustine's in Raleigh "is to be the crown of our Church schools," with a college, training school for nurses, and medical school open to African Americans of both sexes, but with its major emphasis on the "thorough training of women physicians." When the board of the institute formally announced in October 1925 their intention to "develop a full college course" at St. Augustine's, one of the justifications offered was "that our Negro clergy and leaders have long felt the handicap of this situation, and have been urging that it be remedied." Patton strongly encouraged this development, assuring the board in 1926, "It is only natural that Saint Augustine's should place more and more emphasis upon the academic and scholastic." To him, it seemed "the natural center for our only Church College for Negroes." In 1927 the school's name was changed to St. Augustine's College, and its first bachelor's degrees were awarded to twelve candidates in 1931.[18]

As St. Augustine's moved steadily toward becoming an accredited four-year liberal arts college, the institute board considered moving Bishop Payne Divinity School from Petersburg, Virginia, to Raleigh, North Carolina, where it was felt both institutions would be strengthened academically and financially by proximity and association. There was also a strong belief that the divinity school, positioned where it would be a visible model of professional education, would attract some of the better graduates of St. Augustine's. When, in 1928, the National Council of the Episcopal Church forced a prioritization of funding for each of the institute schools, the ACIN board put Payne Divinity School at the top of their list. Robert Patton and the ACIN board were confident that if the school were improved "in outward appearance and . . . equipment," the Episcopal Church, "for the first time," would be in a position "to introduce a method of selecting a high grade Negro young man for the ministry . . . and soon raise up a superior group of Negro clergy." Long-range plans included securing legislation from the denomination's General Convention to make BPDS "a General Seminary for Negroes" and for its relocation. These proposals were strongly supported by the southern Episcopal bishops, who felt a need for additional black clergy, and by the predominantly white trustee board of BPDS, which voted to move the school to Raleigh "to be near St. Augustine's and enjoy closer relation with the College." Off the record, many white church leaders were "bitterly opposed" to the possibility of future black clergyman studying in the north, "lest they become dissatisfied with the GOOD OLD SOUTH," according to Odell Greenleaf Harris, faculty member at BPDS from 1937 to 1949.

18. Trustee Minutes, March 23, 1922, ACIN Papers. Odell Greenleaf Harris, whose writings constitute one of the most important accounts of BPDS's history, recalled that "college graduation" was "the normal entrance requirement" for admission, but for much of its history the seminary admitted "many . . . non-college graduates." Harris, *It Can Be Done*, 40–41. George Foster Peabody to Mrs. B. B. Munford, January 29, 1924, in Peabody Papers. See also Peabody to H. A. Hunt, March 5, 1924, in Peabody Papers. Halliburton, *St. Augustine's*, 53, 57, 65. Robert W. Patton, Report to the ACIN Trustees, October 4, 1926, ACIN Papers.

For these church members, the further south the seminary for Negroes was, the better. But the move never took place, perhaps because of the strong opposition of BPDS alumni. Cecil D. Halliburton, historian of black Episcopal education, explained the failure to relocate as a result of the financial stringencies brought on by the Great Depression. BPDS remained in Petersburg until 1951, when it merged with the Virginia Theological Seminary in Alexandria as an expression of the Episcopal Church's abandonment of segregated theological education in the South.[19]

Under Robert W. Patton, the Episcopal Church increased its funding of ACIN schools, and foundations began to assess the work of the institute and its affiliates more positively. The foundation grants received by a number of the schools were tangible evidence of this. In 1926 the GEB gave grants totaling $77,500 to ACIN schools: $40,000 to St. Augustine's; $25,000 to the Fort Valley School; and $12,000 "toward teachers' salaries in several of our schools." The following year, the GEB awarded a matching grant of $125,000 to Fort Valley High and Industrial School in Georgia and another for $33,000 to St. Paul's Normal and Industrial School in Virginia. By the end of the 1920s, as Patton reported to the Episcopal Church's National Council in 1930, institute schools had received a total of $230,000 in matching grants from foundations: $198,000 from the GEB; $30,000 from the Rosenwald Fund; and $2,000 from the Phelps-Stokes Fund. The foundations' $230,000 and the $425,000 provided by the Episcopal Church from 1925–1928—a total of $655,000—were "used exclusively for [the erection of] modern school buildings and equipment and for the reconstruction of old buildings on a modern basis." The involvement of the GEB went beyond the gift of money, however. Its officers also gave "advice . . . as to the character of the buildings" and "assistance in many ways in our efforts to make the best use of funds committed to our care."[20]

19. Robert W. Patton to George Foster Peabody, January 11, 1926; Robert W. Patton, Report of the Director to the Board of Trustees, December 13, 1927, both in Peabody Papers; Halliburton, St. Augustine's, 63; Harris, It Can Be Done, 41. Harris, Bishop Payne Divinity School: A History, 30; Prichard, A History of the Episcopal Church, 243–44. On the decision to close BPDS, see also Harris, It Can Be Done, 57–58.

20. "American Church Institute for Negroes," The Living Church Annual 1926 (Milwaukee: Morehouse Publishing Company, 1926), 77. Robert W. Patton, "Notable Recognition Accorded Negro Schools. General Education Board Makes Conditional Grants,"

Under Patton's leadership the ACIN paid less attention to the views of the black community, Episcopal or otherwise, than under his predecessor Bishop. No black was invited to join the ACIN board, and Patton and the institute trustees usually communicated only with African Americans who were in subordinate or client relationships with them. According to Patton's daughter, a leading southern advocate of integration, her father's belief "that the squalor of Southern Negroes resulted from poverty and other social pressures" made him "very enlightened for his time." "But what chance," she concluded, "had such stray thoughts against . . . our whole social system." There is no evidence in Patton's papers of correspondence with prominent black leaders, in or outside the Episcopal Church; no signs of any involvement with leaders of the CCWCP or attendance at their meetings. Patton, unlike his predecessor Bishop, who had been almost constantly embattled with James Solomon Russell, avoided conflicts with both Russell and the conservative white southerners who dominated Russell's board of trustees and defended him.[21] When the rector of St. James' Episcopal Church in Wilmington, North Carolina, sent Patton a substantial contribution from his parish to the institute in 1930, the accompanying letter expressed the hope that

> the endorsement of your work by the oldest, and perhaps most conservative, of the larger [white Episcopal] Churches in North Carolina . . . may mean more than a monetary offering. As you know, North Carolina suffered as much as any Southern state through the tragic mishandling of the Negro problem by the Federal Government

---

11–15. "The American Church Institute for Negroes," *The Living Church Annual 1930* (Milwaukee: Morehouse Publishing Company, 1930), 61, 52; "Annual Report for 1929 of the American Church Institute for Negroes" (New York: Church Missions House, 1929), 7, 9.

21. In 1923, according to George Foster Peabody, Bishop Thomas F. Gailor of Tennessee "made a wise suggestion" to the institute trustees, "that we consider having a Negro" on the board. Peabody was a member of the committee appointed "to recommend in that connection." George Foster Peabody to James Hardy Dillard, March 27, 1923, in Peabody Papers. No action resulted from Gailor's suggestion, and the first African American would be elected to the ACIN board in 1945. Sarah Patton Boyle's autobiography makes clear that her parents and extended family firmly supported segregation and white supremacy. See Sarah Patton Boyle, *The Desegregated Heart: A Virginian's Stand in Time of Transition*, 3–42. For specific references to Robert W. Patton, see 1, 7, 12, 14, 15, 19–20, 25, 41. See Patton's 1935 obituary for his "loyal friend" Russell, who "exactly comprehended the essential blend of religion with education to produce character." "Dr. Patton Pays Tribute to a Great Leader," 222.

during the Reconstruction Period; and it should mean much to possible contributors to this work, that such a group of people in the South as St. James congregation should give its hearty approval to the Negro work administered by the Institute.[22]

The paternalism, staunch belief in segregation, and the white supremacist views of Patton and many of the whites who controlled and funded the ACIN and its schools did little to make the ACIN's educational institutions attractive to black Episcopalians or to African Americans in general. To many blacks, it was difficult to imagine that those educated in Episcopal schools for Negroes would be capable of leading their race toward economic, political, religious, and social empowerment.

A major crisis at the Okolona Industrial School in Mississippi in 1925 brought the ACIN board face to face with some of the grim realities encountered by those conducting schools for blacks in certain parts of the South. In a special communication to each member of the board, Robert W. Patton described the murder of Ulysses S. Baskin, a Tuskegee man and World War I veteran who was the superintendent of the school's industries. Angered because two of his dogs had been killed "while attacking livestock on the Okolona Farm," a local white named Hob Anderson shot Baskin eight times with a .44 caliber revolver. Baskin died "two or three days later." Wallace Battle, the "mild and conservative" African American who headed the school, and Captain A. T. Stovall, the white lawyer who was president of the school trustees, "placed different interpretations upon the incident." Battle was convinced "that the killing . . . was a concerted plot on the part of . . . bad white men in the community," while Stovall argued that the murderer or murderers had not been brought to justice because of lack of evidence. Thoroughly discouraged, Battle "tendered his resignation" and met with Patton in Raleigh, North Carolina, where he insisted "there was no use in his returning to the School . . . as the morale of the faculty and of the Negroes in the community was so shattered that the School's usefulness was permanently crippled." Acting on his own authority, Patton gave Battle a leave of absence and appointed his wife acting principal. Eventually Battle was persuaded to return to Mississippi and resume his work at Okolona. But in 1927 he was "forced to flee for his life" when he attempted to have Baskin's

22. William H. Milton to Robert W. Patton, April 13, 1930, in Peabody Papers.

murderer prosecuted. Battle's wife replaced him as principal of the school, and Robert Patton persuaded the institute board to hire Battle as a field agent.[23]

Three special reports in 1929 from Patton to the trustees of the ACIN traced further developments in the situation at Okolona. In July Patton asked for and received permission to cut off funds to Okolona because of a recent attempt to murder W. C. Gilliam, the "only Negro on the [Okolona] Board," by the same group of whites responsible for the murder of the black faculty member in 1924 and for the principal's flight for his life in 1927. The request was accompanied by a description of numerous instances in which the faculty and staff of the school had been attacked and terrorized by whites with the collusion and protection of law officers in the area. Three months later Patton reported on a meeting with representatives of the black community in Okolona, who vigorously protested the institute's withdrawal of funds from the school. Patton's communications with whites in the area must have produced some desire to improve race relations, for two days later he reported that a group of white citizens had met, affirming their support for the school and condemning lawless acts. When the ACIN trustees met in October 1929, they reviewed the three reports and cautiously expressed to the black and white citizens of Okolona their hope that at some time in the future it might be possible to renew support for the school. Almost a year later, Patton made another special report to the ACIN board, in which he stated that "some weeks ago a mass meeting of the citizens of the city of Okolona, Mississippi, called by the Mayor and representing every important business enterprise in the city, passed unanimous resolutions pledging their full protection to the Okolona School in the future. To give practical evidence of their sincerity they pledged about $6000 for new

23. Du Bois, "Wallace Battle, the Episcopal Church and Mississippi," 261. Robert W. Patton to [ACIN] Board of Directors, August 11, 1925, ACIN Papers; Robert W. Patton to George Foster Peabody, July 14, 1925; in Peabody Papers. The following sources contain useful information on Battle and Okolona School: Robert Hayne Leavell, "The Castle That Battle Built," enclosure in R. H. Leavell to Edward R. Ames, April 30, 1923, in Peabody Papers; Bratton, Wanted, 167–68; Neil R. McMillen, Dark Journey: Black Mississippians in the Age of Jim Crow, 94, 350n; Aptheker, ed., The Correspondence of W. E. B. Du Bois: Volume I, Selections 1877–1934, 357–58. Hayden, "The Episcopal Church and Black Education," 33; Trustee Minutes, October 10, 1927, ACIN Papers. Aptheker states that after Baskin's murder "Battle seized a rifle and started after the murderers until his wife and students restrained him" (p. 357).

building and equipment. They asked the Institute to renew its relations with the school." Shortly after, the ACIN resumed its financial support of the Okolona School.[24]

These events in Okolona revealed the limits of the Episcopal Church's race relations policy in the South as expressed through Patton's leadership of the ACIN, specifically, the inability of white paternalists to protect institute schools and the blacks associated with them when they fell victim to implacable white racism and violence. It also exposed the unwillingness of Episcopal Church leaders, including Patton and the board of the American Church Institute, to confront publicly the white perpetrators of violence. Thoughtful and observant African Americans immediately understood the meaning of this, none better than W. E. B. Du Bois, who sought in his report in the *Crisis* to ensure that all his readers shared his assessment of the events at Okolona.

Du Bois described Principal Battle as "the extreme type of the so-called 'white folk's nigger,'" someone "Negroes considered lacking in backbone and self-assertion" and a person "accused" by Mississippi blacks "of going out of his way to condemn black men who stood up for manhood rights and to excuse the South on every occasion." In addition, Du Bois denounced the Episcopal Church for failing to publicize the atrocities in Okolona and for not demanding that justice be done. "The Episcopal Church," the *Crisis* editor observed, "is at a

24. The attempt on Gilliam's life and many of the circumstances surrounding it are vividly described in A. L. Davenport to Wallace A. Battle, July 9, 1929, in Peabody Papers. Patton's movement from a belief that Battle's description of the attacks on him and his coworkers at Okolona was a case of emotional distress that "had temporarily upset his good judgment" to a deeper appreciation of the crisis, as well as a certainty that whites in Okolona and Bishop Theodore Du Bose Bratton of Mississippi were attempting to minimize it, can be traced in Robert W. Patton to Board of Directors, August 11, 1925, ACIN Papers; Patton to George Foster Peabody, July 14, 1925; Patton to Peabody, July 20, 1929; Patton to Theodore Du Bose Bratton, August 9, 1929; Patton to Peabody, August 30, 1929; "My Dear Papa" [Annie Marie Battle] to Wallace Battle, July 13, 1929; Patton to Bratton, July 16, 1929; Bratton to Patton, July 17, 1929; Bratton to Patton, July 18, 1929; Patton to Bratton, July 18, 1929; Patton to Bratton, R. W. Chandler, Bolton Smith, and A. T. Stovall, July 23, 1929; A. T. Stovall to Patton, July 23, 1929; Patton to Stovall, July 23, 1929; all in Peabody Papers. Patton, Report of Director to the Board of Trustees, October 14, 1929; Patton, Report of Director to the Board of Trustees, October 16, 1929, both in ACIN Papers. Patton to Peabody, September 9, 1930, in Peabody Papers. [Robert W. Patton,] "American Church Institute For Negroes," *Spirit of Missions* 97 (June 1931): 434.

serious disadvantage when it tries to deal with the Negro problem. It is the one great church in America which did not split on the subject of slavery. Often it boasts of this fact; and unity is a thing to boast of. Nevertheless, this fact of union spells paralysis on the Negro problem. The Episcopal Church, although the richest in the United States and the first Protestant church among Negroes, has done least for the Negro in America."

Drawing a bead on those white Episcopalians who dominated the ACIN, Du Bois concluded:

> Whenever Episcopalians try to take a high moral stand on any phase of the race problem they find themselves blocked by their Southern white constituents. . . . They still refuse to permit any criticism of the action of the white South toward Negroes and they are determined to pretend that Southern civilization in its attitude toward black folk is the best in the United States if not in the world. When . . . the church faces such an episode as the Okolona murder it suffers moral paralysis.[25]

For African Americans whose children had the option of attending better secondary schools, either public or private, the ACIN's schools were not even competitive. And its one fledgling college was no challenge to older, more-established black undergraduate institutions. Certainly, as news spread through the African American community about the cautious stance taken by local and national white Episcopal leaders in the face of the murder of a black faculty member at the Okolona School and the forced flight of the school's principal when he sought to bring the white murderer to justice, black assessment of ACIN schools must have plummeted. And the widely publicized murder of white Bishop William Alexander Guerry of South Carolina in 1928 added even more to the black community's sense of the ambivalent place occupied by blacks in the life of the Episcopal Church. When Guerry, a strong supporter of the ACIN, asked his diocese to elect a black assistant bishop, he was murdered by one of his white priests, who then committed suicide. During Patton's first sixteen years as ACIN director, discourse within the agency about black education was dominated by white church bureaucrats and conservative southern white Episcopalians, most of whom accepted white supremacy as the norm and were certain that teacher training

25. [W. E. B. Du Bois,] "Wallace Battle," 282.

Wallace Battle, the Episcopal Church and Mississippi

MAY 20, 1925, was commencement day at Okolona Institute. This is a colored school, supported by the Episcopal Church, in northeastern Mississippi, in and near a small Mississippi town of four thousand inhabitants. The plant is valued at about a quarter of a million dollars and the school has been established twenty-five years. The Governor of the state, H. L. Whitfield, was expected to speak on this occasion. The Episcopal Bishop of Mississippi was to be present and many white and colored notables.

Early in the morning, Ulysses S. Baskin, a graduate of the school and of Tuskegee, a world war veteran and for seven years superintendent of mechanical industries, was milking in the pasture ten rods from his home. He saw a white man looking about the pasture, who quickly disappeared. After he had turned his cow back to the pasture and started home, two white men, H. Anderson and his son, came from behind the trees and told him to stop. They asked if he knew anything about the killing of their dog. Mr. Baskin replied that a week before, three dogs had gotten into the pasture and killed a goat. He had shot at the dogs and killed one. The men said that they did not want an explanation; that they wanted to know if he killed the dog. Baskin repeated his story saying he did not know whose dogs they were, but if they were theirs he was ready to adjust the matter to their satisfaction. Immediately the two men shot him eight times, on the side of the head and in Baskin's left thigh. All this was plainly seen by two colored men, by Baskin's wife and by several visitors and teachers at the superintendent's house. The superintendent lived two days after he was shot and then died leaving a widow, three children and a fourth born after his death. The Andersons took the pistol which they found on him with them and went home.

THERE seems to be no dispute about the above facts. They have been well known to the authorities of the Episcopal Church and to the trustees of the school. The story of the conversation is from Baskin's ante-mortem statement. Of his death from the gun shot wounds by the Andersons there is no question.

Wallace Battle, founder and principal of the school, demanded the arrest of the Andersons. The Grand

A Story of Suppressed Truth

Wallace Battle

Jury was about to adjourn, but was held over for a day and the Andersons were arraigned before it. Not a single witness appeared against them. The only witnesses at the trial were the Andersons themselves. Their story was that when they asked Baskin about their dog, he drew a revolver and shot at them twice and that they killed him in self-defense. They had handed Bas-

Ulysses S. Baskin
As he graduated from Okolona

kin's revolver with two cartridges exploded to the chief of police after the murder. They were freed and have not been arrested since.

WALLACE BATTLE has at various times and in various places declared that the above facts are by no means the whole of the story; that the Andersons had a bad reputation and had been in shooting scrapes before and had at least one other murder to their credit; that there were witnesses to the murder of Baskin, colored and white, but that the mob spirit was such in the town, and the feeling against a school for Negroes so strong, that these witnesses dare not testify; that the shooting was a merciless assassination for which no possible excuse could be given; that after the elder Anderson had shot this teacher to death he took from Baskin's pocket a revolver from which no shells had been fired, carried it into the Anderson's garden and within the sight of a white lady, fired two shots so as to make it appear that their story of self-defense was creditable.

Mr. Battle declares that for some time he had seen the mob spirit forming in Okolona. He believes that seventy-five per cent of the white people of the town and vicinity are his firm friends. Many white people say that Battle was the best loved Negro in Mississippi. White Mississippians have given money to the school; have acted upon the Board of Trustees; and have on many occasions, protected the institution.

But these friends find themselves helpless apparently before the other twenty-five per cent, consisting of some poor, illiterate whites, some rich men, some preachers and politicians who were determined the school should go. Mr. Battle declares that twice recently his own life has been threatened and that once he strongly suspected an effort to burn down the school. With his wife and family he was once waylayed in August, 1924, by an automobile full of white men who went by him at great speed and then blocked his road. He escaped by backing his car and fleeing to his campus at the rate of fifty miles an hour. Two weeks later, on a public street opposite the post office, this same H. Anderson stopped Battle and threatened to kill him if he approached the mayor about the case of a Negro whom Anderson had nearly beaten to death. Battle offered to prove that he had said nothing to the mayor about the matter by

The Crisis, October 1927, with W. E. B Du Bois's commentary on the murder of Ulysses S. Baskin of Okolona Industrial School.

and industrial education constituted the best curriculum for Episcopal schools for Negroes.[26]

As we have seen, all of the philanthropic agencies supporting southern black education sought to placate southern white critics. But the ACIN went several steps further, moving, perhaps, from reluctant accommodation to outright collusion. In particular, the institute's slowness in promoting the movement of its few schools toward collegiate status made it distinctive. During the decade the GEB, which assumed the function of evaluating the work of schools and colleges for Negroes, became increasingly concerned about the negative role of private schools whose existence retarded the growth of publicly funded schools for blacks. It was equally concerned to encourage and support the development of a strong black college system capable of educating students prepared to enter postgraduate training programs in the professions or to function as entrepreneurs in the agricultural or service sectors of the black communities in the rural and urban South.[27] Under this scrutiny the efforts of the ACIN seemed increasingly primitive and self-serving. The GEB's doubts about the quality of the oversight exercised by the denominations were reflected in two reports on colleges for Negroes that were presented to the foundation's trustees and officers in 1927. The first, drafted by Jackson Davis, an agent of the foundation, noted, in a section titled "The Missionary Era is Past," that the "moral earnestness" of many denominational schools for Negroes "must be supplemented by sound scholarship and sound common sense." For the "missionary colleges no longer have the field to themselves. They must reckon with the state and with the independent spirit of the colored people. It rests with the church denominations to carry on the work of higher education, the same as with white colleges, but the time has come to place the emphasis more on the college and less on sectarian interests."[28]

---

26. *New York Times*, June 10, 1928; "Bishop Guerry Dies," *Southern Churchman*, June 16, 1928, 14–15, provides a more detailed history. For a description of the kinds of education offered in the ACIN schools, see "Rebirth of an Ancient Race," a 1927 report in the Thomas Montgomery Gregory Papers, Moorland-Spingarn Research Center. Robert W. Patton wrote in 1927: "Our ten Institute Schools are indeed an extension of the Hampton and Tuskegee idea and plan"—ignoring recent changes at Hampton and Tuskegee. Patton, "Notable Recognition Accorded Negro Schools," 14.

27. Fosdick et al., *Adventure in Giving*, 188–211, especially 192–96.

28. Davis, "Recent Developments," 10–12.

Davis's views were affirmed by the second report, which acknowledged that "no serious consideration of Negro colleges in the South can ignore the denominational institutions," but judged "extremely doubtful . . . whether [the] denominations concerned can succeed in developing the . . . institutions in this group which now offer college work."[29] These assessments were not good news for the black educational missionary work of the Episcopal Church, which had been underway since 1867, but by 1927 had produced a total of eleven academically weak, poorly funded secondary schools, only one of which was struggling, with difficulty, to move to collegiate status.

One man had a dramatically different vision for the ACIN. During the 1920s George Foster Peabody, sometimes with and as often without the assistance and support of Robert W. Patton, conducted an intense campaign to persuade the leadership of the Episcopal Church to make its educational work among southern blacks the major domestic mission program of the denomination. He continued to believe, as he had since 1906, that ACIN schools held the key to creating a black leadership class with Christian values and the skills necessary to train the masses of Negroes in cooperative and productive participation in southern society. The decline in the status of southern blacks after Reconstruction and the rise of the white supremacy movement disturbed him because of his "conviction that democracy is the practical exemplification of Christ's teaching, through which the peoples of the world . . . are toq [sic] be gradually given the opportunity to develop their capacity to be true children of God, whom Christ revealed as Father." Peabody found the concept of white supremacy so distasteful that when the Democratic politician William Jennings Bryan purchased a home in Florida and declared himself a supporter of white supremacy, the philanthropist wrote him, protesting Bryan's endorsement of ideas that violated the biblical injunction "that all men are of one blood."[30] Two years later, concerned that an article in a Louisiana newspaper had distorted his views on race, Peabody sent a letter to the editor, in which he denied

29. "Negro Education, Meeting of November 17, 1927," p. 28, GEB Papers.
30. George Foster Peabody to E. R. Hodgson, October 24, 1923; George Foster Peabody to William Jennings Bryan, June 6, 1923, both in Peabody Papers.

that any race has superiority. I think this is clearly demonstrated by my study of the teaching of Jesus Christ who was the One superior Man of all history. . . . While it is true that what we call civilization has made more rapid advance through the evolution of knowledge among the so-called white race, yet it seems to me that it is quite clear that this advance has been very largely due to the clearer apprehension of justice and mercy on the part of those races because of their fuller knowledge of the teaching of Jesus Christ.[31]

Peabody was convinced that the best way to challenge the racism and "ignorance" of the " 'poor whites' " who constituted the great mass of voters in the South was for ACIN schools to provide "efficient teachers with good religious training for the negro public schools scattered over the South and having millions of students. No influence is more compelling to . . . education of white children and the tax money involved than the education of negro children."[32]

Noting with concern the increased level of racial tension in the post–World War I years, Peabody accelerated his efforts to transform the ACIN into a major force in black education. Much of his stimulus came from the belief that if the Episcopal Church failed to make a major investment in black education soon, its opportunity to be a positive force in southern race relations would pass. "One of the sad aspects of the present state of well-nigh chaos throughout the land," he told Oswald Garrison Villard, grandson of the famous abolitionist, "is the lessening interest in the education of the negro in the north and the increasing temper of distaste [for Negroes], to say the least, upon the part of the white population. Alongside of this, there is growing the deepening antipathy to the Jews, which is a discouraging indication. The Klu [sic] Klux Klan, a concentration of race and religious prejudice, is another indication which is disturbing." As Peabody campaigned and lobbied for a multimillion-dollar endowment and budget for the institute, he argued that money invested in ACIN schools would work more "rapidly than any other expenditure" to induce the southern white masses to expand their conception of democracy to include African Americans. He was also "convinced . . . that nothing would be so good for the soul" of the Episcopal Church "as

---

31. George Foster Peabody to Editor of the *Shreveport* (La.) *Sun,* December 17, 1925, in Peabody Papers.
32. George Foster Peabody to Robert Pruyn, March 29, 1923, in Peabody Papers.

to have it aroused to responsibility in the matter of negro education, not only for the negro but for the country as well and the proper development of our democracy."[33]

In 1920 Peabody sought to persuade Bishop Edward Lines of Newark (New Jersey) to join him in locating a sizable group of Episcopalians who "would underwrite" the expansion of the institute's work with pledges of one hundred to one thousand dollars each year "for three years." Writing to another supporter of black Episcopal schools, Peabody stressed that "there should be in each of our [Southern] dioceses one of these [ACIN] normal schools, and the Episcopal Church should raise not less than one million [dollars] a year to see that they are supported properly." In meetings of the ACIN trustees Peabody began to assure his colleagues that once the Episcopal Church committed several million dollars to the institute, the General Education Board "would donate a considerable sum for the support and enlargement of some of the larger [ACIN] industrial schools."[34]

Peabody's comments, directed to Episcopal Church officials and wealthy laity, were part of his effort to prepare the ground for a major capital funds drive for the ACIN and its schools, which he hoped could be launched in 1925 when the Nation-Wide Campaign concluded, and Patton, free of other commitments, would be full-time director of the institute. As long as the Nation-Wide Campaign was underway, however, the institute, like all other Episcopal Church mission programs and agencies, was forbidden to conduct separate fund-raising activities. Peabody urged supporters of the ACIN to make ready for the time when it was their turn, and when it came to "appeal for a ten-million [dollar] endowment, which is what we need and what the church, if it is informed, will be glad to give us."[35]

Like so many of his fellow Episcopalians, Peabody was impressed by the seeming ease with which William Lawrence, the remarkably resourceful bishop of Massachusetts, and a team he assembled raised $6.5 million in a three-year period (1914–1916) to capitalize the Episcopal Church Pension Fund. Peabody, certain that the work of

33. George Foster Peabody to Oswald Garrison Villard, July 28, 1922; Peabody to Ernest M. Stires, April 18, 1922; Peabody to Bishop [Frederick] Burgess, May 22, 1922, all in Peabody Papers.

34. George Foster Peabody to Edward S. Lines, April 6, 1920; Peabody to Frances Farr, April 15, 1920; Trustee Minutes, December 9, 1920, all in ACIN Papers.

35. George Foster Peabody to Robert Pruyn, March 31, 1921, in Peabody Papers.

the institute was of greater importance than a pension fund, had no doubts that if a "clear and strong case" was made, the ACIN could raise even larger sums. For "this work is not for the benefit of the church alone or even mainly, but for the great need of the country for a right education of this [African American] one-tenth of its population, the portion . . . that is liable to prove of greatest hindrance to the advance of the country if right education and proper religious direction are not afforded for the teachers who man the public schools for negroes throughout this country." "If," Peabody warned the treasurer of the Nation-Wide Campaign, "the United States fails during the next 20 years to effectively integrate the negro as an important factor in our economic and political life, the responsibility upon the dominant and influential leaders of the United States will be appalling."[36]

As the Episcopal Church moved toward its triennial General Convention in Portland, Oregon, Peabody made himself into a one-man campaign to secure a multimillion-dollar, long-term commitment for the ACIN. Those ACIN representatives at the convention, he informed another institute trustee, should arouse the Episcopal Church to the realization of the institute's need for a "few million dollars," so the agency could equip its schools for "effective functioning."

> The world is looking to the United States for leadership in the matter of this great problem of race relationship, which is stirring more seriously among the billion people of the yellow, brown, black races than most of us realize. The answer must come from the practical outworking of the situation in the South. . . . The Southern states with their pure Anglo-Saxon stock are the hope of the U.S. for natural, logical evolution and progress of Anglo-Saxon leadership essential to the real success of our democratic experiment.[37]

Peabody's prestige forced Robert W. Patton, who had strong misgivings about the willingness of the convention to make so large an investment in the ACIN, to follow his lead, but with little enthusiasm. Seeking to energize Patton, Peabody issued a constant stream of detailed instructions on convention strategy that would educate the delegates about the importance of the institute's ministry to southern

36. Martin, "*Outlasting Marble and Brass*," 81–105. George Foster Peabody to Robert Pruyn, March 31, 1921; Peabody to Lewis Franklin, April 21, 1921, both in Peabody Papers.
37. George Foster Peabody to Ernest M. Stires, July 1, 1922, in Peabody Papers.

blacks. Presuming to lecture one of the Episcopal Church's best fund-raisers, Peabody identified "the great difficulty" in raising money from Episcopalians for the ACIN. In an explanation that reversed the usual argument made by southern whites of Patton's class, Peabody claimed the problem "is so few people understand the Negroes' qualities and powers and the foundation we have . . . to justify educational gifts on the scale that the country now needs them to come from the Episcopal Church with its billions of wealth rotting the souls of so many of its members." Patton and others whom Peabody bombarded with his arguments and instructions found it irritating that despite the great importance the philanthropist placed on lobbying the General Convention, he refused to join them in Portland, bluntly explaining: "I could not spare the time. . . . one's patience is so strained in listening to the feeble discussions and foolish expressions which fill up the time." Outraged by the news in 1922 that a wealthy Episcopalian had left a legacy of $1 million to Tuskegee and nothing to the institute for its schools, he was certain "this instance . . . is one that should be made use of to reach the minds of thousands of churchmen and women who have millions of the Lord's money entrusted to their stewardship."[38] "We must stress," Peabody repeatedly reminded Patton, the institute trustees, and other prominent church leaders,

> the matter of endowments and particularly the fact that great endowments are needed for this. Hampton now has nearly five million of endowment and Tuskegee, with the one million just received by legacy, will have between three and four million. This would mean our Church Institute, to properly carry forward the schools to the point of greatest efficiency, should have an endowment of over ten million and at least five million to spend during the next ten years on building.[39]

Referring to the million-dollar legacy left to Tuskegee, Peabody frankly told Bishop Frederick Burgess of Long Island "the only safe way for a churchman to leave a large sum [for the education of southern blacks] is to bequeath it to the American Church Institute for Negroes." And responding to a letter from the bishop of southern Virginia

38. George Foster Peabody to Robert W. Patton, July 18, 1922; Peabody to Isabel Carter, May 30, 1922, both in Peabody Papers. Peabody lamented that "imperative obligations" prevented him from personally helping to raise several million dollars for the ACIN. Peabody to Arthur Selden Lloyd, July 21, 1922; Peabody to Robert W. Patton, May 22, 1922, both in Peabody Papers.

39. George Foster Peabody to Isabel Carter, May 22, 1922, in Peabody Papers.

regarding black education, Peabody declared, "We can no longer found new Hamptons or new Tuskegees. The future of development along those lines . . . must reast [sic] with the churches. . . . Hampton and Tuskegee have always received important and large gifts from members of the Episcopal church who believe in investing on an assured basis of permanence."[40]

As things turned out, little attention was paid to the ACIN at the Portland Convention, which was preoccupied with the ups and downs of the Nation-Wide Campaign, and nothing occurred to move the agency closer to receiving the millions of dollars Peabody believed it merited. Undaunted, Peabody suggested that a way be found to circumvent the restriction on fund-raising by gathering an independent group of "some few hundred men and women of the [Episcopal] church "willing to give some of their principal as well as income to the Institute."[41] It seemed not to occur to him that most people would have seen this as an indefensible violation of the prohibition against fund-raising that competed with the Nation-Wide Campaign.

Once this was brought to his attention, Peabody began to concentrate on securing support for a $20 million capital funds drive from the General Convention of 1925, scheduled to meet in New Orleans. Cautioning Peabody as he did before the 1922 Portland Convention, Robert Patton expressed strong doubts that the Episcopal Church would commit to raise so large a sum for Negro education, urging him to settle on a smaller figure of perhaps $2 million or $3 million, and suggesting that anything larger would not have the support of the church's National Council prior to the convention. But even pursuit of a smaller amount would be rejected, Patton warned, unless Peabody came to the convention "with these sums practically so guaranteed in advance under financial leadership as to insure success of the whole objective." Was there any possibility, Patton queried, with little doubt what the answer would be, that Bishop Lawrence of Massachusetts and "his following" would endorse the campaign and provide leadership for it? When Peabody sought to interest Lawrence in leading an appeal for the institute, the bishop of Massachusetts told him that as far as

40. Peabody to Burgess, May 22, 1922; Peabody to Beverly Tucker, May 23, 1923, both in Peabody Papers.
41. "September Eighteenth, Monday," *Spirit of Missions* 87 (November 1922): 725–26. George Foster Peabody to Louis J. Hunter, December 30, 1922, in Peabody Papers.

raising money for Episcopal Church programs went, he had done his part and "the call for future effort must be answered by the younger men." Lawrence offered no advice, nor did he encourage a meeting to discuss the matter.[42]

In 1924, with the New Orleans General Convention a year away, Peabody and Patton began to clash in institute board meetings over Peabody's insistence that the ACIN seek a resolution from the convention endorsing a $20 million campaign for the ACIN. Patton stressed that the Episcopal Church's commitments to other mission enterprises made it unwise to do anything more than "start a limited campaign to raise money by appealing to a selected list of individuals and old friends of the Institute." Patton won the debate, for when a vote was taken, the trustees empowered him, "in consultation with the president of the board," Bishop Gailor, "to act as might seem best in the circumstances."[43]

Undaunted, Peabody pressed on, firing off letters to trustees, bishops, and wealthy laity in which he literally demanded they back him in seeking a resolution from the New Orleans Convention to support, at minimum, a $10 million campaign for the ACIN. "I think," he told Patton's friend and ally Bishop Gailor,

> the rectors of the rich parishes have come to be in essence cowardly with respect to making an appeal for what the Lord has shown our Church we need to expend. . . . if the vaults of Tiffany and other safe keeping places are opened to take out of them jewelry and silverware that has not been used for ten years belonging to the members of perhaps twenty congregations in our Church, the value of them would carry on the work of the National Council at one hundred per cent of its program for some years. . . . I know that it is an utterly unsound program for the National Council to provide only $130,000 for The Church Institute for Negroes as compared with the millions for the outside missionary work.[44]

42. Ware, *Peabody*, 215–16. Robert W. Patton to George Foster Peabody, July 24, 1923, in Peabody Papers. Patton's warnings were shaped by painful experience, for Lawrence had publicly opposed the Nation-Wide Campaign because he thought it poorly conceived and bound to fail, contributing, in Patton's opinion, to its shortfall. See Martin, *"Outlasting Marble and Brass,"* 134. For the specific objections raised by Lawrence and others, see "Editorial Correspondence From General Convention-II," *The Living Church* 61 (October 25, 1919): 903. George Foster Peabody to William Lawrence, July 2, 1923, in Peabody Papers.

43. Trustee Minutes, ACIN, February 18, 1924, Peabody Papers.

44. George Foster Peabody to Thomas F. Gailor, March 3, 1924, in Peabody Papers.

Brushing aside warnings from Patton and Bishop Lloyd that he would find little support in the convention for his proposal, especially since it would come with no endorsement from the institute trustees or the National Council, Peabody decided to attend the October 1925 New Orleans meeting and force it through. In New Orleans Peabody demonstrated himself to be an intrepid lobbyist as he repeatedly told leaders of the Episcopal Church: "The South is entitled to have the most generous aid from the wealth of the North and West to help it educate the negro to an understanding of agriculture and the coincident production of wealth. The need is vaster than has ever been stated. It is a good investment for hundreds of millions [of dollars] when wisely planned."[45]

Peabody's remarks usually concluded with references to James B. Duke's gift of $40 million in 1924 to establish the Duke Endowment as a perpetual educational and charitable trust for the benefit of whites and blacks in the Carolinas and George Eastman's contribution the same year of $1 million to Hampton Institute and $1 million to Tuskegee Institute. These allusions were intended to stimulate both guilt and competition on the part of affluent Episcopalians. Peabody's seriousness of purpose was underscored by the common knowledge that he had been a major figure in the successful national campaign to raise $8 million for Hampton and Tuskegee.[46]

But it was all to no avail. Because Peabody's proposed resolution had not been affirmed by the ACIN board or approved by the Episcopal Church's National Council, it was not even submitted. Leading members of the convention's two houses declared "that it was wholly improper to introduce it. . . . since the passage of a resolution of this character might cut athwart and, possibly, jeopardize the whole Program of the National Council." Peabody's hope that the General Convention's meeting in the South would work in his favor did not prove true. A delegate from Massachusetts recalled many years later that the "convention was in a reactionary mood" on most issues, a

45. George Foster Peabody to Arthur Selden Lloyd, January 10, 1925; Peabody to Robert Pruyn, January 14, 1925; Robert W. Patton to Peabody, October 20, 1925; all in Peabody Papers. Peabody, "Letter to the Editor," *New York Times*, July 17, 1925.

46. "James Buchanan Duke," *The National Cyclopedia of American Biography* 17 (New York: James T. White and Company, 1927): 382–83; Robert R. Moton, *Principal's Annual Report*, 1924–1925, 18–19; Robert R. Moton, *Principal's Annual Report*, 1925–1926, Tuskegee Institute. Ware, *Peabody*, 215.

mood compounded by "a debt of over a million dollars due to the over-optimism of some in missionary expansion and to the failure of others to meet their share of the cost. There was, therefore, an enthusiastic movement to liquidate the debt." Although Peabody's efforts to get the General Convention to launch a $20 million campaign for the institute went nowhere, the two houses did approve a voluntary fund-raising "program of extension and equipment" for the ACIN, with a goal of $655,000. "Frankly," Robert Patton smugly told Peabody after the convention, "the thing that happened was just what I expected." Disappointed, Peabody observed disgustedly to a southern bishop, "When we think of the many multi-millionaires in our church, men and women, and realize that Hampton and Tuskegee will have raised . . . five millions within the year . . . twenty millions for the church is a small sum."[47]

During the next two years, Peabody struggled to come to terms with the ending of a dream. It was only with the greatest difficulty that he finally relinquished his hope that the ACIN would someday become an Episcopal Church foundation for the education of southern blacks, surpassing in vision, wealth, and impact the Rockefeller-funded General Education Board. His slow process of realization can be traced in the series of letters he continued to direct to leaders of the Episcopal Church, asserting over and over, as he had done since 1906, the religious and political imperatives he believed called the institute and Episcopalians to use black education as a tool to redeem, reform, and democratize the South. By the end of 1927, Peabody finally accepted the reality that the ACIN would remain an underfunded agency, charged with oversight of a small number of financially weak, academically marginal, church-affiliated schools, most having limited respect and small impact on both the black and white communities of the South. On December 13, 1927, he notified Robert Patton and the ACIN board of his resignation for reasons of health. In view of

47. Robert W. Patton to George Foster Peabody, October 20, 1925, in Peabody Papers. Peabody was not a delegate to the General Convention and therefore was unable personally to submit proposed legislation to either house of the assembly. Henry Knox Sherrill, *Among Friends: An Autobiography*, 131, 132; "Fiscal Problems at General Convention. Program for Triennium, Proposed Budget Reduction, and Present Deficit Will Be Considered," *Spirit of Missions* 90 (September 1925): 527–30. Robert W. Patton, "The American Church Institute for Negroes," *Spirit of Missions* 93 (June 1928): 417. Robert W. Patton to George Foster Peabody, October 20, 1925; Peabody to Thomas F. Gailor, November 2, 1925, both in Peabody Papers.

his role as a founder of the agency and his many years of service, the board made him an "honorary Vice-President." "Though forced to take care of his health because of a heart condition and complications," Peabody, who was seventy-five when he resigned, lived to be eighty-six and was an active public citizen until two years before his death in 1938. After ceasing to be a trustee of the ACIN, he continued to serve on the boards of Hampton Institute, Fort Valley High and Industrial School, Penn School, Colorado College, Skidmore College, and the University of Georgia; he actively supported his friend Alfred E. Smith's bid for the U.S. presidency as the Democratic nominee in 1928; in 1929 he accepted appointment from another friend, New York Governor Franklin D. Roosevelt, as chair of a state commission; and, once FDR was elected president, Peabody became one of his informal advisers and a lobbyist for passage of New Deal legislation.[48]

Between Peabody's departure from the institute board and the onset of the Great Depression in December 1929, the ACIN and its schools limped along financially as they had since 1906. Funds from the Episcopal Church to some of the schools actually declined in 1927, when the National Council informed the institute board it did not have the money to meet "the building and equipment needs of all of them." At this point, the trustees, following the recommendations of the director, prioritized the needs of all the institutions, with the intention of meeting the requests of one or perhaps two of them year by year, as resources permitted. Despite the prospect of reduced appropriations from the National Council, Patton sought to convince the trustees at this same meeting that the planting of ACIN schools in Florida, Maryland, and the Southwest was long overdue. In addition, he also asked them to endorse his plan to extend the work of the institute "beyond the limits of the Southern states," through establishment of ACIN schools in the U.S. territories of Puerto Rico and the Virgin Islands, and in the country of Panama, with its American Canal Zone and sizable Negro population. The board, doubtful about the wisdom of new schools in the South at a time when it was facing a reduction in funds, rejected the first proposal. They endorsed the second suggestion, however,

48. George Foster Peabody to Arthur Selden Lloyd, February 12, 1926; Lloyd to Peabody, February 23, 1926; Peabody to Lloyd, February 25, 1926; Peabody to John Gilbert Murray, May 7, 1926; Peabody to William Andrew Leonard, April 29, 1927; Peabody to Murray, July 14, 1927; Trustee Minutes, ACIN, December 13, 1927, all in Peabody Papers. Ware, *Peabody*, 224, 225, 228, 230–44.

hoping that a move into overseas educational missionary work would generate income. In 1929, again at the urging of Patton, a committee of the ACIN board explored the possibility of establishing an institute school in the West African country of Liberia.[49] Nothing was done to implement these schemes before the fiscal constraints created two years later by the Great Depression rendered their possibility moot.

From 1926 until 1930, when the Depression reduced spending in all of the Episcopal Church's agencies and programs, according to Robert W. Patton's estimates, the ACIN distributed "approximately" $250,000 per year to its schools.[50] Patton's estimate, however, is contradicted by the section on finances in the extant annual reports of the ACIN. Carelessness, or perhaps craftiness, characterized Patton's accounting of institute expenditures, as he admitted in his history of the ACIN: "Omitting year by year detail, I submit a total of the financial history of the Institute in the period 1906 to 1939. I should perhaps have asked the treasurer to check my figures but did not wish to subject him to the trouble, and, moreover, I was confident that even if I made some mistakes, they would not materially alter the purpose of my approximate summary and argument."[51]

The [ACIN] Annual Report for 1927 lists $226,714.77 as the total expenditure on schools for that year. Annual reports for 1929 and 1932, however, list total expenditure on schools as $508,672.33 and $495,605.03, respectively.[52] Unfortunately, annual reports with comparable expenditure figures for 1928, 1930, and 1931 have not survived. Though the 1927 expenditure was $226,714.177, gifts in 1929 were slightly more than $500,000 and in 1932 only slightly less than $500,000. If expenditures in 1928, 1930, and 1931 were at or near $500,000, then the ACIN contributed considerably more than "$250,000 per year to its schools" and Patton's estimate is incorrect. Without complete figures, however, these remain speculations.

49. Robert W. Patton, Report of the Director to the Board of Trustees, December 13, 1927; Trustee Minutes, ACIN, December 13, 1927, both in Peabody Papers. "American Church Institute for Negroes," The Living Church Annual 1929 (Milwaukee: Morehouse Publishing Company, 1929), 76.

50. In his 1931 report Patton estimates "approximately $900,000" was expended by the ACIN on its schools from 1926 to 1930. "American Church Institute for Negroes," The Living Church Annual 1931 (Milwaukee: Morehouse Publishing Company, 1931), 53.

51. Patton, An Inspiring Record, 13.

52. The [ACIN] Annual Report for 1929, 15; The [ACIN] Annual Report for 1931 and 1932, 17–18, ACIN Papers.

The bulk of this money came as direct grants from the National Council to the ACIN, and was supplemented by individual gifts and fund-raising events such as the one Patton put together in March 1928 for the agency and all its schools at New York City's Carnegie Hall. The event, cosponsored by William T. Manning, bishop of New York, was an effort to solicit contributions from wealthy New York Episcopalians and their parishes.[53] This level of giving was a marked improvement on what the ACIN had done for its schools from 1906 to 1919, prior to the Nation-Wide Campaign. Nevertheless, it brought the institute and its schools no closer to realizing the grand schemes of the ACIN's founders than in 1906.

In March 1930, with the Depression ravaging the financial health of every institution in the United States, Patton had Wallace Battle, the ACIN's black field agent, write to the African American clergy of the Episcopal Church, pointing "out the importance of the Negroes themselves taking a larger and more definite responsibility in supporting and advertising the Church's ten Negro schools in the South." This was a unique step, for previously appeals had only been addressed to white clergy. The response was heartening—pledges totaling twenty-five thousand dollars were received—but not enough to make up for the steady decline in funds from the Episcopal Church and individual donors. As 1930 drew to a close, Robert W. Patton began to stress the need for the ACIN to secure a significant endowment and larger annual appropriations from the Episcopal Church if the institute was to be of material assistance in ensuring that its schools fulfilled their mission.[54] George Foster Peabody had made similar arguments throughout most of the 1920s.

53. Robert W. Patton, "American Church Institute for Negroes," *Spirit of Missions* 92 (January 1928): 65; *New York Times*, March 13, 1928; Halliburton, *St. Augustine's*, 57.

54. Robert W. Patton, "The American Church Institute for Negroes," *Spirit of Missions* 95 (March 1930): 197. Patton provides a running commentary on the steady decline in Episcopal Church funds for the ACIN as a result of the Depression in Robert W. Patton to George Foster Peabody, June 16, 1930; Patton to Peabody, June 25, 1930; Patton to Peabody, November 10, 1930; all in Peabody Papers. In his 1927 published report to the Episcopal Church, Patton gave the amount of the ACIN endowment as $255,749.33, noting that to be of material assistance to the work of the institute it "should be twenty times that sum" or approximately $5 million. Patton's 1931 report gave the amount of the endowment as $400,000. And he again stressed the need for a minimum endowment of $5 million. "American Church Institute for Negroes," *The Living Church Annual 1927*, 75; "American Church Institute for Negroes," *The Living Church Annual 1931*, 53. Robert W. Patton to George W. Peabody, September 9, 1930, in Peabody Papers.

Under both Bishop and Patton all ACIN schools continued to conduct individual fund-raising drives (even during the Nation-Wide Campaign), in which they solicited direct gifts from their alumni and longtime friends. What each institute school received from the ACIN was supplemental. None could have survived on this subsidy.

The relatively small amounts of money that came to the ACIN during the years 1906 to 1925 explain the restless quest of Bishop, Peabody, and Patton for major gifts from individuals of great wealth, the GEB, and the Episcopal Church. Without resources in the multi-million-dollar range, the grand ambitions of the ACIN's founders could never be realized. Peabody's eventual realization that multi-million-dollar gifts would not be forthcoming from the more vastly wealthy of his fellow philanthropists or from their foundations sent him on a hopeless quest to secure $20 million from the Episcopal Church. Patton also turned to the Episcopal Church for help, but by a different route.

During the early years of Robert Patton's directorship, there was no improvement in ACIN income. Indeed, until the Nation-Wide Campaign began to generate funds for domestic and foreign missionary programs after 1919, the situation probably worsened. This seems to be corroborated by Thomas Jesse Jones's Report of 1917, which comments on the "small proportion of its wealth" the Episcopal Church was contributing to its "colored schools." A steady increase in appropriations to the ACIN from the Episcopal Church did begin once the Nation-Wide Campaign was underway, however. There is documentary evidence that from 1920 to 1922 ACIN disbursements to its affiliated schools rose: in 1920 they totaled $98,135.27; in 1921 $120,346; and in 1922 $120,000. One of Robert Patton's achievements was ensuring that the ACIN was a designated beneficiary of the NWC.[55] Unfortunately, no records survive that indicate the specific amount the campaign brought to the institute.

After the Nation-Wide Campaign concluded in the mid-1920s and its monies were all disbursed, the Episcopal Church began to relate to

55. Jones, *Negro Education*, vol. 1, 146–48. "Bulletin No. 39, Report of Income and Expenditures for 1922 with Comparative Figures for 1920 and 1921," *Official Bulletins of the National Council of the Protestant Episcopal Church, Series of 1923* (New York: Issued by the Department of Finance. Published by the Department of Publicity, 1923), 10. Patton's crucial role in using the NWC to secure funds for the ACIN is discussed in "Robert Patton, Father of the Nation-Wide Campaign," 16–17, 31; R. Bland Mitchell, "R. W. Patton Gave Church New Vision," 10–11.

the ACIN as a national denominational program entitled to an annual appropriation. From 1925 on the officers of the ACIN expected a regular subsidy from the national Episcopal Church. This was assumed by Patton in his 1926 annual report, in which he stated, "The National Council [of the Episcopal Church] makes an annual appropriation toward the budget of the Institute and the latter regularly renders a report of its trusteeship to the National Council and the General Convention." By 1935, "the total annual budget of the institute was about $450,000, with nearly a third of this [$150,000] appropriated by the National Council. For the remaining two thirds [$300,000], the Institute was dependent upon the gifts of friends, upon student fees, and an income of $26,000 from endowments totaling $625,000." There was steady movement toward this level of income from 1919 to 1925, due to the inflow of funds from the NWC reserved for the institute, which, when exhausted, were replaced by an annual appropriation from the National Council and a growing ACIN endowment.[56] Robert W. Patton did more than anyone to produce this increase in the Episcopal Church's financial support for the institute.

Historians have ignored the ACIN. Their neglect goes beyond the usual erroneous dismissal of the missionary societies as waning or irrelevant in the twentieth century, because even those who comment on the church missionary societies restrict themselves to the Congregational, Baptist, Presbyterian, and Methodist organizations, leaving the Episcopalians out. This case study is both a corrective to that omission and an examination of the intersection between the southern black educational work of a significant religious agency and the GEB, the most important of the northern secular foundations active in the field. Unlike other Protestant denominations, the Episcopal Church entered the twentieth century without a long-established missionary organization dedicated to southern black educational philanthropy. The ACIN, which replaced the various failed Episcopal Church Commissions on "Colored Work," was established by men who saw the General Education Board as the model for their work. And because the institute came into being much later than most other denominational

56. "The American Church Institute for Negroes," *The Living Church Annual 1926* (Milwaukee: Morehouse Publishing Company, 1926), 171. See also H. A. Hunt to E. C. Sage, October 18, 1925, in Peabody Papers. Blanton, *Voorhees*, 114. In 1926 the ACIN endowment was $255,749.33. By 1931 it was $400,000. See footnote 54.

agencies for black educational mission work—thus lacking a tradition of independent operation—it was especially receptive to influence by the GEB, which sought to standardize and regulate all forms of southern black education. Patton understood more quickly than either Bishop or Peabody that if the ACIN was to derive any benefit from the GEB, it must accept GEB procedures and policies. For GEB money was available to specific institute schools, but not to the ACIN as an independent center of power.[57] Patton accepted this and brought the institute and its schools into a cooperative client relationship with the GEB.

With Bishop's death and Patton's succession as his replacement, the ACIN gained a very different kind of director. Bishop was educated, trained, and socialized into ministry and social work by northern Progressives whom James M. McPherson and Ralph E. Luker have described as keeping alive important elements of the "abolitionist legacy" in their attitudes toward and concern for African Americans. Patton, on the other hand, was educated, trained, and socialized into ministry through the cultural prism of southern Episcopalianism, with its conservative, paternalistic, and defensive view of blacks and black-white relations. None of his professional training or experience took place outside the institutional context of the Episcopal Church, which generally reflected the racial attitudes of the white South.

Patton had no interest in working to make the ACIN a major Christian educational foundation, one affiliated with the Episcopal Church but independent of it. He moved the institute from quasi-independence to full integration into the institutional structure of his denomination. To him, the agency was a specialized domestic missionary program of the Episcopal Church, whose chief purposes were to assist the southern dioceses in their educational and social

57. This is made clear in the following correspondence: Louis J. Hunter to Robert W. Patton, February 4, 1925; Robert W. Patton to Hunter, February 10, 1925; Patton to Edgar H. Goold, July 20, 1929; Hunter to Joseph Blunt Cheshire, July 28, 1929; Peabody Papers. GEB grants went to specific schools. If the school chose to designate the ACIN as the custodian of its grant, then the check was forwarded to the institute treasurer. Since this was the arrangement the ACIN trustees favored, most institute affiliates complied. Edgar Goold, the principal of St. Augustine's School, did not like this procedure, however. He preferred to have his school's foundation grants sent to him and resisted requests from the ACIN treasurer to relinquish them. See Robert W. Patton to Edgar H. Goold, July 20, 1929; Louis J. Hunter to Joseph Blunt Cheshire, July 28, 1929, Peabody Papers.

service ministry among African Americans, and to draw blacks educated at institute schools into the Episcopal Church. As director of the Nation-Wide Campaign, Patton successfully pushed the Episcopal Church to invest in the institute at a level that eventually caused the GEB and other foundations to begin to respect the Episcopal Church's efforts in black education. He also worked in partnership with GEB program officers and those of other foundations to persuade the Episcopal Church to match grants to specific schools, thus assuring that ACIN schools received more money from both the Episcopal Church and foundations. As a result, the institute began to secure significant sums for its schools from secular foundations and undertook a major building program in the late 1920s. To Patton, the GEB was a source of additional support for the schools and an important source of secular validation for his agency's work in black education. The early Patton years (1914–1929) were also critical for the ACIN in another way. During these years Patton brought the institute under the effective control of southern whites.

7

The Transformation of Northern Philanthropy for the Black South

Mr. Rosenwald's subscription to our school means more than $2,500 for it will bring to us the recognition of other persons and agencies that are interested in the welfare work among our people.

—Charlotte Hawkins Brown[1]

As we proceed along the lines of standardization, . . . we are in grave danger from over-emphasis of the public school as the only way out. . . .

—George Foster Peabody[2]

I t is easy to find dramatic progress in southern black education between 1900 and 1930. By almost every measurement, including the number (and proportion) of black children in school, literacy rates, educational expenditure, and the quality of buildings and equipment, the school system for black southerners was markedly better thirty years after Robert Ogden launched his crusade for southern education.

In the South and the border states in 1900, only about half the black children between the ages of ten and fourteen attended school. The educational statistics were far worse in certain states, with, for example, Louisiana reporting 35 percent of the black children in this age group in school and Alabama 41 percent. By 1930 nearly 90 percent of black girls ages ten to fourteen were enrolled in school, and the proportion of boys in school was nearly as high. In 1900 a majority of the black population was illiterate in Alabama, Georgia, Louisiana, and South Carolina, and black illiteracy exceeded 40 percent in all the former Confederate states except Texas and Florida. Over the next three decades, these figures shrank so dramatically that in the state

1. Charlotte Hawkins Brown to W. C. Graves, July 14, 1916, in Julius Rosenwald Papers, University of Chicago.
2. Peabody to James H. Dillard, June 12, 1926, in Peabody Papers.

with the worst statistics, South Carolina, nearly three-quarters of the black population over the age of ten could read and write in 1930. In the region as whole, only one in five African Americans was illiterate in 1930.[3]

Across the South, even in states in which Negrophobic demagoguery flourished, spending for black schools increased sharply. Measuring progress from a pathetically low baseline, Mississippi's per pupil expenditure for black education nearly doubled between 1910 and 1935, while South Carolina tripled its support (in constant dollars) for black learning. Other states, including North Carolina, Tennessee, Virginia, Florida, and Texas offered more substantial support to black education. In some cases the gap between whites and blacks had narrowed by the 1930s. In North Carolina, for instance, the state spent $32.92 per black pupil in 1935, about 64 percent of the expenditure for a white student. These figures represented significant improvement over 1910, when per pupil expenditures for Negroes were only 54 percent of the spending on whites. In other states, including Texas and Tennessee, a distinct advance for blacks was overshadowed by an even bigger increase for whites.[4]

Even more striking progress can be seen in higher education. Many schools that in 1900 were "colleges" in name only had, by the 1930s, realized the hopes of their founders. Public higher education, virtually unknown in 1900, was rapidly growing in significance. More than 40 percent of the 29,269 black college students in the South (including the border states and the District of Columbia) in 1935 attended public colleges.[5]

Yet there was an inconsistent, even deceptive quality to this educational progress. Without resorting to Dickens's paradox about the "best of times" also being "the worst of times," and the "season of Light" coexisting with the "season of Darkness," the historian can only notice something dubious about "progress" that increased black dependence on white oversight and regulation, and be skeptical of "advances" that

3. Anderson, *The Education of Blacks in the South*, 151. Robert A. Margo, *Race and Schooling in the South, 1880–1950: An Economic History*, 10, 7. Grantham, *Southern Progressivism*, 258; Monroe N. Work, ed., *Negro Year Book: An Annual Encyclopedia of the Negro, 1937–1938*, 163.

4. Margo, *Race and Schooling*, 21.

5. Anderson, *The Education of Blacks in the South*, 275.

destroyed private schools and cut autonomous communication with the North.

No black educator could in 1930 exercise the influence—the independent power, one is tempted to say—that Booker T. Washington wielded three decades earlier. Those who had tried to follow in his footsteps by creating private, nonsectarian, industrial schools were, by 1930, failing. The new black educators were better qualified— if qualifications are measured by credentials and graduate degrees— yet more dependent on the southern political system. The model of success, for them as well as for northern philanthropists, became a state-employed administrator presiding over a once-private school incorporated into the public school system, or the president of a nominally private college gradually adjusting to secular and national patterns.

Speaking through the Southern Education Association, southern white educators in 1907 had deplored the "isolation" of many black schools founded by northern philanthropy "from the life and the sympathies of the communities in which they are located." They recommended that "all such schools" be supervised by the state so that "their work and their methods" would be "adjusted to the civilization in which they exist."[6] By one means and another, these goals had been achieved in 1930, though one might well describe the earlier "isolation" of the philanthropically backed schools as "independence" and their "adjustment" as really "accommodation," or even a form of "surrender."

Increasingly active in the South during this period, northern philanthropy cannot be accused of simply ignoring the needs of Negroes. Though more could have been done for black southerners, what was attempted and achieved was remarkable. The General Education Board, which at first spent very little for black education, sharply increased its spending in the 1920s. By the end of fiscal year 1931 the GEB had appropriated nearly $31 million for the education of African Americans. Julius Rosenwald's benefactions stimulated the building of nearly five thousand black rural schools by 1932. Though they were less influential than the secular foundations, church missionary societies continued to be active in the South, supporting black schools at all levels. Between 1916 and 1930, for example, the American

6. W. D. Weatherford, *Negro Life in the South: Present Conditions and Needs*, 111–12.

Missionary Association increased its spending on black education fivefold.[7]

The transformation of northern philanthropy for black education that took place between 1900 and 1930 was not the direct result of a farsighted plan, though new approaches to giving had been advocated by philanthropic planners and foundation executives for many years. Some features of educational philanthropy in 1930 were unintended results of a series of decisions taken years earlier, often with much different objectives in mind. Philanthropists who prided themselves on their scientific methods and ruthless objectivity sometimes accepted uncritically the reigning assumptions of their day, failing to anticipate such significant social changes as the large-scale migration of blacks into the North. "Students of the Negro problem," declared Samuel H. Bishop in 1906, "are more and more coming to the conclusion that the immediate *terminus ad quem* for the Negro is agriculture." Three decades later, Jackson Davis of the GEB was repeating the same message—despite the pessimistic conclusion of "some of our best sociologists" that in twenty years "the Negro will be an urban man." In a Founder's Day Address at Tuskegee, Davis declared: "Now if you and I do not believe this, it is up to us to do something about it and not let it happen."[8]

In other cases, in which the results clearly were *intended*, the philanthropists did not necessarily understand the full implications of their goals. Northern educational theorists, for example, did not seem to appreciate fully the implications of their policy of closing missionary schools as soon as adequate public schools were available. Though they insisted that their work was nonpolitical, there were unavoidable political implications to relying on public education in an era of systematic disfranchisement.

In the end, the philanthropic enterprise was radically altered by three decades of gradual, quiet changes. The heart of the change lay in the reduced practical influence of religiously motivated individual donors and church-sponsored missionary education. By 1930 modern

7. General Education Board, *Annual Report, 1930–31*, 36. For a table summarizing Rosenwald's gifts up to 1932, see Anderson, *The Education of Blacks in the South*, 155. For AMA expenditures on black education, see Appendix.

8. Samuel H. Bishop, "Report to the Board of Directors, American Church Institute for Negroes" [1906], in ACIN Papers; Jackson Davis, "Founder's Day Address, Tuskegee Institute, April 3, 1938," in Rosenwald Fund Papers, Fisk University.

foundations such as the General Education Board were able to set the philanthropic agenda for the South, though religious givers still donated large amounts for the education of African Americans. The influence of the foundations was enhanced both by carefully prepared, widely disseminated reports, and by a hard-headed politics which excluded religious philanthropy from most educational planning and directed grants to specific schools, rather than through denominational agencies. The ambitious, confident foundation administrators of the time thought they had managed the transition from unplanned philanthropy to planned. In fact, the changes involved *who* did the planning and how it was done. The success of the philanthropic bureaucrats lay in their ability to persuade most other givers to accept their perspectives on what the problems of black education were—and how these problems might be solved.

The transformation of northern philanthropy for southern blacks is illustrated particularly well in the career of Julius Rosenwald. In the beginning Rosenwald was an old-fashioned individual donor, inspired by the examples of William H. Baldwin, Jr., and Booker T. Washington, but by 1930 his giving had been organized in a thoroughly modern manner. The charitable Mr. Rosenwald had become the Rosenwald Fund, an incorporated social agency, directed by a veteran of the Rockefeller Foundation.

Rosenwald's interest in southern black education was sparked in 1910 when he read *An American Citizen*, John Graham Brooks's biography of Baldwin.[9] In the following year, Rosenwald met Washington, who would have a decisive influence upon his understanding of the needs of black education. In 1912 Rosenwald agreed to serve as a member of the Tuskegee Institute's board of trustees. His first ventures in large-scale aid for black education were shaped by Washington, administered by Tuskegee, and committed to the goal of spreading the "Tuskegee idea." He celebrated his fiftieth birthday in August 1912 by creating a twenty-five-thousand-dollar fund to benefit "colored schools that have grown out of Tuskegee Institute, or are doing the same kind of work as Tuskegee branch schools," with Washington empowered to decide how the money should be distributed. In 1913 Rosenwald began his program in support of the

9. Julius Rosenwald to Lessing Rosenwald, October 5, 1910; Julius Rosenwald to Mrs. William H. Baldwin, Jr., August 30, 1912, in Julius Rosenwald Papers.

Julius Rosenwald. Moorland-Spingarn Research
Center, Howard University Archives.

construction of buildings for rural black public schools; once again
the plan showed the influence of Washington—and Tuskegee administered the gifts.[10]

Between 1913 and the early 1920s Rosenwald experimented with
several schemes of giving, all of them oriented toward small, un-
federated individual donors scattered across the North and in tune
with the educational assumptions of such patrons. His help went to
many schools, most of them independent industrial schools modeled,
directly or indirectly, on Tuskegee. His favorite formula, the five-year
plan, featured a Rosenwald conditional gift, usually one-fifth of a
total goal, to be coordinated with a specific group of donors who also
promised to give a certain amount for a school's operating expenses for

10. Washington to Rosenwald, June 21 and July 20, 1912; Rosenwald to Washington,
August 5, 1912, in *The Booker T. Washington Papers*, vol. 11, 552–54, 562–63, 576–77.

five consecutive years. The idea was to build up a corps of committed, long-term donors to these schools, thus making their survival less precarious and their educational planning less haphazard. Most of those who matched Rosenwald's gifts were small donors (with gifts of $50 to $100) who were impressed, no doubt, by the imprimatur of the famous Chicago philanthropist.[11]

In about 1920 Rosenwald began to move in a new direction. Concerned about inefficient management, he relieved Tuskegee of the task of administering the school construction program. Although Principal Robert R. Moton strongly protested, noting "the moral effect on the whole Southern situation" of having "this Fund administered through a Negro school," Rosenwald decided to channel all future giving for this purpose through a recently established foundation— the Rosenwald Fund.[12] He began to turn down the requests of schools that he had helped before, such as Utica, Palmer Memorial, Snow Hill, Manassas, and Calhoun Colored, often after consulting with other philanthropic agencies, particularly the GEB.

For example, Rosenwald gave Utica Normal and Industrial Institute thirteen thousand dollars between 1913 and 1922, then refused further aid after being advised by Abraham Flexner of the GEB: "The General Education Board has made no appropriations to Utica mainly because we have never felt clear in our own minds that the future of the school is assured. It lacks backing. It has no religious or other organization particularly interested in it, but lives through the exertions of the principal." Flexner added that the school was on too ambitious a scale to be absorbed into the public school system. (This criticism would have mystified Utica's principal, a Tuskegee man who, no doubt, saw himself as simply following the pattern set by his mentor.) A few days later, Rosenwald's chief assistant wrote to Utica, announcing the end of aid to the school, and apologizing if Rosenwald's action resulted in "anyone else dropping out from the support of Utica Institute."[13]

---

11. The Rosenwald Papers contain voluminous material on Rosenwald's schemes of coordinated giving in this period.

12. R. R. Moton to Abraham Flexner, July 19, 1919; Moton to Rosenwald, July 21, 1919, both in Rosenwald Fund Papers, Fisk University.

13. W. C. Graves to Rosenwald, December 4, 1917; Rosenwald to Graves, December 8, 1917; "K." to A. K. Stern, November 4, 1926; Abraham Flexner to Graves, March 30, 1923; Graves to William H. Holtzclaw, April 14, 1923; all in Rosenwald Papers.

To cite another example, Rosenwald gave a last contribution of one thousand dollars to Manassas Industrial Institute in 1926 "against his judgment" and "with the understanding that it is not to be continued." No doubt he would have halted gifts to Manassas earlier, if it had not been for the powerful pressure exerted by Oswald Garrison Villard, NAACP trustee, influential editor, and president of the Manassas trustees for many years. "Mr. Rosenwald believes," wrote his chief aide, "that the state should take over the school if it is worthy." Rosenwald was unmoved by a later appeal from a trustee, couched in the language of an earlier style of philanthropy: "Manassas is a character-building institution, and we are hoping that you will help us continue this process." Rosenwald's last word on the subject came in 1928, through Rosenwald's assistant (and son-in-law) Alfred K. Stern, who stated that Rosenwald and the Rosenwald Fund planned to limit their support "to a carefully selected group of independent institutions but largely to State Colleges."[14]

The reorientation of Rosenwald's philanthropy can be seen very clearly in his reaction to a proposal made in 1925 by Tuskegee trustees Anson Phelps Stokes, secretary of the Phelps-Stokes Fund, and pharmaceuticals heir William Jay Schieffelin. After a successful endowment campaign for Tuskegee, Stokes and Schieffelin urged that the school use its new wealth to help "schools that are patterned after Tuskegee." Why not "devote the income from a part of our endowment toward extending the Tuskegee influence and spreading the Tuskegee idea throughout the country"? The plan proposed that Tuskegee help selected independent industrial schools by paying the salaries of certain Tuskegee graduates on their staffs, regularly examining their financial records, providing expert supervision of the teaching and curriculum at such schools, and evaluating all new construction. The plan was designed with one eye on Snow Hill Institute's deteriorating financial situation, and had the benefit of advice of several educational experts, including Thomas Jesse Jones of the Phelps-Stokes Fund.[15]

Ten years earlier Rosenwald would have undoubtedly endorsed such a plan, but now he had only reservations. He did not like the idea that

14. W. C. Graves to Oswald Garrison Villard, June 1, 1926; T. C. Walker to Alfred K. Stern, November 30, 1927; Alfred K. Stern to Edna Porter, July 10, 1928; all in Rosenwald Papers.

15. William Jay Schieffelin to Rosenwald, December 28, 1925, in Rosenwald Papers.

Tuskegee's new, larger endowment could greatly increase the duties of the board of trustees. "If getting this large endowment is going to place upon us such obligations as your letter would indicate," he wrote to his fellow trustee, "I would feel that we have been presented with a *liability* instead of an *asset.*"[16]

The transformation of Julius Rosenwald's philanthropy from individual donations to social agency was completed in 1928, when the Rosenwald Fund was reorganized into an imitation of the Rockefeller Foundation, with a former vice president of the Rockefeller Foundation, Edwin Embree, at its head. Embree explained years later that Rosenwald "came to believe that a philanthropic foundation, to be truly a social agency rather than a personal convenience, had to have a policy-forming body made up of men and women of wide interests and knowledge, who had no direct connection with the founder's fortune, and a staff which could give all their time to the work."[17]

Scornful of foundation timidity, Embree always advocated innovation in Rosenwald Fund programs. "There is a real danger," he wrote in a confidential memorandum in 1930, "that the whole foundation movement . . . may break down by becoming timid, bureaucratic and routinized." He moved quickly to scale back the Fund's school-building program, halting all aid for one-room schools in 1930. He was inflexible in his belief that there were too many small, independent or parochial schools for blacks, insisting that most of these schools were at best irrelevant to the basic educational problems of the South. In 1932 he welcomed the "selective force" of the Depression, which was forcing many schools "to go under." He wrote to another foundation executive: "That, on the whole, I think, is not a bad thing."[18]

Embree expressed his own philosophy—and revealed philanthropy's new direction—in his response to a 1929 appeal from a friend of Rosenwald, urging aid for Mississippi's Piney Woods School, headed

16. Rosenwald to Schieffelin, January 6, 1926, in Rosenwald Papers.
17. Edwin R. Embree and Julia Waxman, *Investment in People: The Story of the Julius Rosenwald Fund,* 29.
18. "Special Confidential Memorandum on the Kinds of Things That Should Be Supported by Foundations" (July 30, 1930); "Conspectus of Present and Future Activities of the Julius Rosenwald Fund" (July 23, 1930); both in Rosenwald Papers. Edwin R. Embree to James H. Dillard, January 15, 1932, in Rosenwald Fund Papers.

by one of the most flamboyant of the Booker Washington imitators, "little professor" Lawrence C. Jones.

"As you know," wrote Embree, "the South is honey-combed with these little private Negro schools. They do not meet the problem of education. This must be assumed by the public funds of the states and localities." Embree had no lingering affection for the structure of philanthropy created by individual donors in the years before the domination of the large foundations. "The Piney Woods people are notorious beggars," he declared, "and they succeed in interesting a good many people who are simply sentimental about the Negro without trying to find out what will really meet his problems." He conceded that at "several of these schools there are picturesque personalities who are sincerely trying to do their best," but he maintained that they made little difference in the overall picture. He was even more direct in a letter to Rosenwald: "I see no reason why you or any other Northern friend should give anything to this kind of school."[19]

Embree's judgment of Piney Wood's significance was in sharp contrast to the assessment of an older philanthropic executive, James Hardy Dillard. In 1934 he described the school as "doing a very important job" in an extremely backward area of the South. "I cannot help thinking that at the present stage of the game nothing better can be done than the improvement of the schools of this type," which were likely to reach far more students "than the higher-up efforts for the intelligentia [sic]." Indeed, averred Dillard, "the general uplift of the race depends on bringing up just the class of students who are attending these humbler schools." But Dillard was a voice from the past, at least on this subject, enunciating views that would have made sense to Washington, Baldwin, and even Julius Rosenwald in an earlier time.[20]

Black education cannot be studied in isolation, since the same reformers and educational fashions affected all schools. Apparently distinctive features of black education, praised and damned in the

19. Embree to Rush C. Butler, October 11, 1929; Embree to Rosenwald, October 10, 1929; both in Rosenwald Papers.

20. James H. Dillard to Trevor Arnett, April 7, 1934, Box 268, GEB Papers. Professor Mabel Carney of Columbia University judged Piney Woods worthy of support, though she recognized that it was more of a "welfare center" than a school, thanks to Jones's policy of "outrageously" neglecting academic work. Carney to George Foster Peabody, January 17, 1933, in Peabody Papers.

Edwin Embree. Rockefeller Archive Center.

context of American race relations, were, in most cases, not unique at all. The history of New York City's recurring political battles over public education, for example, is replete with themes familiar in southern black education. At a time when New York had a small black population, reformers were advocating educational reforms that would later be promoted in the South as especially suited to Negroes. Beginning in 1881 with the Kitchen Garden Association, and continuing in the Industrial Education Association and the later Public Education Association, New York reformers sought to improve the city's schools by introducing manual and vocational training, downplaying the role of rote memory in classes, and building a course of study "around human problems, emphasizing important aspects of commercial and industrial life, and incorporating the customs, activities, and pursuits familiar to their pupils." During the height of the reform effort in the years 1915–1917, the president of the Board of Education was William G. Willcox, former president of Tuskegee's board, and GEB staffers Abraham Flexner and Raymond B. Fosdick were influential board members. Much like southern critics of northern philanthropy, critics of the Progressive reformers in New York deplored "the attempt of corporations and foundations to control our school system," specifically condemning the power of "the Rockefeller crowd," and suspected "that businessmen were trying to convert the schools into cheap labor-training programs."[21]

This larger context is particularly important to understanding the Jones Report of 1917—a controversial document central to the transformation of northern philanthropy for black schools. Now best known, perhaps, as the object of one of W. E. B. Du Bois's brilliant polemical attacks, the report once had a broader, more nuanced significance than Du Bois and other critics found in it. Thomas Jesse Jones and his report on Negro education deserve a second look from scholars studying black educational history.

The son of a rural Welsh blacksmith, Jones came to the United States at the age of eleven, speaking only Welsh. Anson Phelps Stokes later claimed that Jones's status as an immigrant gave him "a certain detached point of view" on American race relations. After a year at Washington and Lee University, and two years as a public school teacher and principal, he enrolled at a small Ohio school, Marietta College, where he earned a bachelor's degree in 1897. Among those who influenced him at Marietta were social gospel advocate Washington Gladden, trustee and occasional lecturer, and J. Allen Smith, an economist whose bold critiques of American society produced an "awakening," Jones remembered, in his "economic and sociological knowledge." After college, Jones moved to New York City, concurrently registering as a graduate student in sociology at Columbia University and a divinity student at Union Theological Seminary, a stronghold of the social gospel. A deeply religious man, Jones worked in a New York social settlement house and considered entering the ministry. He was granted a master's degree in sociology in 1899 and

21. Ravitch, *The Great School Wars*, 112–13, 115, 167–69, 182–83, 191, 212–18. See also Cremin, *The Transformation of the School*, 154–60.

a Bachelor of Divinity in 1900. Deciding ultimately against a career in the ministry, he won a fellowship and completed a doctorate in sociology, writing his dissertation on "The Sociology of a New York City Block" under the direction of Columbia's pioneering sociologist Franklin H. Giddings. His study focused on conflicts between Jewish and Italian immigrants and the problem of their assimilation into American life. (He fancied that his swarthy complexion made him more trustworthy in Italian eyes.)[22]

When the trustees of the Phelps-Stokes Fund decided in 1912 to sponsor a study of black education in cooperation with the federal Bureau of Education, Jones was an obvious candidate to direct the study. He had been a staff member at Hampton Institute for eight years, developing an influential "social studies" curriculum. In addition, he had served with the Census Bureau as the supervisor of the collection of "Negro statistics" for the Census of 1910. By 1912 he was employed at the Bureau of Education as a "specialist in the education of racial groups." He was a part-time sociology professor at Howard University and had agreed to chair the Committee on Social Studies, part of the Commission on the Reorganization of Secondary Education sponsored by the National Education Association. Jones saw himself as a person familiar with workingmen, with a basic "sympathy with labor unions and resentment against capitalists."[23]

The research of Jones and his associates was published in two large volumes in 1917, complete with numerous photographs, statistical tables, maps, and school-by-school evaluations. Widely praised among white sociologists and philanthropists, the Jones Report eventually became intensely unpopular with many black educators and activists. "He was detested by the majority of thinking Negroes," claimed

22. Stephen T. Correia, "Thomas Jesse Jones—Doing God's Work and the 1916 Report," 94–101; Herbert M. Kliebard, " 'That Evil Genius of the Negro Race': Thomas Jesse Jones and Educational Reform," 5–8; William H. Watkins, "Thomas Jesse Jones, Social Studies, and Race," 124–27; Kenneth James King, Pan-Africanism and Education: A Study of Race Philanthropy and Education in the Southern States of America and East Africa, 21–23. (King is incorrect in his assertion that Jones "had his undergraduate education largely in the South.") Anson Phelps Stokes briefly summarizes Jones's background in the introduction to Jones, Negro Education, xii-xiii.

23. Watkins, "Thomas Jesse Jones," 126–27; King, Pan-Africanism and Education, 23–31; Correia, "Doing God's Work," 105; Kliebard, "Evil Genius," 14. Jones is quoted in Correia, 95.

historian Carter G. Woodson a few years later. "Among them his name was mentioned only to be condemned."[24]

Since his report challenged the academic claims of many black schools, exposing a few frauds and puncturing numerous inflated claims, Jones was bound to be feared or disliked by some educators. It was the eloquent opposition of Du Bois, however, that permanently marked Jones's reputation. Shortly after the Jones Report appeared, Du Bois wrote a lengthy denunciation of *Negro Education* in the *Crisis*. Although "the ordinary reader . . . will hail this report with unstinted praise," Du Bois wrote, "thinking Negroes" and well-informed whites would see it as "dangerous" despite its "many praiseworthy features."

Du Bois accused Jones of promoting three unwise goals: seeking to restrict higher education for blacks, using the concept of "cooperation" to surrender black private schools "to the domination of the white South," and advocating that the philanthropic foundations have a unified policy toward black education—a particularly "unfortunate and dangerous proposal" since the most important philanthropic organization, the GEB, had "long ago surrendered to the white South."

Denying that he opposed either manual training "as a means of education" or the Progressive principle of "adaptation of educational activities . . . to the needs of the pupils and the community," Du Bois objected to an elementary education so thoroughly industrial that it precluded conventional high school and college training, even for gifted students. Though Du Bois was considered a "radical" and Jones has sometimes been inaccurately described as a "conservative," it was Du Bois who offered a qualified defense of the traditional college

---

24. Carter G. Woodson and Charles H. Wesley, *The Negro in Our History*, 506. Woodson's first reactions to the Jones Report were positive. He began publicly attacking Jones in 1921, after Jones's confidential advice was blamed for the South African government's decision to bar Max Yergan, a popular and effective black YMCA worker, from entering the country for missionary work. August Meier and Elliott Rudwick, *Black History and the Historical Profession, 1915–1980*, 22, 37–40. In fact, Jones had merely advised caution, while he sought to find out whether Yergan was a Du Bois–style radical or a believer in "co-operation." After controversy erupted, Jones "went to considerable trouble to have the decision . . . reversed," and Yergan was allowed to go to South Africa. According to Kenneth James King, Jones's reputation was damaged by critics who believed that his action in this case was part of a broader yet unprovable pattern of interference with black missionary activity. He observes that "the fictitious aspects of the [Yergan] case were as firmly believed in as those admitting of some proof." King, *Pan-Africanism and Education*, 81–85.

curriculum: "Anyone who suggests by sneering at books and 'literary courses' that the great heritage of human thought ought to be displaced simply for the reason of teaching the technique of modern industry is pitifully wrong and, if the comparison must be made, more wrong than the man who would sacrifice modern technique to the heritage of ancient thought."

The Jones Report's repeated calls for educational "cooperation" to promote racial harmony, praising schools that had gained the confidence of their white neighbors, ignored the political facts of southern life, according to Du Bois. Although Jones assumed that black private schools should eventually be taken over by the public school authorities, Du Bois strongly dissented. "Until the southern Negro has a vote and representation on school boards," he declared, "public control of his education will mean his spiritual and economic death."[25]

Most historians have depended upon Du Bois's polemical judgments for their assessments of the Jones Report. David Lewis, for example, claims that the Jones Report had the effect of intensifying the "isolation" of black higher education from "the academic mainstream" for "more than a decade." He accepts uncritically Du Bois's claim that the Jones Report was part of a "master plan" by foundation philanthropists to restrict higher education among blacks, though he admits that the problem with the report was not so much "what the report stated" as "the *tone* of its argument and ulterior purpose."[26]

Forewarned by such criticisms, a reader is unprepared for some features of the Jones Report. For example, Jones candidly admitted that recent initiatives of northern philanthropy had failed to help the black South. Instead of presenting a skillful apology for the Ogden movement, as he might have been expected to do, Jones recognized that this educational revival had stimulated "unsurpassed progress" only for whites: "Unfortunately direct benefit to the Negroes from this great advance has been limited."[27]

On the subject of college education, Jones not only issued the predictable Progressive educator's warnings against unnecessary duplication, dead languages, and the neglect of "scientific gardening,"

25. W. E. B. Du Bois, "Negro Education," 173–78.

26. Lewis, *W. E. B. Du Bois*, 547–50. For similar judgments of the Jones Report, see Wolters, *The New Negro on Campus*, 14–15; King, *Pan-Africanism and Education*, 31–43.

27. Jones, *Negro Education*, vol. 1, 19.

he also advocated the development of Fisk and Howard as "institutions of university grade." He recommended five "first-class colleges" for blacks—in Richmond, Atlanta, and Marshall, Texas, along with Lincoln University and Wilberforce University in the North. He saw twenty-five other institutions, including St. Augustine's, Talladega, and Tougaloo, as appropriately junior colleges, with a strong focus on teacher training.[28]

He did not advocate turning black colleges into industrial education schools, as one might conclude from reading Du Bois's critique. Black colleges needed consistently enforced admission standards, according to Jones, and such "modern standards" in curriculum as "adequate courses in the physical sciences," courses in economics and social conditions, the possibility of substituting modern languages for Greek and Latin, and minimally acceptable libraries and laboratories.[29]

The Jones Report's comments on specific schools are revealing. Although Atlanta University, for instance, has often been described as a school systematically rejected by the GEB and kindred philanthropies, Jones wrote a strongly positive report about the school. "In spirit and aim it resembles the old-fashioned small college," he observed, "but departs from this type in the recognition of recent movements in social studies and manual training." He praised AU's capable board of trustees, "high standards of character in the pupils," and thorough classroom work. Not an easy man to please, Jones was impressed with AU's high school curriculum: "The selection of subjects indicates a regard for the needs of the pupils and a commendable freedom from the despotism of ancient languages." He did question the efficiency of two separate college programs (classics and philosophy; science and mathematics) for only forty-four college students. Though Lewis states that the philanthropists tried to ignore Du Bois's work on "The College-Bred Negro" and "The Negro Common School," Jones went out of his way to mention the Atlanta University Conferences and note the value of the reports produced by them. Along with his usual recommendations about gardening and other agricultural pursuits, he recommended that teacher training "be made the central work of this institution," that the manual training department receive "financial support," and that "college instruction" be conducted

28. Ibid., 61–65.
29. Ibid., 58–61.

in cooperation with nearby colleges, to avoid duplication of small courses.[30]

On the other hand, Snow Hill Institute, an offshoot of Tuskegee and a favorite of many philanthropists, received a rather negative review from Jones. Though the school owned a great deal of land, exerted "much influence" on its community, and had "won the friendship of its white neighbors," Jones saw major problems. The school was poorly organized, handicapped by an "ineffective administration" and poorly trained teachers, according to Jones. He noted "the insufficient preparation of the pupils for the work they are endeavoring to do," and questioned the grand and expensive brick building being erected on campus. "A few of the night pupils are permitted to spend the entire day at their trades," he observed with disapproval. He recommended that the school sell off much of its farmland, keeping just enough "for instruction in agriculture."[31]

Jones's comments on black education were part of a comprehensive philosophy of educational reform. Though Du Bois—and the scholars who have followed his lead—described Jones as a man with a distinctive program of caste education, in fact he repeatedly based his arguments on general theories of "modern" or "progressive" education. Speaking of the "striking results" that "might be obtained in the teaching of English, geography, and history, as well as the introduction of such subjects as gardening, industrial work, and hygiene," Jones made an argument that usually has been overlooked: "These are the adaptations that are being introduced in the school work for white pupils. Surely the Negro schools are equally in need of similar adaptations."[32] In other words, Jones was not assuming that the traditional high school and college curriculum was appropriate for whites but beyond the limited abilities of black students.

He was advocating for black schools a series of reforms that he was energetically promoting in all schools. An emphasis on Greek and Latin, for example, caused "colored schools" to adhere "to a tradition fast vanishing elsewhere." Black educators needed to catch up with the rest of the country: "It seems extraordinary . . . that private secondary schools for colored people should give more time

30. Ibid., vol. 2, 213–15; Lewis, *W. E. B. Du Bois,* 547–48.
31. Jones, *Negro Education,* vol. 2, 94–96.
32. Ibid., vol. 1, 35.

to these languages than the high schools of a progressive State like Massachusetts."[33]

Condemning the "traditional high school" as "preparation for college rather than preparation for life," Jones advocated, in the standard language of Progressive educators, "democracy in education," and a curriculum "adapted to the needs of the pupils and the community." He agreed with those educators who advocated more science in the secondary curriculum, since "The great achievements of modern times are largely in the realm of the social sciences." Like other Progressives, Jones assumed that "modern languages are generally to be preferred to ancient languages," and questioned the practical value of advanced mathematics. He believed that history, civics, and economics should be taught to all students as integrated "social studies," with the goal of creating "good citizenship." Recent American history was more valuable to students than ancient history, he believed, and social history ("the labors and pains of the multitudes") more appropriate than a history focused on "the pleasures and dreams of the few." All schools needed to change their curricula to provide "a more intelligent appreciation of the mechanical activities and household arts of the masses of the people." His proposals for black education merely echoed the reforms he sought for education in general: "If these are necessary elements in the education of the white youth of the country, surely the colored youth should have every opportunity to acquire them."[34]

The pervasive racism of the earlier twentieth century was evident not in the specific curriculum Jones supported but in the benefits Jones expected from applying this curriculum to African Americans. The manual training mandated by "modern educational practice," for example, was "even more necessary for the Negro than for the white," he declared, "since the Negro's highly emotional nature requires for balance as much as possible of the concrete and definite." The mathematical training that "all pupils should have," was even more vital for "emotional groups, prone to action without adequate thought."[35]

The fact that such arguments were used in reference to black schools should not obscure the fact that Jones and his supporters sought similar "reforms" in all schools. Far from designing a program that tried to

33. Ibid., vol. 2, 23.
34. Ibid., vol. 1, 39, 48–51.
35. Ibid., vol. 2, 23; vol. 1, 49.

isolate black schools or made sense only as means of controlling a subordinate caste, Jones's ideas developed in the other direction. His curriculum grew from being a specific attempt to educate black southerners to being a general program, applicable across the nation. As one educational scholar has put it, "The new social studies designed by Jones for the rehabilitation of African Americans in the South became the model for the social studies for the nation at large."[36]

Jones's biases are evident enough and easy to caricature. His glib assumptions about racial and ethnic differences were hardly unique—he was not the only "social scientist" to make sweeping generalizations about the "impulsive" Italian, the "phlegmatic" German, the "steady, plodding" Jew, and the "emotional" Negro. What distinguished Jones from many other commentators on American race relations was his explanation of the differences between black and white. He did not regard any of the group characteristics that he observed as "fixed or innate." Specifically, as he examined the problems of black southerners, he did not explain the source of these problems as "inherent deficiencies," but rather "the product of historical circumstances and an evolutionary lag," and *therefore remediable through education.*"[37]

The claim that Jones sought to brainwash young Negroes into accepting second-class status is not true, although he was undeniably a Washingtonian optimist, readier to praise faint signs of progress than to excoriate racist outrages. Even as a faculty member at Hampton, however, Jones was prepared to protest some aspects of the southern racial order. In 1907 he wrote an essay in the influential northern journal the *Outlook,* describing "The Power of the Southern Election Registrar." As a "noteworthy" example of "the extremely arbitrary power" of white election officials, Jones reported his own unsuccessful effort to register in Virginia. An ignorant officer blocked Jones with petty, irrelevant objections. The sociologist underlined the moral of the tale for his northern readers: if a white man could be treated in such an unfair way, "one can imagine with what ease colored men, however worthy, are disenfranchised."[38]

Like Washington, Jones saw the future of black Americans as rooted in the South and the farm, not based in the city and the factory. His

36. Kliebard, "Evil Genius," 20.
37. Ibid., 8–11, emphasis added.
38. Thomas Jesse Jones, "The Power of the Southern Election Registrar," 52–53.

model Negro citizen was not an obedient factory worker, but a patient, skillful, self-reliant yeoman farmer. "As a farmer owning his own land," Jones argued in *Social Studies in the Hampton Curriculum*, "the colored man suffers less from prejudice of those who do not like him than he does in any other occupation." He admitted that rural Negroes suffered from "poor roads, inadequate school facilities, and, worst of all, lack of police protection." Despite all this, and "too frequent" lynchings and other acts of violence against them, Jones believed that rural blacks were making substantial economic gains, especially in the number of farm owners. Jones can more fairly be accused of failing to anticipate the future, particularly the impact of the "great migration" already underway as he wrote *Negro Education*, than he can be condemned for providing "the intellectual foundation for minorities to understand, then accept their second-class citizenship."[39] The Welsh sociologist was too complacent, no doubt, about the slow pace of evolutionary progress, but he showed no desire to preserve permanently the status quo of the early twentieth century.

In addition to relentlessly promoting the Progressive vision of education, *Negro Education* strongly emphasized a change in the organization of black schools. Unlike earlier supporters of southern black education, Jones saw no value in the proliferation of independent Tuskegee offshoots and imitations. "It is the emphatic conclusion of this study," wrote Jones, employing the ponderous and authoritative passive voice, "that the organizing of additional independent schools is to be seriously questioned." Quoting Booker T. Washington himself, Jones urged that existing institutions be strengthened, rather than new ones created. Many of the independent schools "should be transferred to public or private educational boards" as soon as possible, he asserted. "The founding of new independent schools should be vigorously discouraged."[40]

If the Jones Report was part of a master plan to restrict black higher education, it failed miserably. Almost as soon as the ink was dry on the report, a spectacular expansion in the number of black college students began. Jones and researchers found only thirty-three black schools "teaching any subject of college grade" and only 1,643

---

39. Quoted in Kliebard, "Evil Genius," 12. Jones, *Negro Education*, vol. 1, 99. Correia, "Doing God's Work," 103.
40. Jones, *Negro Education*, vol. 1, 15, 127.

students enrolled in these courses.[41] By the 1926–1927 school year, ten years after the publication of *Negro Education*, the number of college students in black colleges had jumped to 13,860—an eightfold increase. Schools once solely committed to industrial education enrolled large numbers of students in their collegiate programs. At Hampton Institute, for example, the college students increased from 47 to 382 in five years. Even St. Paul's Normal and Industrial School opened a junior college division in 1924, and by the 1926–1927 school year claimed more than 50 college students. Eight years after Booker T. Washington's death, Tuskegee Institute added a collegiate division, which enrolled nearly a hundred students in 1927.[42]

Despite its unpopularity among black educators, the Jones Report may have helped stimulate the expansion of college education for black Americans. More than one black college, no doubt, responded in the manner of Talladega College, where school officials in 1917 were "indignant" at the description of their school as "an institution of high school and college grade"—rather than simply a college. But the criticism helped to produce change. Ten years later, after Talladega's curriculum and faculty had been greatly strengthened, James T. Cater, the school's first black academic dean, "admitted that Jones's evaluation of Talladega had been correct."[43]

In 1928, the Bureau of Education sponsored another report on black higher education, this time without the collaboration of the Phelps-Stokes Fund. Written by Arthur J. Klein, chief of the division of higher education, *Survey of Negro Colleges and Universities* was much more positively received among black educators and intellectuals than the Jones Report. Du Bois described the Klein Report as "distinctly favorable to real Negro education," unlike the "incomplete and unfair" Jones Report, which was marred "by a prejudice against Negro colleges."[44]

He overlooked the ways in which Klein's work was a continuation of Jones's—with similar assumptions and judgments about black education. It was Klein, for example, and not Jones, who said: "The

41. Ibid., vol. 2, 16.
42. Arthur J. Klein, *Survey of Negro Colleges and Universities*, 946–47.
43. Maxine D. Jones and Joe M. Richardson, *Talladega College: The First Century*, 107. One black educator with a positive view of Jones was John Hope. See Davis, *A Clashing of the Soul*, 286.
44. "A Government Survey of Negro Colleges," 261.

economic salvation of the Negro is dependent to a great degree upon his training in the fields of agriculture, mechanic arts, and crafts." Like Jones, Klein strongly supported cooperation between black schools and southern whites, suggesting that colleges operated by northern religious groups needed to give up "long-distance administration of their institutions," and cede control to local "boards of trustees made up chiefly of prominent white citizens and business men of the communities in which the institutions are located." Like Jones, Klein warned of "pretentious" curricula, "thin" in substance, and subject to the "disdain" of knowledgeable whites and blacks. Klein found "a number of institutions" which, in the transition from high school to college programs, had "spread the work of their teachers to an absurd degree in order to offer a minimum college program." Like Jones before him, Klein clearly described various educational deficits, including poorly organized and overworked faculties, inadequate libraries and laboratories, and high dropout rates.[45]

Yet his report did not provoke similar ire. Unlike Jones, Klein had not been accused of engaging in heavy-handed, behind-the-scenes power politics, in order to promote the success of a carefully selected group of black leaders. What made Jones anathema to "thinking Negroes" was not so much his educational ideas as his alleged attempt after 1917 to set himself up, in Du Bois's words, as "arbiter and patron of the Negro race in America."[46]

By the time Klein's work was published, many of Jones's educational judgments of a decade earlier were widely accepted, even taken for granted. Despite the personal unpopularity of Jones among black educators, his report had a major impact on black education—though not in the way his critics expected. Rather than restricting college education for blacks or isolating black colleges, the Jones Report helped to kill the kind of school that Booker T. Washington and William H. Baldwin had once seen as the future of black education, the private secondary school devoted to industrial education. Such schools were increasingly irrelevant by 1930, and many of them were forced to close during the Depression.

When in 1939 Jackson Davis of the GEB sought to discover the fate of schools listed in the Jones Report, he received revealing answers

45. Klein, *Survey of Negro Colleges and Universities*, 3, 20, 36, 40–43, 46–50, 54.
46. W. E. B. Du Bois, "Thomas Jesse Jones," 252–56.

from several state superintendents of education. In North Carolina, only five private secondary schools survived, out of more than sixty institutions, mostly private, visited by Jones and his associates. In a long list of schools, the superintendent repeatedly wrote after the names of once-thriving "academies" or "industrial institutes": "Discontinued. Field served by public accredited high school." Successful colleges, such as Scotia Seminary, Bennett College, Johnson C. Smith University, Livingstone College, and Shaw University, had all dropped their high school departments. Several relatively strong secondary schools continued as public schools, though private organizations might own the school buildings. There were more private industrial schools in Alabama, where public education lagged behind North Carolina, though about half of the schools mentioned by Jones had been absorbed into the public systems or simply closed. Independent schools, such as Kowaliga Academic and Industrial Institute, the Industrial Missionary Association School, and Snow Hill, were least likely to have maintained their operations.[47]

Black educational history in the years between 1902 and 1930 is full of paradoxical developments if one assumes that northern philanthropists followed a policy of consistently supporting "the Hampton-Tuskegee idea" as it existed at the turn of the century. The actual aftermath of the Jones Report—a dramatic expansion of black collegiate education combined with the disappearance of small private industrial schools—is but one example. If outside donors single-mindedly promoted "the Hampton-Tuskegee idea," how do we account for significant changes in that idea, including the transformation of both Hampton and Tuskegee into colleges rather than teacher training centers for industrial education? Why did foundation philanthropy, allegedly inspired by dreams of social control, steadily refuse to give significant, long-term aid to the Tuskegee offshoots—and why did the Association of Negro Rural and Industrial Schools have such patrons as W. E. B. Du Bois and Oswald Garrison Villard? Why were key philanthropists having doubts, by 1930, about the utility of vocational education for blacks or whites? Vocational education, declared Edwin Embree in a memo to Julius Rosenwald, was "a very questionable movement," drawing too much support from philanthropy. "Huge

47. N. C. Newbold to Jackson Davis, July 1, 1939; J. S. Lambert to Jackson Davis, June 12, 1939; Box 17, in GEB Papers.

expenditures" and "busy activity" had produced "astonishingly little evidence" of practical results, he asserted in another memo.[48]

Black educational history in this period makes more sense, on the other hand, if the choices of black people are taken seriously. Historians may have devoted too much attention to the motives of distant philanthropists and their agents, relegating the decisions of black folk to the background and margins of the story. The plans of the General Education Board, the American Church Institute for Negroes, the Rosenwald Fund, and kindred philanthropies were shaped, even stymied on occasion, by the actions of black students and parents. Regardless of the farsighted plans of men such as Abraham Flexner or Edwin Embree or James Hardy Dillard, black students had their own demands, and African American families steadily moved away from terror and proscription, ignoring the experts who insisted that the South and the countryside were the ideal home for the Negro.

The rapid expansion of black education after 1915, especially the explosive growth of public high schools and related progress in collegiate education, were tied to actions beyond the control of the northern philanthropists, including black population movements, changing white southern attitudes and policies, and rising expectations of black students. Hampton Institute, for example, did not become a college because a foundation expert in New York decreed it. Black students were ready to disrupt their campuses if certain changes were not made.[49] Nor did young black southerners rush off to college in a mysterious enthusiasm. Rather, they were making a practical response to decisions belatedly made in southern cities and states to build black high schools. Similarly, the private industrial schools' long and generally unsuccessful struggle for survival cannot be explained merely as one educational philosophy supplanting another. The issue was black autonomy, and the black educators who operated these schools were willing to seek allies without regard for the fine points of educational theory or political ideology. By some interpretations, of course, the foundation philanthropists *should* have provided timely

48. Edwin R. Embree to Julius Rosenwald, October 16, 1931; "Conspectus of Present and Future Activities of the Julius Rosenwald Fund," October 31, 1930, both in Rosenwald Papers.
49. See Wolters, *The New Negro on Campus*.

and extensive aid to these schools, but the inconvenient fact is that they did not do so.[50]

Rather than being consistently wrongheaded and malicious, philanthropic attention to black education was wavering and shaped by many assumptions that had little to do with race. Studying black education as a direct extension of the racial beliefs of the philanthropists is a little like studying United States–Canadian relations solely on the basis of State Department documents on Canada. In fact, the United States has often affected Canada absentmindedly, shaping a weak neighbor even while ignoring it or dealing with another subject. In a similar way, the prejudices and presuppositions of the foundation planners went well beyond black-white relations.

The history of black education must take this "conventional wisdom" into account. Philanthropists approached the reform of American education—North or South, white or Negro—with a distinct mentality. In addition to their program of curricular reform, they were almost instinctively suspicious of certain ways of organizing education. Without always justifying their choices, they were skeptical of local institutions, religious or sectarian motivation, what they called "nonscientific" or "sentimental" approaches, competition (or "unnecessary duplication"), and tradition. These prejudices, rather than simply white racism, explain important aspects of the transformation of philanthropy for black education from 1902 to 1930.

Even those who might have been expected to defend tradition, sentiment, and missionary motives were, by 1930, more and more likely to accept the worldview of the GEB. For example, the Protestant missionary societies steadily withdrew from secondary education, encouraged directly and indirectly by the secular foundations. The process of actually closing schools was painful and difficult to justify to their black patrons. Only the steady reassurance of unexamined assumptions enabled the northern religious philanthropies to push ahead against all objections, certain that simply seeking denominational adherents was an atavistic goal, that private schools were inferior to public institutions, that distant central planners were more

50. Thus James Anderson writes that after 1916 the General Education Board "moved immediately to provide financial support for the smaller industrial schools," though, as we have seen, the GEB in fact encouraged donors to cut support for schools such as Utica. *The Education of Blacks in the South*, 260.

likely to create a useful curriculum than local parents, and that long-established loyalties could be readily transferred to new organizations.

Looking backward from 1950, the head of the American Missionary Association, Frederick Brownlee, saw the process of turning over missionary schools to the public school authorities as a painful and "hazardous" experience: "The parents looked askance at every step the A. M. A. took toward public schools. It was difficult for them to admit that such a step was even in the right direction. From our end it was always easier to make decisions in New York than on the ground in conference with principals, teachers, parents, and patrons." In order to close an AMA school, he admitted: "I had to steel my emotions." But since the goal of expanding public education seemed right, "I took a long look, drew a long breath," and urged the AMA executive committee to go ahead with turning another school over to a white public school board: "And every time the Committee vote read like a death sentence to the people. To me the decision meant extended life; to the people it meant death. Invariably it was impossible to carry the people with us in our conclusions."[51]

This missionary philanthropist remembered one such "transition" with particular clarity—the closing of Burrell School in Florence, Alabama, in the 1930s. A white Presbyterian minister who was a member of the public school board said:

> Mr. Brownlee, I know that it is the city's duty to operate an accredited high school for Negro students. I shall vote to take over your Burrell School, but I shall do so reluctantly. There is a quality about your school that is lacking in all our schools, white as well as colored. We need that quality, but, with the passing of Burrell it will be gone.

Despite his educational ideology, Brownlee knew that "to the parents of our students Burrell meant more than it did to that minister." The AMA school had been "a house of freedom, a house of refuge." Brownlee understood how hard the withdrawal of northern missionary support hit supporters of the Burrell School: "It was as if the bottom had fallen out of the universe when 'those who cared' passed and 'those who must' took hold."[52]

51. Frederick Brownlee, "The American Missionary Association, Yesterday and Tomorrow" (private memorandum, 1950), 68–69, in Brownlee Papers, Amistad Center, Tulane University, New Orleans.
52. Ibid.

Both secular and religious philanthropists missed the basic problem with public schools in the era of disfranchisement. "Public" institutions serving a voteless population were bound to be inattentive at best, egregiously unfair at worst, since their constituents had no direct sanction against hostile policies. As William J. Edwards put the matter in 1928, after he had been forced out as principal of Snow Hill Institute: "I do not think the time is ripe for the Negro to give his private institutions in the South over to the state. That time will not be until the Negro is given a chance to vote like other men." (Eight years later Snow Hill would become a public school, completely under the control of local white voters.)[53]

One wonders how many of the philanthropists of the 1920s saw black education as an end in itself. Were weak and underfunded black schools simply convenient places to carry out educational innovations? Was the primary purpose of philanthropy to solve the pressing problem of American race relations? Or were the foundation planners more interested in black educational experiments for their relevance to a larger agenda of social change? To William H. Baldwin, Jr., or Booker T. Washington or George Foster Peabody, the answer was clear—black education was important because it held the key to racial justice, as they understood it. For a later generation, there are hints that "solving the Negro problem" was a step to something more central. Edwin Embree reported the conclusions of a dinner he had with "an amazing group" of University of Chicago professors—a "selection of brains" Embree called them—invited to comment on a paper he was writing on "the social implications" of foundation activity. "The most interesting outcome of the discussion," according to Embree, "was that the group recommended unanimously that the Fund's best approach to all social problems would be through the Negro." An intelligent attack on "Negro problems" would open the way "to the solution of many general social problems." Embree found this opinion "very reassuring," clear evidence that the Rosenwald Fund was on the right track.[54]

Thanks partly to northern philanthropists, but shaped also by the actions of southerners, black and white, southern black education

53. W. J. Edwards to Julius Rosenwald, May 26, 1928, in Rosenwald Papers; Arnold Cooper, *Between Struggle and Hope: Four Black Educators in the South, 1894–1915*, 17.
54. Edwin R. Embree to Julius Rosenwald, October 30, 1931, in Rosenwald Papers.

had been transformed by 1930. The notion that blacks could be essentially excluded from education, a plausible idea in 1902, had been thoroughly discredited. The idea that white taxpayers had little or no obligation to Negro schools was fading extremist folly, rather than public policy in any southern state. Equally moribund, however, was the concept of southern black education as a special project of northern missionaries or the idea that northern donors were the primary constituency of black educational leaders. Black public education had dramatically expanded, even as "the Hampton-Tuskegee idea" faded (or evolved) into something that would have been unrecognizable to Robert C. Ogden or Booker T. Washington. Though black education enjoyed better funding and more systematic organization than three decades earlier, it was, somehow, much further from the top of the national agenda in 1930 than in 1902. Most educators had long forgotten, if they ever knew, that the mighty General Education Board had once been a John D. Rockefeller, Jr., brainstorm called the Negro Education Board.

A keen observer might well have predicted in 1930 that the expansion of southern black education almost guaranteed a future challenge to white supremacy and Jim Crow. At the same time, any careful student of American race relations could also see that the present organization of education made it highly unlikely that any future protest would be led by black educators. But only a true prophet could have foreseen that a revolutionary challenge to segregation would come from the one institution still controlled by black southerners—the seemingly weak, insular, divided, corrupt black church. But that is another story.

Northern Philanthropic Spending for Southern Black Education

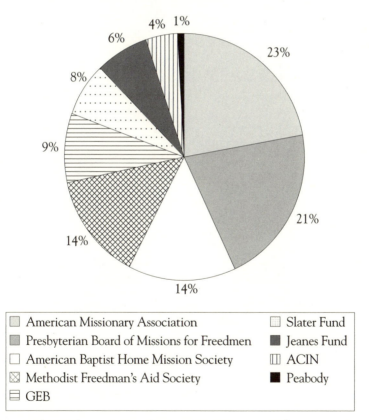

Gifts for Black Education, Fiscal 1910

4% 1%

6%

8%

9%

14%

14%

23%

21%

▢ American Missionary Association	▦ Slater Fund
▨ Presbyterian Board of Missions for Freedmen	■ Jeanes Fund
▢ American Baptist Home Mission Society	▥ ACIN
▨ Methodist Freedman's Aid Society	■ Peabody
▤ GEB	

1. Gifts for Black Education, Fiscal Year 1910. The total value represented is $944,646. Exhibit B, General Education Board Dockets, 1910–1913, vol. 2, 254–59, General Education Board Papers.

219

GEB Appropriations in Black and White, 1902–1918

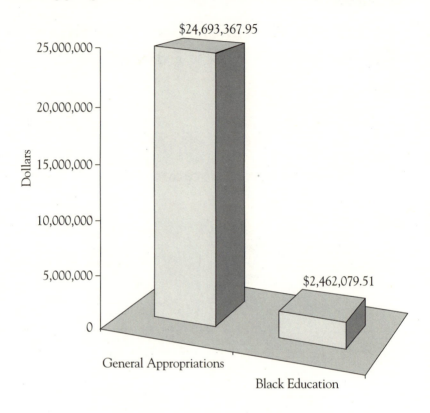

General Appropriations Black Education

2. General Education Board Appropriations in Black and White, 1902–1918. General Education Board, *Annual Report, 1918–19,* 68–70.

GEB Appropriations, Black Education

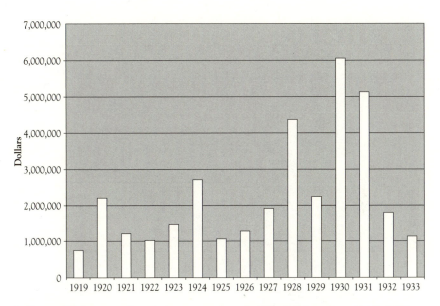

3. General Education Board Appropriations for Black Education, 1919–1933. General Education Board, *Annual Reports*.

Total Aid to Black Education (AMA and Hand Fund)

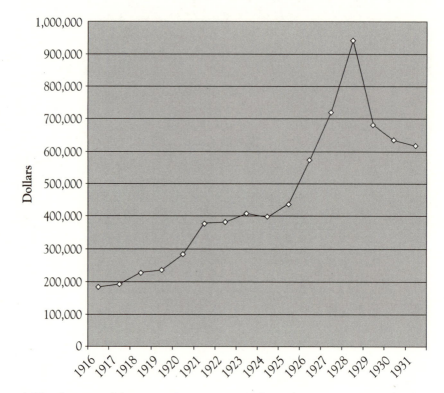

4. The American Missionary Association's Aid to African American Schools, 1916–1931. American Missionary Association, *Annual Reports*.

Bibliography

Primary Sources

Manuscripts
Amistad Center, Tulane University
    American Missionary Association Archives
    Beam-Douglass Papers
    Frederick Brownlee Papers
    Francis Louis Cardozo Papers
Archives of the Episcopal Church, Austin, Texas
    American Church Institute for Negroes Papers
Archives of the Episcopal Diocese of New York, New York City
    David Hummell Greer Papers
Atlanta University
    Archives of the Freedmen's Aid Society
Duke University, Perkins Library
    Hemphill Family Papers
    Charles Norfleet Hunter Papers
    T. S. Inborden Papers
Fisk University
    Rosenwald Fund Papers
General Theological Seminary, New York City
    Howard Chandler Robbins Papers
Harvard University, Houghton Library
    Walter Hines Page Papers
    Oswald Garrison Villard Papers
Library of Congress
    Jabez L. M. Curry Papers
    William E. Dodd Papers
    W. E. B. Du Bois Papers
    Robert C. Ogden Papers

George Foster Peabody Papers
Booker T. Washington Papers
Moorland-Spingarn Research Center, Howard University
Mary E. Branch Papers
Benjamin G. Brawley Papers
Roscoe Conkling Bruce Papers
George William Cook Papers
Anna Julia Cooper Papers
James Stanley Durkee Papers
Ernest E. Just Papers
John Mercer Langston Papers
Thomas Montgomery Gregory Papers
Kelly Miller Papers
National Archives
Office of Education, Historical File
North Carolina State Archives
Superintendent's Papers, Department of Public Instruction
Rockefeller Archive Center, North Tarrytown, New York
General Education Board Papers
Schomburg Research Center, New York Public Library
Alexander Crummell Papers
Southern Historical Collection, University of North Carolina at
Chapel Hill
A. P. Bourland Collection, Southern Education Papers
Joseph Blunt Cheshire Papers
Charles L. Coon Papers
Charles W. Dabney Collection, Southern Education Papers
G. S. Dickerman Scrapbooks, Southern Education Papers
J. Y. Joyner Collection, Southern Education Papers
State Historical Society of Wisconsin
William H. Baldwin [III] Papers
University of Chicago
Julius Rosenwald Papers
University of Massachusetts at Amherst
W. E. B. Du Bois Papers
University of Tennessee, Knoxville
Philander P. Claxton Papers

Convention Proceedings

American Association of Educators of Colored Youth, Minutes of Meeting Held at Baltimore, July 24–27, 1895. Raleigh, N.C.: Barnes Brothers, 1895.

North Carolina Teachers Association, Proceedings of the 20th Annual Session Held at Kittrell College, Kittrell, North Carolina, June 12–17, 1901. Elizabeth City, N.C.: E. F. Snakenburg, 1901.

Proceeding of the Conference for Education in the South, the Sixth Session. New York: Committee on Publication, 1903.

Proceedings of the First Capon Springs Conference on Christian Education in the South, 1898. N.p., n.d.

Proceedings of the Second Capon Springs Conference on Christian Education in the South, 1899. N.p., n.d.

Proceedings of the Third Capon Springs Conference on Christian Education in the South, 1900. N.p., n.d.

Periodicals and Serials

A. M. E. Christian Recorder
Atlanta University Bulletin
Charities
Charleston News and Courier
Crisis
Independent, The
Journal of Social Science
Manufacturers' Record
New York Times
New York Evening Post
Southern Churchman
Southern Workman
Spirit of Missions
Voice of the Negro

Articles in Periodicals and Edited Works

Baldwin, William H., Jr. "Present Problem of Negro Education." *Southern Workman* 28 (October 1899): 399–404.

———. "The Present Problem of Negro Education." *Journal of Social Science* 37 (1899): 52–68.

Bassett, John Spencer. "Stirring Up the Fires of Race Antipathy." *South Atlantic Quarterly* 2 (October 1903): 297–305.

Bishop, Samuel H. "The Church and the City Negro." *Spirit of Missions* 76 (February 1911): 297–99.

———. "The Negro and the Church." *Spirit of Missions* 75 (June 1910): 437–41.

———. "A New Movement in Charity." *Charities* (November 23, 1901): 446–47.

———. "The Psychology of Charity Organization Work." *Charities* (July 6, 1901): 21–28.

———. "Romance of the Negro." *Spirit of Missions* 75 (March 1910): 204–5.

———. "The Struggle." *Crisis* 7 (March 1914): 244–46.

———. "In Topsy-Turvy Land." *Spirit of Missions* 78 (February 1913): 127–29.

Carter, Isabel. "American Church Institute for Negroes." *Spirit of Missions* 86 (October 1921): 667–68.

Crummell, Alexander. "Common Sense in Common Schooling." In *Alexander Crummell: Africa and America.* Springfield, Mass.: Wiley and Company, 1891.

———. "The Destined Superiority of the Negro." In *Alexander Crummell: The Greatness of Christ and Other Sermons.* New York: T. Whittaker, 1882.

Du Bois, W. E. B. "The Episcopal Church." *Crisis* 7 (December 1912): 83–84.

———. "The General Education Board." *Crisis* 37 (July 1930): 229–30.

———. "A Graduate School." In Meyer Weinberg: *W. E. B. Du Bois: A Reader.* New York: Harper and Row, 1970.

———. "Negro Education." *Crisis* 15 (February 1918): 173–78.

———. "The Negro since 1900: Progress Report." In Meyer Weinberg: *W. E. B. Du Bois: A Reader.* New York: Harper and Row, 1970.

———. "Samuel Henry Bishop." *Crisis* 8 (July 1914): 127.

———. "Thomas Jesse Jones." *Crisis* 20 (October 1921): 252–56.

———. "Wallace Battle, the Episcopal Church and Mississippi." *Crisis* 34 (October 1927): 261–62, 282–83.

Dudley, Thomas Underwood. "How Shall We Help the Negro?" *Century* 30 (June 1885): 273–80.

Franklin, Lewis B. "The Nation-Wide Campaign." *Spirit of Missions* 85 (March 1920): 185.

Jones, Thomas Jesse. "The Power of the Southern Election Registrar." *Outlook* 39 (November 1907): 52–53.

"King Theological Hall (for Colored Students)." In *Inventory of Church Archives in the District of Columbia*, 285–87. Washington, D.C.: District of Columbia Historical Records Survey, 1940.

McGuire, George Alexander. "Things Done and to Be Done." *Spirit of Missions* 76 (December 1911): 1020–21.

Mitchell, R. Bland. "R. W. Patton Gave Church New Vision." *Forth* 110 (January 1945): 10–11.

Patton, Robert W. "Dr. Patton Pays Tribute to [James Solomon Russell] a Great Leader." *Spirit of Missions* 100 (May 1935): 222.

———. "Notable Recognition Accorded Negro Schools. General Education Board Makes Conditional Grants." *Spirit of Missions* 92 (January 1927): 11–15.

———. "Objectives of the Centennial Offering, I. The Bishop Payne Divinity School." *Spirit of Missions* 87 (January 1922): 26.

"Robert Patton, Father of the Nation-Wide Campaign." *Forth* 105 (August 1940): 16–17, 31.

Schurz, Carl. "Can the South Solve the Negro Problem?" *McClure's* 22 (January 1904): 258–75.

Washington, Booker T. "The Future of the American Negro." In *The Booker T. Washington Papers*, ed. Louis R. Harlan and Raymond W. Smock; Barbara Kraft, G. McTigue, and N. E. Woodruff, asst. eds., vol. 5, 299–392. Urbana: University of Illinois Press, 1976.

Books and Pamphlets

Bragg, George Freeman. *Afro-American Church Work and Workers*. Baltimore: Church Advocate Press, 1904.

———. *History of the Afro-American Group of the Episcopal Church*. Baltimore: Church Advocate Press, 1922.

Bratton, Theodore Du Bose. *Wanted Leaders! A Study of Negro Development*. New York: Presiding Bishop and Council. Department of Missions and Church Extension, 1922.

Candler, Warren A. *Dangerous Donations and Degrading Doles, or A Vast Scheme for Capturing and Controlling the Colleges and Universities of the Country*. N.p. [1909].

Chesnutt, Charles W. *The Journals of Charles W. Chesnutt*. Ed. Richard Brodhead. Durham: Duke University Press, 1993.

Cooper, Anna Julia. *A Voice from the South*. Xenia, Ohio: Aldine Printing Company, 1892.

Dixon, Thomas. *The Sins of the Father: Romance of the South*. New York: Grosset and Dunlap, 1912.

Douglass, Frederick. *The Frederick Douglass Papers*. Ed. John W. Blassingame. Vols. 1–5. New Haven: Yale University Press, 1979–1992.

Douglass, H. Paul. *Christian Reconstruction in the South*. Boston: Pilgrim Press, 1909.

Du Bois, W. E. B. *The Correspondence of W. E. B. Du Bois*. Ed. Herbert Aptheker. Vol. 1, *Selections 1877–1934*. Amherst: University of Massachusetts Press, 1973.

———. *The Education of Black People*. Amherst: University of Massachusetts Press, 1973.

———. *The Quest of the Silver Fleece*. Reprint of 1911 ed. Boston: Northeastern University Press, 1989.

———. *The Souls of Black Folk*. Chicago: A. G. McClurg, 1903.

———, ed. *The College-Bred Negro*. Atlanta: Atlanta University Publication, 1900.

Flexner, Abraham. *A Modern School*. General Education Board Occasional Papers, no. 3. New York: General Education Board, 1921.

Forten, Charlotte. *The Journals of Charlotte Forten*. Ed. Brenda Stevenson. New York: Oxford University Press, 1988.

General Education Board: An Account of Its Activities, The. New York: General Education Board, 1915.

Grimké, Francis J. *Address of Rev. F. J. Grimké In Memoriam Prof. Wiley Lane of the Howard University, Washington, D. C.* Washington, D.C.: Judd and Detweiler, 1885.

Harlan, Louis R., and Raymond W. Smock, eds., Barbara Kraft, G. McTigue, and N. E. Woodruff, asst. eds. *The Booker T. Washington Papers*. Vols. 1–14. Urbana: University of Illinois Press, 1972–1989.

Harris, Odell Greenleaf. *It Can Be Done: The Autobiography of a Black Priest*. Alexandria, Va.: Protestant Episcopal Theological Seminary, 1985.

Jones, Thomas Jesse. *Negro Education: A Study of the Private and Higher Schools for Colored People in the United States*. Vols. 1–2. Washington, D.C.: Government Printing Office, 1917.

Klein, Arthur J. *Survey of Negro Colleges and Universities*. Washington, D.C.: Government Printing Office, 1929.

Lawrence, William. *Memories of a Happy Life*. Boston: Houghton Mifflin Company, 1926.

Murphy, Edgar Gardner. *Problems of the Present South*. New York: Macmillen Company, 1904.

Page, Thomas Nelson. *The Negro: The Southerner's Problem*. New York: Charles Scribner's Sons, 1904.

——. *The Old South: Essays Social and Political*. New York: Charles Scribner's Sons, 1906.

——. *Red Rock: A Chronicle of Reconstruction*. New York: Charles Scribner's Sons, 1904.

Patton, Robert W. *An Inspiring Record in Negro Education*. New York: National Council Protestant Episcopal Church, 1940.

Rubin, Louis D., Jr. *Teach the Freeman: The Correspondence of Rutherford B. Hayes and the Slater Fund for Negro Education, 1881–1887*. Vol. 1. Baton Rouge: Louisiana State University Press, 1959.

Russell, James Solomon. *Adventure in Faith: An Autobiographic Story of St. Paul's Normal and Industrial School, Lawrenceville, Virginia and James S. Russell, Founder*. New York: Morehouse, 1936.

Scarborough, William S. *The Educated Negro and His Mission*. American Negro Academy Occasional Papers, no. 8. Washington, D.C.: American Negro Academy, 1903.

Sherrill, Henry Knox. *Among Friends: An Autobiography*. Boston: Little, Brown and Company, 1962.

Southern Education: Whither? Baltimore: Manufacturers' Record Publishing Company, 1908.

Washington, Booker T. *Black-Belt Diamonds: Gems from the Speeches, Addresses, and Talks to Students of Booker T. Washington*. Ed. Victoria Earle Matthews. New York: Fortune and Scott, 1898.

——. *My Larger Education: Being Chapters from My Experience*. New York: Doubleday, Page and Company, 1911.

Weatherford, W. D. *Negro Life in the South: Present Conditions and Needs*. New York: Young Men's Christian Association, 1910.

Wells, Ida B. *The Memphis Diary of Ida B. Wells: An Intimate Portrait of the Activist as a Young Woman*. Ed. Miriam Decosta-Willis. Boston: Beacon Press, 1995.

Work, Monroe N., ed. *The Negro Yearbook, 1915*. Tuskegee: Tuskegee Institute, 1915.

————. *Negro Year Book: An Annual Encyclopedia of the Negro, 1937–1938.* Tuskegee Institute: Negro Year Book Publishing Company, 1938.

Secondary Sources

Articles in Periodicals and Edited Works

Anderson, James D. "Northern Foundations and the Shaping of Southern Black Rural Education, 1902–1935." *History of Education Quarterly* (winter 1978): 371–96.

————. "Northern Philanthropy and the Training of the Black Leadership: Fisk University, A Case Study, 1915–1930." In *New Perspectives on Black Educational History*, ed. Vincent P. Franklin and James D. Anderson, 97–111. Boston: G. K. Hall, 1978.

Caution, Tollie L. "The Protestant Episcopal Church: Policies and Rationale upon which Support of Its Negro Colleges Is Predicated." *Journal of Negro Education* (summer 1960): 274–83.

Cooke, Paul Phillips. "Anna J. Cooper, Educator and Humanitarian." *Negro History Bulletin* 45 (January–February–March 1982): 5–7.

Correia, Stephen T. "Thomas Jesse Jones—Doing God's Work and the 1916 Report." In *The Social Studies in Secondary Education: A Reprint of the Seminal 1916 Report with Annotation and Commentaries*, ed. Murry R. Nelson, 94–101. ERIC Clearinghouse for Social Studies/Social Science Education, 1994.

Davis, Lenwood G. "Livingstone College: The Epitome of Self-Help in Black Higher Education." *Negro History Bulletin* 43 (April–May–June 1980): 34–36.

Enck, Henry S. "Tuskegee Institute and Northern White Philanthropy: A Case Study in Fund Raising, 1900–1915." *Journal of Negro History* 65 (fall 1980): 336–48.

Fleming, Cynthia Griggs. "The Plight of Black Educators in Postwar Tennessee, 1865–1920." *Journal of Negro History* 64 (fall 1979): 355–64.

Fultz, Michael. "African American Teachers in the South, 1890–1940: Powerlessness and the Ironies of Expectations and Protest." *History of Education Quarterly* 35 (winter 1995): 401–22.

Hanchett, Thomas W. "The Rosenwald Schools and Black Education in North Carolina." *North Carolina Historical Review* 65 (October 1988): 387–444.

Hayden, J. Carleton. "Different Names but the Same Agenda: Precursors to the Union of Black Episcopalians." In *The Episcopal Church*, n.a. Cincinnati: Union of Black Episcopalians, n.d.

———. "The Episcopal Church and Black Education." In *1979 Directory: Black Episcopal Clergy and the Episcopal Church*, 31–34. New York: Commission on Black Ministries. Executive Council of the Episcopal Church, 1979.

———. "George Alexander McGuire." In *Dictionary of American Negro Biography*, ed. Rayford W. Logan and Michael R. Winston, 416–17. New York: W. W. Norton and Company, 1982.

———. "James Solomon Russell (1857–1935): Missionary and Founder of St. Paul's College." *Linkage* (March 1987): 10–11.

"Henry Laird Phillips Wanted Cannibals." *Forth* 112 (June 1947): 10, 28.

Karl, Barry D., and Stanley N. Katz. "The American Private Philanthropic Foundation and the Public Sphere, 1890–1930." *Minerva* 19 (1981): 236–70.

———. "Foundations and Ruling Class Elites." *Daedalus* 116 (winter 1987): 1–40.

Kliebard, Herbert M. " 'That Evil Genius of the Negro Race': Thomas Jesse Jones and Educational Reform." *Journal of Curriculum and Supervision* 10 (fall 1994): 124–27.

Marable, Manning. "Tuskegee Institute in the 1920s." *Negro History Bulletin* 40 (November–December 1977): 764–68.

Morris, Robert C. "Educational Reconstruction." In *The Facts of Reconstruction: Essays in Honor of John Hope Franklin*, ed. Eric Anderson and Alfred A. Moss, Jr., 141–66. Baton Rouge: Louisiana State University Press, 1991.

Moss, Alfred. "Alexander Crummell: Black Nationalist and Apostle of Western Civilization." In *Black Leaders of the Nineteenth Century*, ed. Leon Litwack and August Meier, 237–52. Urbana: University of Illinois Press, 1988.

Patton, James W. "The Southern Reaction to the Ogden Movement." In *Education in the South: Institute of Southern Culture Lectures at Longwood College, 1959*, ed. R. C. Simonini, Jr., 63–82. Farmville, Va.: Longwood College, 1959.

Patton, June O. "The Black Community of Augusta [Georgia] and the Struggle for Ware High School, 1880–1899." In *New Perspectives on Black Educational History,* ed. Vincent P. Franklin and James D. Anderson. Boston: G. K. Hall, 1978.

Rabinowitz, Howard. "Half a Loaf: The Shift from White to Black Teachers in the Negro Schools of the Urban South, 1865–1890." *Journal of Southern History* 40 (November 1974): 565–94.

Smallwood, James M. "Early 'Freedom Schools': Black Self-Help and Education in Reconstruction Texas, a Case Study." *Negro History Bulletin* 41 (January–February 1978): 790–93.

Watkins, William H. "Thomas Jesse Jones, Social Studies, and Race." *International Journal of Social Education* 10 (fall 1995): 124–27.

Wheatley, Steven C. "Abraham Flexner and the Politics of Educational Reform." *History of Higher Education Annual* 8 (1988).

White, Gavin. "Patriarch McGuire and the Episcopal Church." In *Black Apostles: Afro-American Clergy Confront the Twentieth Century,* ed. Randall K. Burkett and Richard Newman, 151–80. Boston: G. K. Hall, 1978.

Yandle, Paul. "Joseph Charles Price and His Peculiar Work, Part II." *North Carolina Historical Review* 70 (April 1993): 130–52.

Books and Pamphlets

Anderson, Eric. *Race and Politics in North Carolina, 1872–1901.* Baton Rouge: Louisiana State University Press, 1981.

Anderson, James D. *The Education of Blacks in the South: 1860–1935.* Chapel Hill: University of North Carolina Press, 1988.

Ayers, Edward L. *The Promise of the New South: Life after Reconstruction.* New York: Oxford University Press, 1992.

Berlin, Ira, Barbara J. Fields, Steven F. Miller, Joseph Reidy, and Leslie S. Rowland. *Slaves No More: Three Essays on Emancipation and the Civil War.* Cambridge: Cambridge University Press, 1992.

Blanton, Robert J. *The Story of Voorhees College from 1897 to 1982.* Denmark, S.C.: Voorhees College, 1983.

Bond, Horace Mann. *The Education of the Negro in the American Social Order.* New York: Prentice-Hall, Inc., 1934.

Boyle, Sarah Patton. *The Desegregated Heart: A Virginian's Stand in Time of Transition.* New York: William Morrow and Company, 1962.

Brawley, Benjamin. *Dr. Dillard of the Jeanes Fund.* New York: Fleming H. Revell Company, 1930.

Brent, Charles H. *A Master Builder: Being the Life and Letters of Henry Yates Satterlee, First Bishop of Washington [D.C.]*. New York: Longmans, Green and Company, 1916.

Brooks, John Graham. *An American Citizen: The Life of William Henry Baldwin, Jr.* New York: Houghton Mifflin Company, 1910.

Bullock, Henry Allen. *A History of Negro Education in the South: From 1619 to the Present*. Cambridge: Harvard University Press, 1967.

Burkett, Randall K. *Black Redemption: Churchmen Speak for the Garvey Movement*. Philadelphia: Temple University Press, 1978.

Butchart, Ronald E. *Northern Schools, Southern Blacks, and Reconstruction: Freedmen's Education, 1862–1875*. Westport, Conn.: Greenwood Press, 1980.

Chernow, Ron. *The House of Morgan: An American Banking Dynasty and the Rise of Modern Finance*. New York: Atlantic Monthly Press, 1990.

———. *Titan: The Life of John D. Rockefeller, Sr.* New York: Random House, 1998.

Clayton, Bruce. *The Savage Ideal: Intolerance and Intellectual Leadership in the South, 1890–1914*. Baltimore: Johns Hopkins University Press, 1972.

Cooper, Arnold. *Between Struggle and Hope: Four Black Educators in the South, 1894–1915*. Ames: Iowa State University, 1989.

Cremin, Lawrence A. *The Transformation of the School: Progressivism in American Education, 1876–1957*. New York: Alfred A. Knopf, 1961.

Curti, Merle. *The Social Ideas of American Educators*. Paterson, N.J.: Littlefield, Adams and Company, 1963.

Dabney, Charles W. *Universal Education in the South*. 2 vols. Chapel Hill: University of North Carolina Press, 1936.

Davis, Leroy. *A Clashing of the Soul: John Hope and the Dilemma of African American Leadership and Higher Education in the Early Twentieth Century*. Athens: University of Georgia Press, 1998.

Drago, Edmund L. *Initiative, Paternalism, and Race Relations: Charleston's Avery Normal Institute*. Athens: University of Georgia Press, 1990.

Embree, Edwin R., and Julia Waxman. *Investment in People: The Story of the Julius Rosenwald Fund*. New York: Harper and Row, 1949.

Fosdick, Raymond B., Henry F. Pringle, and Katherine Douglas Pringle. *Adventure in Giving: The Story of the General Education*

Board, a Foundation Established by John D. Rockefeller. New York: Harper and Row, 1962.

Franklin, John Hope, and Alfred A. Moss, Jr. *From Slavery to Freedom: A History of African Americans*. 7th ed. New York: McGraw-Hill, Inc., 1994.

Frederickson, George. *The Black Image in the White Mind: The Debate on Afro-American Character and Destiny, 1817–1914*. New York: Harper, 1971.

Gatewood, Willard B. *Aristocrats of Color: The Black Elite, 1880–1920*. Bloomington: Indiana University Press, 1990.

Gilmore, Glenda Elizabeth. *Gender and Jim Crow: Women and the Politics of White Supremacy in North Carolina, 1896–1920*. Chapel Hill: University of North Carolina Press, 1996.

Grantham, Dewey W. *Southern Progressivism: The Reconciliation of Progress and Tradition*. Knoxville: University of Tennessee Press, 1983.

Haley, John. *Charles N. Hunter and Race Relations in North Carolina*. Chapel Hill: University of North Carolina Press, 1987.

Halliburton, Cecil D. *A History of St. Augustine's College, 1867–1937*. Raleigh, N.C.: St. Augustine's College, 1937.

Harlan, Louis R. *Booker T. Washington: The Making of a Black Leader, 1856–1901*. New York: Oxford University Press, 1972.

———. *Booker T. Washington: The Wizard of Tuskegee, 1901–1915*. New York: Oxford University Press, 1983.

———. *Separate and Unequal: Public School Campaigns and Racism in the Southern Seaboard States, 1901–1915*. New York: Atheneum, 1968.

Harris, Odell Greenleaf. *The Bishop Payne Divinity School: A History*. Alexandria, Va.: Protestant Episcopal Theological Seminary, 1980.

Hildebrand, Reginald F. *The Times Were Strange and Stirring: Methodist Preachers and the Crisis of Emancipation*. Durham: Duke University Press, 1995.

Holmes, David L. *A Brief History of the Episcopal Church*. Valley Forge, Pa.: Trinity Press International, 1993.

Holmes, Dwight Oliver Wendell. *The Evolution of the Negro College*. New York: Bureau of Publications, Teachers College, Columbia University, 1934.

Jacoway, Elizabeth. *Yankee Missionaries in the South: The Penn School Experiment*. Baton Rouge: Louisiana State University Press, 1980.

Jones, Edward A. *A Candle in the Dark: A History of Morehouse College*. Valley Forge, Pa.: Judson Press, 1967.

Jones, Jacqueline. *Soldiers of Light and Love: Northern Teachers and Georgia Blacks, 1865–1873*. Chapel Hill: University of North Carolina Press, 1980.

Jones, Maxine D., and Joe M. Richardson. *Talladega College: The First Century*. Tuscaloosa: University of Alabama Press, 1990.

Kerman, Cynthia Earl, and Richard Eldridge. *The Lives of Jean Toomer: A Hunger for Wholeness*. Baton Rouge: Louisiana State University Press, 1987.

King, Kenneth James. *Pan-Africanism and Education: A Study of Race Philanthropy and Education in the Southern States of America and East Africa*. Oxford: Oxford University Press, 1971.

Lagemann, Ellen Condliffe. *The Politics of Knowledge: The Carnegie Corporation, Philanthropy, and Public Policy*. Middletown, Conn.: Wesleyan University Press, 1989.

Leavell, Ullin Whitney. *Philanthropy in Negro Education*. Westport, Conn.: Negro Universities Press, 1970. Reprinted.

Leloudis, James L. *Schooling the New South: Pedagogy, Self, and Society in North Carolina, 1880–1920*. Chapel Hill: University of North Carolina Press, 1996.

Lewis, David Levering. *W. E. B. Du Bois: Biography of a Race*. New York: Henry Holt and Company, 1993.

[Lewis, Harold T]. *"Whose Service Is Perfect Freedom." The Episcopal [Church's] Commission for Black Ministries*. New York: Office for Black Ministries. Episcopal Church Center, 1987.

———. *Yet with a Steady Beat: The African American Struggle for Recognition in the Episcopal Church*. Valley Forge, Pa.: Trinity Press International, 1996.

Linnemann, Russell, ed. *Alaine Locke: Reflections on a Modern Renaissance Man*. Baton Rouge: Louisiana State University Press, 1982.

Logan, Rayford W. *Howard University: The First Hundred Years, 1867–1967*. New York: New York University Press, 1969.

Luker, Ralph E. *The Social Gospel in Black and White: American Racial Reform, 1885–1912*. Chapel Hill: University of North Carolina Press, 1991.

————. *A Southern Tradition in Theology and Social Criticism, 1830–1930*. New York: Edward Mellon Press, 1984.

McFeeley, William S. *Frederick Douglass*. New York: W. W. Norton and Company, 1991.

McMillen, Neil R. *Dark Journey: Black Mississippians in the Age of Jim Crow*. Urbana: University of Illinois, 1989.

McPherson, James M. *The Abolitionist Legacy: From Reconstruction to the NAACP*. Princeton: Princeton University Press, 1975.

Manross, William Wilson. *A History of the Episcopal Church*. New York: Morehouse-Gorham, 1950.

Margo, Robert A. *Race and Schooling in the South, 1880–1950: An Economic History*. Chicago: University of Chicago Press, 1990.

Marrin, Albert. *Nicholas Murray Butler*. Boston: Twayne Publishers, 1976.

Martin, Harold. *"Outlasting Marble and Brass": The History of the Church Pension Fund*. New York: Church Hymnal Corporation, 1986.

Meier, August. *Negro Thought in America, 1880–1915*. Ann Arbor: University of Michigan Press, 1968.

Meier, August, and Elliott Rudwick. *Black History and the Historical Profession, 1915–1980*. Urbana: University of Illinois Press, 1986.

————. *From Plantation to Ghetto*. 3d ed. New York: Hill and Wang, 1976.

Montgomery, William E. *Under Their Own Vine and Fig Tree: The African American Church in the South, 1865–1900*. Baton Rouge: Louisiana State University Press, 1993.

Morris, Robert C. *Reading, 'Riting, and Reconstruction: The Education of Freedmen in the South, 1861–1870*. Chicago: University of Chicago Press, 1976.

Moses, Wilson Jeremiah. *Alexander Crummell: A Study of Civilization and Discontent*. New York: Oxford University Press, 1989.

————. *The Golden Age of Black Nationalism, 1850–1925*. Hamden, Conn.: Archon Books, 1978.

Moss, Alfred A., Jr. *The American Negro Academy: Voice of the Talented Tenth*. Baton Rouge: Louisiana State University Press, 1981.

Parris, Guichard, and Lester Brooks. *Blacks in the City: A History of the National Urban League*. Boston: Little, Brown and Company, 1971.

Prichard, Robert. *A History of the Episcopal Church*. Harrisburg, Pa.: Morehouse, 1991.

Puleston, W. D. *Mahan: The Life and Work of Captain Alfred Thayer Mahan, U.S.N.* New Haven: Yale University Press, 1939.

Ravitch, Diane. *The Great School Wars: A History of the New York City Public Schools*. New York: Basic Books, Inc., 1988.

———. *The Revisionists Revised: A Critique of the Radical Attack on the Schools*. New York: Basic Books, 1978.

Read, Florence M. *The Story of Spelman College*. Princeton: Princeton University Press, 1961.

Richardson, Joe M. *Christian Reconstruction: The American Missionary Association and Southern Blacks: 1861–1890*. Athens: University of Georgia Press, 1986.

Schrieke, B. *Alien Americans: A Study of Race Relations*. New York: Viking Press, 1936.

Sealander, Judith. *Private Wealth, Public Life: Foundation Philanthropy and the Reshaping of American Social Policy from the Progressive Era to the New Deal*. Baltimore: Johns Hopkins University Press, 1997.

Sears, Jesse Brundage. *Philanthropy in the History of American Higher Education*. Washington, D.C.: Government Printing Office, 1928.

Sherer, Robert C. *Subordination or Liberation?: The Development and Conflicting Theories of Education in Nineteenth Century Alabama*. University: University of Alabama Press, 1977.

Slattery, Charles Lewis. *David Hummell Greer, Eighth Bishop of New York*. New York: Longmans, Green and Company, 1921.

Sosland, Jeffrey. *A School in Every County: The Partnership of Jewish Philanthropist Julius Rosenwald and American Black Communities*. Washington, D.C.: Economics and Science Planning, 1995.

Spivey, Donald. *Schooling for the New Slavery: Black Industrial Education, 1865–1915*. Westport, Conn.: Greenwood Press, 1978.

Stanfield, John H. *Philanthropy and Jim Crow in American Social Science*. Westport, Conn.: Greenwood Press, 1985.

Trattner, Walter I. *From Poor Law to Welfare State: A History of Social Welfare in America*. New York: Free Press, 1974.

Urban, Wayne J. *Black Scholar: Horace Mann Bond, 1904–1972*. Athens: University of Georgia Press, 1992.

Walls, William J. *The African Methodist Episcopal Zion Church: Reality of the Black Church*. Charlotte, N.C.: A.M.E. Zion Publishing House, 1974.

Ware, Louise. *George Foster Peabody, Banker, Philanthropist, Publicist.* Athens: University of Georgia Press, 1951.

Weiss, Nancy J. *The National Urban League, 1910–1940.* New York: Oxford University Press, 1974.

Werner, M. R. *Julius Rosenwald: The Life of a Practical Humanitarian.* New York: Harper and Brothers, 1939.

Wheatley, Steven C. *The Politics of Philanthropy: Abraham Flexner and Medical Education.* Madison: University of Wisconsin Press, 1988.

Williamson, Joel. *The Crucible of Race: Black-White Relations in the American South since Emancipation.* New York: Oxford University Press, 1984.

Wilson, Philip Whitwell. *An Unofficial Statesman—Robert C. Ogden.* New York: Doubleday, Page and Company, 1924.

Wolters, Raymond. *The New Negro on Campus: Black College Rebellions of the 1920s.* Princeton: Princeton University Press, 1975.

Woodson, Carter G., and Charles H. Wesley. *The Negro in Our History.* 10th ed. Washington, D.C.: The Associated Publishers, Inc., 1962.

Zabriskie, A. C. *Arthur Selden Lloyd.* New York: Morehouse-Gorham, 1942.

Dissertations

Anderson, James D. "Education for Servitude: The Social Purposes of Schooling in the Black South, 1870–1930." Ph.D. diss., University of Illinois, 1973.

Bauman, Mark Keith. "Warren Akin Candler: Conservative amidst Change." Ph.D. diss., Emory University, 1975.

Belles, Alfred G. "The Julius Rosenwald Fund: Efforts in Race Relations, 1928–1948." Ph.D. diss., Vanderbilt University, 1972.

Enck, Henry Snyder. "The Burden Borne: Northern White Philanthropy and Southern Black Industrial Education, 1900–1915." Ph.D. diss., University of Cincinnati, 1970.

Thurman, Frances A. "The History of St. Paul's College, Lawrenceville, Virginia, 1888–1959." Ph.D. diss., Howard University, 1978.

Index

Abolitionists, 9, 66, 188

Adams, Charles Francis, Jr., 66, 75

African American community: attitudes toward education at the end of slavery, ix, 13–15; Baptist Churches, 17, 19, 93, 105; colleges, 104–5, 210–11, 213, 214; criticisms of philanthropists, 9–10, 41, 45, 49, 56–57, 58–59, 104, 214; denominations, 16–19, 26, 36, 93, 101–2; educational development, 10, 11, 15, 16, 19, 20, 41, 191–218; educational goals, 3–4, 5, 13–14, 37–38, 214; educational history, ix–xi, 1–12, 213–18; efforts to control black schools, ix, 13–14, 20, 38, 214; high schools, 9, 20, 61, 99–100, 105, 213, 214; ministers, 15; opposition to distinctive black curriculum, 13–14, 23, 37–38, 91; philanthropy to black schools, 36–37; poverty, 35–36

African American teachers, 10, 14–16, 21–24, 38, 100, 130, 193; commitment to "civilization," 25, 27–28, 38; commitment to racial pride, 24–25; commitment to Victorian behavior, 25; concern for their own well-being, 31–32; educate for racial leadership and racial uplift, 31, 38; stress Christian beliefs, 26, 38; views on industrial and liberal arts education, 28–31, 38

African Civilization Society (ACS), 17–18

African Methodist Episcopal Church (AME), 17–19, 36

African Methodist Episcopal Zion Church (AMEZ), 17–19

African Orthodox Church, 141

Allen University, 18

American Association of Educators of Colored Youth (AAECY), 22–23, 24, 36

American Baptist Home Mission Society, 87, 102, 103–4

American Church Institute for Negroes (ACIN), xi, 5–7, 31, 53, 109–54, 155–90, 214; appeals for funds, 111–13, 133–39, 147–50; board goals, 122–23, 173–74; criticized by Du Bois, 119–20, 148–50, 170–71; distrusted by white southerners, 128–33, 135, 138, 139–40, 143–44; fund-raising under Bishop, 135–39, 141–54; fund-raising under Patton, 166, 183–89; GEB concerns about effectiveness, 173–74; gifts to black schools under Bishop, 138, 152; gifts to black schools under Patton, 166, 183–89; ignored by historians, xi, 5–6, 187–89; imitates GEB, 109–10, 111, 113, 122; Jones Report gives negative assessment, 162–63; Okolona crisis and limits of its southern racial policy, 168–73; origins, 110–23. *See also* Episcopal Church

American Citizen, An, 64, 73–74, 82, 195

American Missionary Association, 5, 29, 77, 87, 103, 152, 193–94, 216, 222

American Negro Academy, 19, 32–34

American Social Science Association, 68, 74

Anderson, Hob, 168

Anderson, James D., 47, 64, 69*n,* 89–90, 215*n*

Armstrong, Samuel C., 42, 84, 115

Association of Negro Rural and Industrial Schools, 106, 213

Atlanta Baptist College, 105. *See also* Morehouse College

Atlanta Independent, 59, 68

239